The Edinburgh Companion to
Liz Lochhead

Edinburgh Companions to Scottish Literature

Series Editors: Ian Brown and Thomas Owen Clancy

Titles in the series include:

The Edinburgh Companion to Robert Burns
Edited by Gerard Carruthers
978 0 7486 3648 8 (hardback)
978 0 7486 3649 5 (paperback)

*The Edinburgh Companion to Twentieth-
Century Scottish Literature*
Edited by Ian Brown and Alan Riach
978 0 7486 3693 8 (hardback)
978 0 7486 3694 5 (paperback)

*The Edinburgh Companion to Contemporary
Scottish Poetry*
Edited by Matt McGuire and Colin
Nicholson
978 0 7486 3625 9 (hardback)
978 0 7486 3626 6 (paperback)

The Edinburgh Companion to Muriel Spark
Edited by Michael Gardiner and Willy
Maley
978 0 7486 3768 3 (hardback)
978 0 7486 3769 0 (paperback)

*The Edinburgh Companion to Robert Louis
Stevenson*
Edited by Penny Fielding
978 0 7486 3554 2 (hardback)
978 0 7486 3555 9 (paperback)

The Edinburgh Companion to Irvine Welsh
Edited by Berthold Schoene
978 0 7486 3917 5 (hardback)
978 0 7486 3918 2 (paperback)

The Edinburgh Companion to James Kelman
Edited by Scott Hames
978 0 7486 3963 2 (hardback)
978 0 7486 3964 9 (paperback)

*The Edinburgh Companion to Scottish
Romanticism*
Edited by Murray Pittock
978 0 7486 3845 1 (hardback)
978 0 7486 3846 8 (paperback)

The Edinburgh Companion to Scottish Drama
Edited by Ian Brown
978 0 7486 4108 6 (hardback)
978 0 7486 4107 9 (paperback)

The Edinburgh Companion to Sir Walter Scott
Edited by Fiona Robertson
978 0 7486 4130 7 (hardback)
978 0 7486 4129 1 (paperback)

*The Edinburgh Companion to Hugh
MacDiarmid*
Edited by Scott Lyall and Margery Palmer
McCulloch
978 0 7486 4190 1 (hardback)
978 0 7486 4189 5 (paperback)

The Edinburgh Companion to James Hogg
Edited by Ian Duncan and Douglas Mack
978 0 7486 4124 6 (hardback)
978 0 7486 4123 9 (paperback)

*The Edinburgh Companion to Scottish
Women's Writing*
Edited by Glenda Norquay
978 0 7486 4432 2 (hardback)
978 0 7486 4431 5 (paperback)

*The Edinburgh Companion to Scottish
Traditional Literatures*
Edited by Sarah Dunnigan and Suzanne
Gilbert
978 0 7486 4540 4 (hardback)
978 0 7486 4539 8 (paperback)

The Edinburgh Companion to Liz Lochhead
Edited by Anne Varty
978 0 7486 5472 7 (hardback)
978 0 7486 5471 0 (paperback)

Visit the Edinburgh Companions to Scottish Literature website at
www.euppublishing.com/series/ecsl

The Edinburgh Companion to Liz Lochhead

Edited by Anne Varty

EDINBURGH
University Press

Edinburgh University Press Ltd
22 George Square, Edinburgh EH8 9LF

www.euppublishing.com

Typeset in 10.5/12.5 Adobe Goudy
by Servis Filmsetting Ltd, Stockport, Cheshire, and
printed and bound in Great Britain by
CPI Group (UK) Ltd, Croydon CR0 4YY

A CIP record for this book is available from the British Library

ISBN 978 0 7486 5472 7 (hardback)
ISBN 978 0 7486 5471 0 (paperback)
ISBN 978 0 7486 5473 4 (webready PDF)
ISBN 978 0 7486 5475 8 (epub)
ISBN 978 0 7486 5474 1 (Amazon ebook)

Contents

Series Editors' Preface

In the preface to the first tranche of volumes in this series, the series editors argued that, while recognising that some literary canons can conceive of a single 'Great Tradition', there is no such simple way of conceiving of Scottish literature's variousness. This year's tranche, the fifth, illustrates that variousness in two ways.

The subject of this year's author volume, Liz Lochhead, currently Scotland's Makar, illustrates the variousness of her talents as poet, playwright and, in a broader sense, figure of cultural significance. As she moves between poetry and playwriting, her work brings lessons from each genre to the other, highlighting the generic slipperiness and interpenetration that is such a feature of Scottish literature. Her work also illuminates relationships between Scotland's languages and dialects, particularly between the Scots and English languages – but also the varieties of dialect and register in Scots usage – as she brings her sharp eye and insightful wit to bear. In her art, Lochhead exemplifies even wider artform interaction as her painting, poetry and playwriting each shape aspects of her creative output.

The second volume this year is one of the series' topic volumes. In its own way, it also illustrates the variousness of the elements in the canon of Scottish literature, sliding between the oral and literary traditions – and their interaction – and voyaging among a wide variety of genres, including story, song, ballad and poetry. This is part of the reason it is entitled a Companion not to 'Scottish Traditional Literature', but to 'Scottish Traditional Literatures'. It considers the impact of traditional literatures in Scotland's several languages both on one another and on what is often more commonly, if in a more limited (and limiting) sense, defined as the Scottish literary tradition. In fact, this volume, like the rest of the series, challenges just what is meant by such a term. The volume pays particular attention to the role of tradition-bearers and those who collected traditional material and made it available to us. In doing so, it raises important and pressing questions about the nature of collecting and the conception of authenticity of tradition.

Ian Brown Thomas Owen Clancy

Brief Biography of Liz Lochhead

Liz Lochhead was born in Motherwell, Lanarkshire on 26 December 1947, the first child of John Lochhead who worked as a local government clerk and his wife Margaret Forrest. The family moved to Newarthill in 1952 where Lochhead went to primary school and her sister was born in 1957. As a secondary school pupil she went to Dalziel High School in Motherwell and in 1965 matriculated in the Glasgow School of Art, graduating in 1970. During her time as an art student Lochhead began to attend Stephen Mulrine's writers' workshop and to write poetry. From there she worked as an art teacher in Glasgow, Bristol and Cumbernauld until the watershed year of 1978 when she was awarded the first Scottish/Canadian Writers' Exchange Fellowship and left Scotland for Toronto and America. Her first collection of poetry, *Memo for Spring*, which won a Scottish Arts Council Book Award, was published in 1972, and her second, *Islands*, in 1978 which was also the year in which she wrote and performed, with Marcella Evaristi, her feminist revue *Sugar and Spite* at the Traverse Theatre in Edinburgh.

Lochhead married the architect Tom Logan in 1986 and they settled in the West End of Glasgow. She continued to publish poetry throughout the 1980s, with *The Grimm Sisters* in 1981, *Dreaming Frankenstein & Collected Poems* in 1984 and a new collection of performance pieces, *True Confessions and New Clichés* in 1985. At the same time, she was experimenting in full-length theatre, adapting *Frankenstein* for the stage as *Blood and Ice* (Traverse Theatre, Edinburgh and Belgrade Theatre, Coventry) in 1982; *Shanghaied* for the Ayrshire-based Borderline Theatre in 1982; *Rosaleen's Baby* for the Scottish Youth Theatre in 1983; and *Dracula* for the Royal Lyceum Theatre, Edinburgh in 1985. Her Scots adaptation of Molière's *Tartuffe* premièred at the Royal Lyceum Theatre in 1986. *Mary Queen of Scots Got Her Head Chopped Off*, to mark the 400th anniversary of Mary's death, was performed by Communicado Theatre Company at the Edinburgh Festival in 1987.

From here, Lochhead's work branched in several directions. She published three further collections of poetry, *Bagpipe Muzak* in 1991, *The Colour of Black and White: Poems 1984–2003* in 2003 and *A Choosing* in 2011. Her more recent adaptation of theatrical classics started with Theatre Babel's *Medea* in 2000, which gained the Saltire Society Scottish Book of the Year award. This was followed by *Miseryguts*, a version of Molière's *Le Misanthrope* set around the Scottish Parliament and performed at the Royal Lyceum in 2002, *Thebans* (after Sophocles) in 2003 and *Educating Agnes*, a version of Molière's *School for Wives/L'École des Femmes* in 2008, the latter two with Theatre Babel. She also wrote a sequence of original dramas: *Cuba* (1997, for the 35th anniversary of the Cuban missile crisis), a play for young people commissioned by the Royal National Theatre; *Elizabeth* (1998), a sequel to *Shanghaied*, for the Royal Lyceum, where both were played together under the joint title *Britannia Rules*; the romantic comedies *Perfect Days* (1998) and *Good Things* (2004); and the 'theatrical event' *Edwin Morgan's Dreams and Other Nightmares* for Glasgay! (2011).

Her husband died after a short illness in 2010.

She was appointed an honorary fellow of the Association for Scottish Literary Studies in 2010 and Scotland's Makar, its national Poet Laureate, in 2011.

Introduction

Anne Varty

'Country: Scotland. What like is it?' Few today have greater authority to answer that question than Liz Lochhead. Loved and lauded, she has rarely been out of the public eye since the publication of her first volume of poetry, *Memo for Spring*, over forty years ago. Succeeding Edwin Morgan to the role of Poet Laureate for the city of Glasgow in 2005, and again to the role of Scotland's Makar in 2011, Liz Lochhead's astonishing creativity, its plurality, its intimacy, its unassuming power, recognised by public honours, is gathering momentum. Yet it is twenty years since the last, and indeed first, publication of a volume devoted exclusively to the study of Liz Lochhead's work.[1] This new collection could be seen as long overdue.

Taken together, the essays here confirm two major things. Firstly, they demonstrate the exceptional range and versatility of Liz Lochhead's craft; secondly, they show the extraordinary reach of her imagination. No less than early emigrants from Scotland, she has taken Scotland beyond its borders and brought home new worlds, transforming both her native landscape and its global position. And as contributor after contributor attests, it is the strength of her poetry that achieves these things. 'It comes through, as leaves do.'[2] Just as this line speaks with an echo of Keats, so this volume also seeks to draw out Liz Lochhead's dynamic connection with the past, to explore traditions she puts to such resonant use. Whether these are traditions of story, evinced in *Medea* or *The Grimm Sisters*; history, seen in *Mary Queen of Scots Got Her Head Chopped Off* or *Shanghaied*; the Gothic, in *Dracula* but also in *Cuba*; or language itself, the absolute foundation of Liz Lochhead's work, seen perhaps at its most dazzling in *Tartuffe* and at its seemingly simplest in 'Kidspoem/ Bairnsang', the vision she communicates is always layered. The palimpsest of past and present informs everything she writes. The past, whether ghostly, ghastly, or just unavoidably there, shines through and is seen afresh, even as the contours of the present are seen with an adjusting perspicacity through her particular lens.

Liz Lochhead's contribution to cultural life goes well beyond her publica- tions, and her determination to define the role of Makar for herself has simply intensified, made more visible perhaps, her life-long drive to communicate the value of poetry. And this commitment comes not from a belief in the worthy acquisition of an inner museum of cultural capital – far from it. It comes from the passionate conviction that poetry, and access to a poetic sensibility, sharpens perception of the self, of politics, of human experience and the experience of being human. She has been particularly outspoken about the importance of reaching young audiences for poetry in schools, and she has supported this by conducting readings and workshops in schools throughout her career as a poet.[3] She is motivated primarily by the desire to share the pleasure which poetry can bring, and there are three underpinning elements to what she hopes to achieve by this engagement with young people. She wishes to offer a broader experience of poetry than is afforded by the curriculum, to encourage the recitation of poetry and to facilitate the writing of poetry. Her emphasis on learning by heart links with her belief in the value of internalising the voices of others, to encourage a sense of individual ownership and shared community through poetic expression. But it is also by listening, and really hearing, the voices of others that one's own voice can be developed. Recitation, for Liz Lochhead, leads directly to composition. She has stated her own early enthusiasm for Louis MacNeice, and the 1960s Liverpool voice poets, Patten, Henri and McGough,[4] and it is to enable young people to make their own journeys into voice, language and form that she pursues her work in schools with such dedication. The dynamic range of her impact over the decades is suggested by David Barnett's recollection of a visit she made to his school in Wigan in 1981, and by the publication in 2011 of poetry by school pupils from nine different education authorities, *The Liz Lochhead Collection*, following her creative writing workshops.[5] The priority which she gives to such work is evident in her recently stated ambition to write a new piece to perform herself in schools, incorporating some of her own youthful favourites, Alfred Noyes's 'The Highwayman', Keats's 'Old Meg She Was a Gypsy' and 'La Belle Dame sans Merci' (the recitation of which she stages in *Cuba*), Burns's 'To A Mouse' and Border ballads such as 'The Twa Corbies', all of which, she states, are strong narratives and have 'a bit of magic in them'.[6]

Most of all Liz Lochhead communicates her enthusiasm for poetry by the example of her own practice, as Carol Ann Duffy asserted in greeting Liz Lochhead's new appointment:

> Since her early work in the 1970s, she has been an inspirational presence in British poetry – funny, feisty, female, full of feeling; a fantastic performer of her work and a writer who has tirelessly brought poetry to the drama and drama into poetry.[7]

These features of Liz Lochhead's writing draw on her mastery of the language of her community and its different registers. In the past – for example in a major interview given in 1984 – she has resisted a simple classification of her in terms of a specific regional or national community, asserting 'I think my country is women.' Nevertheless, she undoubtedly finds linguistic and creative energy from her Glasgow and West of Scotland environment. She continues in the 1984 interview by saying:

> I'm not all female chauvinist and I don't want my work limited to women, but I feel that the things I've got to say are specific and that mine come from wanting to delineate that territory rather than the physical territory of Glasgow – which I feel very much at home in. I do like to use Glasgow and West of Scotland register, but that's only because it's part of my own childhood and private register that I know intimately. I'm certainly interested in Scottishness, but I feel that the territory that gets delineated is a macho William McIlvanney and Tom Leonard world and that's what Glasgowness feeds into. I'm quite interested in writing Glasgow or Scottish material, but really femaleness seems to be my country.[8]

What emerges clearly is that Liz Lochhead has a nuanced sense of her cultural homeland, and that, just as she says she is not a female chauvinist, so she is not a chauvinist at all. There is, nonetheless, a lively strand in her work that derives great strength from her linguistic, geographical and social roots and that strength serves her as she sets about, particularly in her drama, reimagining and reshaping a 'Glasgowness' that escapes the machismo to which she refers. The women in her *Tartuffe* (1986), for example, are strong, and Dorine speaks with a Glaswegian vitality that exceeds even that of the original. Randall Stevenson[9] draws attention to one example of this when he analyses the way Lochhead deals with and expands on Molière's original speech when in Act III Dorine rebuffs Tartuffe:

> *je ne suis point si prompte,*
> *Et je vous verrais nu du haut jusques en bas*
> *Que tout votre peau ne me tenterait pas*
>   (I am not so hasty:
> I might see you naked from head to foot
> And all your skin would not tempt me)

Liz Lochhead's rendition of this stark put-down uses Scots (spelled – 'proaper', 'lukk ett' – to suggest Glaswegian dialect) to enliven the rejection and she adds powerfully to its vividness by a certain frankness in addressing the ineffectiveness of the impact of Tartuffe's state of sexual arousal, 'staunin' hoat'.

As fur masel', Ah'm no that easy steered.
If you were barescud-nakit, aye and geared
Up guid and proaper, stauning' hoat for houghmagandie [sexual congress]
I could lukk and lukk ett you, and no get randy.

As Stevenson observes, 'An emphatic, terminal position in the line helps assert the gallus colloquialism of the term "randy", but celebrates even more strongly the suggestively wild-sounding "houghmagandie".'[10] Stevenson's use here of the word 'gallus', a word especially associated with Glaswegian dialect, reinforces the sense that here we are relishing language derived from Lochhead's linguistic heartland.

Lochhead uses this language in her drama – *Perfect Days* (1998), in particular – to resist, challenge and subvert macho 'Glasgowness'. In this play, her central character Barbs is a successful business-woman, though one whose public agency is haunted by her desire to have a child as she approaches the age of forty. Barbs's friend Brendan Boyle, like her a hair-dresser, is a clear-eyed and scatologically witty gay man. In one speech he undermines a received vision of Glasgow, referring in short order to the classic novel of Glasgow violence, *No Mean City* (1935), female respectability, the city as home of 'hardmen' and the religiosity that at times can topple over into bigotry. Brendan talks of his gay identity:

> But then you see, growing up a Glesca Boy in No Mean City – yeah, among all the easy-affrontit Mammies and all the Daddies that were pure frozen arsed hardmen wi jaws made oot of girders, well, I found out very early that the world and its wife were quite happy and totally tane oan wi the local token Wee-Bit-of-a-Mary-Anne-God-Love-Him. Even Father Hugh and Father Thomas used to pure crease themsels at my antics when I took centre stage crossdressed at the Legion of Mary Conversazzione.[11]

Within this satirical speech on Glaswegian mores are further hidden jokes. It is well-known in Scotland, for example, as a result of advertising campaigns, that the soft drink Barr's Irn-Bru is made 'out of girders'. The cross-dressing at the Catholic church social event raises unanswered questions about the sexuality of Fathers Hugh and Thomas as they 'pure crease themsels', with the hidden hint of 'cross themsels', while the crossing here is done by the cross-dressing Brendan, with his Irish explorer-saint's name. As is clear from this example, Liz Lochhead is capable of the most acutely observed comedy full of dense ideas and motifs and yet lightly delivered. Sometimes her comedy is based on her sense of a changing Glasgow as when Barbs, talking of the recently gentrified central zone, says, 'Merchant City! As my auld mammy calls it, the Back o' Goldberg's.'[12] Her mention of a defunct department store, much loved by the older generation, allows a dismissively sardonic reference to adjustments representing, but often superficially, economic and social change, while reminding us of Glasgow's intercultural nature in which the Jewish community has played, and plays, an important role. Lochhead is aware too of the nuances of class and of snobbery, both simple and reverse, when Brendan says of a customer 'Bonny lookin lassie . . . Pleasant to talk to . . . A bit kinna . . . Kilmalcolm'.[13] The emphasis on the final syllable of Kilmacolm speaks volumes about the city would-be sophisticate's attitude to the aspirational inhabitants of a small nearby town. Lochhead avoids Glaswegian chauvinism, often expressed by others in Glasgow–Edinburgh rivalry, but again her sharp eye and ear allow her, writing in 1998 when the Scottish Parliament was yet to be reopened, to present Brendan commenting sharply on aspects of the Scottish capital's gay community. Talking of Edinburgh, where he has been working, he says, 'I was thinking of flitting [moving house] through, but then I thought do I want to live in a gay scene dominated by Q.C.'s [sic] and candidates for the new Scottish Parliament . . .?'[14] Lochhead presents a Glasgow and Glaswegians that are changing, which cannot be simply seen in a macho light, but are, in a modern Scotland, complex and capable of progressive social and cultural attitudes.[15]

A powerful element in complex progressiveness is, however, an openness to what lies beyond the local and familiar. This volume demonstrates the extent to which Liz Lochhead aligns her resources, those of language, place and gender, with the unfamiliar and distant, contributing, it is hoped, to a change in the landscape of criticism. To suggest the unique inspiration Liz Lochhead has brought to those working alongside her, this volume opens with the voices of her colleagues. Robyn Marsack, director of the Scottish Poetry Library, assesses the political complexities of her first year as Makar; Andrew Greig salutes her infectious generosity to her fellow poets; and Robert Crawford offers a close reading of 'Something I'm Not' which captures features of what a younger generation of poets have learned from her. Liz Lochhead's influence on dramatic forms is as diverse as it is compelling: Marilyn Imrie writes from extensive experience of producing her radio drama; Joe Ahearne, director of her short film *Latin for a Dark Room* describes the impact of her screenwriting technique; and Graham McLaren speaks intimately about Liz Lochhead's collaborations at Theatre Babel.

The second chapter of this volume engages with her publication of poetry over four decades. Dorothy McMillan shows how Liz Lochhead's poetry has grown out of a consuming intellectual curiosity to explore and express the unknown. She reminds us of the transforming moment when Liz Lochhead stepped through the cupboard door in the English classroom at the school where she was teaching art in the early 1970s, to discover the wonderland of Geoffrey Summerfield's anthologies of world poetry. Her spirit of intellectual and emotional adventure drives her bold encounters with the fearful, the

dangerous, the politically contentious, and with ourselves at our most vulner-
able. Taking the long view, McMillan considers how issues of feminism or
nationalism, certainly real, may, when given exclusive focus, diminish our
understanding of the larger enterprise and wider ambition of Liz Lochhead's
oeuvre.

McMillan's noticing of the moment when the art teacher opened the
English teacher's cupboard also points to Liz Lochhead's flair for both trans-
gression and auto-didacticism. These features link her enterprise with that
of the Romantics, not only with Mary Shelley, but also with Wordsworth,
sharing with him the determination to tune the language people really speak
to poetry, and sharing with Keats the belief that poetry comes 'as leaves to a
tree'. And just as the Gothic flourished first in the Romantic era of political
turbulence, so she too deploys the Gothic to address aspects of disturbance
in our own times. As Stuart Kelly stated on her appointment as Makar, 'the
easy flow of her lines belies a very intense gothic preoccupation with sexual-
ity, monstrosity and the dark myths of gender'.[16] Her subject matter, her
language, her modes of treatment, authentically owned, always answer an
immediate need as she speaks not just for herself but for her contemporaries,
and the culture of her country.

Trained as a visual artist, yet practising in the written word, her sensitiv-
ity to the complementary resources of these media has always been acute,
is evident throughout her theatre, poetry and performance pieces, and is
reflected in every chapter of this volume. The visual/verbal complexity of
her work is given particular attention by Laura Severin in Chapter 3, in the
consideration of *The Colour of Black and White* as an artefact created from
the interplay of word and image. At the same time, Severin attends to the
cumulative narrative of that collection and is alert to its embedded story of
maturation, bringing artist, woman and nation into view. The narrative is
told not simply through juxtaposition and what happens next, but also, more
profoundly, through language, or languages. Joyce McMillan responded to Liz
Lochhead's appointment as Makar with the assertion,

> in the intensity of her engagement with feminism, and with the cultural nation-
> alism of a re-emerging nation, she reflects some of the key cultural and political
> shifts of recent history; and at her best, she uses poetry, and the fluid energy of
> a changing language, to shape new theatrical worlds in a way that seems almost
> Shakespearean.[17]

McMillan identified a timely excitement about Liz Lochhead's use of lan-
guage, and this is the focus of Chapter 4. Taking *Mary Queen of Scots Got Her
Head Chopped Off* as her primary example, Nancy Gish focuses on the wide
spectrum of language, both English and Scots Standard English, literary and

demotic Scots, deployed by Liz Lochhead. She suggests how her manipulation of this range, at once contemporary and historicised, creates a new medium of expression and in turn opens up fresh perspectives and modes of perception at a period of political renaissance.

In Chapter 5, Susanne Hagemann looks at Liz Lochhead's work through the other end of the telescope, and reflects on the challenges posed to translators by Liz Lochhead's uniquely forged language. She examines how Lochhead's material is translated into other languages and traditions. By contrast, looking at what Liz Lochhead has brought in to British culture rather than what of hers has been disseminated further afield, John Corbett (Chapter 6) explores Liz Lochhead's stage translations or adaptations of the neo-classical French of Molière and the ancient Greek of Euripides and Sophocles. Translations of course always offer the translator or adapter the opportunity to 'make it new', but in Liz Lochhead's case this is where her ability to create links between past and present, between communities, to think both historically and ahistorically, become vividly real. Interviewed about Thebans by Mark Brown in 2003 she stated:

> It became obvious that Thebans is what it had to be called. It's very much about a set of people who live in a place where they are waiting for a war to start. It felt very timely working on it. The whole rewriting of these stories has been so informed by contemporary events. I was just starting work on it in September 2001. There's been this whole sense of cities suddenly being precarious places. I was thinking about the people of Iraq sitting there waiting for it to happen, while I was also thinking about the Thebans waiting for one of their own to come and besiege the city.
>
> I don't think of the Thebans as being different from us. I don't think of them as people set in olden days.[18]

Lochhead's acute sense of the spirit of the times and her ambition to intervene are evident both in her selection of material for adaptation and in the language in which it is conveyed. She illuminates the past by the present just as these myths express the magnitude of the immediate.

One further aspect of major significance for Liz Lochhead's ability to interpret zeitgeist so accurately is her relish and wealthy knowledge of popular culture. While her command of the colloquial can be seen as one dimension of popular culture – we remember Norman MacCaig's assessment, 'Liz doesn't use clichés, she flypes them [turns them inside out]'[19] – she is equally adept at manipulating the material world of commodity (we noted earlier her sly hidden reference to Barr's Irn Bru), celebrity and events. This is nowhere more in evidence than in her use of the Gothic. Benjamin Poore in Chapter 7 addresses Liz Lochhead's thoroughgoing treatment of the Gothic through the materiality of popular culture as a context for Dracula before demonstrating how, again, she augments her version of the contemporary by deliberate and playful entertainment of the Scottish traditions of the Gothic. Several of these themes: the use of the uncanny, the anchorage of popular culture, the desire to rebel, the confusions of limited understanding, run through my own chapter (8) on Lochhead's theatre for young people. In this, she renders accurately an archetypal experience of being young while also locating that experience within specific periods of history.

The volume closes with Adrienne Scullion's appraisal of Liz Lochhead's representation of women's voices over the thirty-year period of her career as a dramatist. She argues for Lochhead's role in internationalising feminist debate in Scotland, both from the stage and through academic critical response. Yet, Scullion pauses over Liz Lochhead's apparent move from epic theatre to domestic drama evident in the trajectory from *Blood and Ice* to *Good Things*, and notes the increasing dominance of her unmediated voice in public debate. Scullion's account of this trajectory may, of course, be altered, if Lochhead's stage translations of the first decade of this century – major interventions in creating a porous relationship between Scotland and the past, the international, and the masculinities of classical culture – are drawn into play. Nevertheless, what emerges from this and the other chapters in the volume is the vigour of debate provoked by Liz Lochhead's work, and an affirmation of the centrality of her place in the changing Scottish culture of today.

Answering the question with which this introduction began, La Corbie, the choral voice of *Mary Queen of Scots Got Her Head Chopped Off*, says, 'Ah dinna ken whit like *your* Scotland is. Here's mines.' Above all, this volume suggests the exuberant plurality of Liz Lochhead's vision.

CHAPTER ONE

Poet and Performer: Practitioners Speak

Robyn Marsack, Andrew Greig, Robert Crawford,
Marilyn Imrie, Joe Ahearne, Graham McLaren

On the National Poet's First Year
Robyn Marsack

What does it mean for a modern nation to have a poet laureate? What does it say about tradition, language, ambition? Or indeed, politics?

> In 1668, King Charles II gave John Dryden the official titles of Poet Laureate and Historiographer Royal in a formal Royal warrant.

> In some ways Dryden and his eighteenth century successors were 'spin doctors' in verse. Charles II created the post hoping that Dryden would act as advocate for him in the turbulent decades following his restoration to the throne in 1660.[1]

The Poet Laureate of the United Kingdom, appointed by the Queen on the prime minister's advice, can now use the post as she or he sees fit: 'Recent holders of the post have sought to champion the reading and writing of poetry as well as addressing whichever public issues have seemed of importance to them, not simply Royal events.'[2]

In Scotland's case, this is a new position. It began with the notion of paying homage to Scotland's most distinguished living poet, Edwin Morgan, who was given the title 'Scots Makar' in February 2004. It was conferred on him by the Scottish Parliament under First Minister Jack McConnell. The requirements were left fairly vague except for an urgent first request: a poem for the opening of the Scottish Parliament in October 2004. Morgan came through – despite age and illness – with a brilliant public poem that set a very high bar for anyone following, a poem that articulated the history, challenges and hopes for Scotland's newly devolved government in their controversial new building.[3] Very typically, it was about openness, energy, moving forward. It gave a sense of the confidence of the Scottish people, and the need for parliamentarians to live up to the restoration of self-determination. On the day of the opening it was read by Liz Lochhead, as Morgan was unable to manage a public performance. He rehearsed her, though, and she delivered it with great panache and conviction, providing one of the highlights of the day.

Morgan did not feel it was right to be both Poet Laureate of Glasgow – a position also created for him, in October 1999 – and Scots Makar, so resigned from the former post. The City Council asked Lochhead to be his successor, and Lord Provost Liz Cameron confirmed the new Poet Laureate at the opening of the city's book festival, Aye Write, in February 2005. Having a younger, more physically active laureate, the Council nevertheless had little notion of the best use to be made of the position, and Lochhead has expressed her frustration at this lack of clarity and definition.[4]

After Edwin Morgan's death in August 2010, the post of Scots Makar could perhaps have lapsed, but the Parliament decided to continue and to fund the post – or at least, through Creative Scotland, to give the Scots Makar an annual stipend of £10,000 and to pay the Scottish Poetry Library £2,000 annually for administrative support. A representative committee mulled over possible candidates and sent a list to the group of three first ministers – Alex Salmond, Jack McConnell and Henry McLeish – meeting to decide who should be offered the post. They also agreed that the position should be held for five years. The offer was made to and accepted by Liz Lochhead, and announced by Alex Salmond on 19 January 2011, at the National Library of Scotland:

> In creating the post of national poet, the communities of Scotland demonstrated the importance it places on the many aspects of culture which lie at the heart of our identity. As an author, translator, playwright, stage performer, broadcaster and grande dame of Scottish theatre, Ms Lochhead embodies everything a nation would want from its national poet.
>
> With a natural ability to reach all ages and touch both sexes through her writing, Ms Lochhead has also been immensely successful at championing the Scots language. She continues to reach out to school pupils through her work which is widely read in Scotland's schools and she is also a much valued role model, advocate and inspiration for women who are given a strong voice in her writing.

Lochhead said in her reply:

> I am as delighted as I am surprised by this enormous honour. I accept it on behalf of poetry itself, which is, and always has been, the core of our culture, and in grateful recognition of the truth that poetry – the reading of it, the writing of it, the saying it out loud, the learning of it off by heart – all of this matters deeply to ordinary Scottish people everywhere.[5]

So from the politicians, a fudged first sentence: the 'communities of Scotland' did not create the post, although the literary community through some strong organisational representation (particularly from the Association for Scottish Literary Studies) contributed to its making; and the almost meaningless 'many aspects of culture which lie at the heart of our identity'. Perhaps it was meant to indicate that poetry, playwriting and (unexpectedly) translation are at 'the heart' of Scottish identity, but this claim would need a lot of unpacking. More obvious aims emerge from the second paragraph of Salmond's statement: that the national poet (Morgan thought the title 'Scots Makar' very backward looking)[6] should champion the Scots language, provide work that can be used in the classroom, inspire the young and provide a voice for the marginalised – in this case, women.

Lochhead saved the occasion by bringing the honour back to the art, clearly and unequivocally, with a sense of its long heritage and its immediate presence for 'ordinary Scottish people'. This is where she can most powerfully use her position, and wants to: in speaking for the people, and in restoring a pleasure she increasingly feels has been lost in the grind of exam-led examination of poetry.

Thus, in the first year or so of holding the position, she has been assailed by requests to read and not a few to write. Her first official act was to open the Robert Burns Birthplace Museum in Alloway on 21 January, saying: 'His work is, was, and ever shall be, the greatest monument to him, but his life of passion, pleasure, poverty and contradiction will never fail to fascinate, infuriate, challenge and engage with us, whether we're young or old, scholar or ordinary enthusiast, Scot or citizen of somewhere else.' She has read at schools, where she has also been glad to encounter some inspired teachers of literature. She was a member of the Scottish Studies Working Group, exploring the role of Scottish language, history and literature in the curriculum. She has read at festivals from Plockton to Pitlochry, Colonsay to Dunfermline, and in England and Ireland. Festival organisers have especially relished the fact that the three current national laureates of Great Britain are women, and have programmed them together: Carol Ann Duffy (born in Scotland) was appointed the UK's Poet Laureate in 2009, and Gillian Clarke the National Poet of Wales in 2008. Lochhead worked on the new production of her *Educating Agnes* at the Lyceum,[7] and wrote a new play, in tribute to Morgan and his biographer James McGonigal, *Edwin Morgan's Dreams and Other Nightmares*, premièred at the Tron during the Glasgay! festival in 2011.[8]

Preceding the first commissions was an act of choosing, assembling a new collection of her work that would serve as the ideal source for her readings. *A Choosing* was published by Polygon in the summer of 2011 in a special edition for the Edinburgh International Book Festival, and subsequently in an edition featuring one of her own paintings on the cover. The first commission was for the opening of the fourth Parliament in 2011, and her poem paid homage to her predecessor, focusing on Morgan's call for the Parliament to be open-minded:

> Now 'Justice' is a fine and bonny word
> To engrave upon a mace
> As are 'Integrity' 'Compassion' and 'Wisdom' –
> Grand Concepts, qualities to grace
> Every last thinking person of our Parliament –
> But above all: Open-ness.[9]

The insistence in this poem that words were fine but meaningless if not acted upon was even more strongly and persuasively expressed in the poem commissioned for Commonwealth Observance Day on 12 March 2012. Lochhead delivered this at a service in Westminster Abbey, attended by the Queen, and alongside an international cast of performers including Canadian singer-songwriter Rufus Wainwright, Nigerian novelist Chimamanda Ngozi Adichie and South African musician Hugh Masakela. She was given 'Connecting Cultures' as her theme, and concluded the poem:

> *Commonwealth* means
> *A free association of independent member nations bound by*
> *Friendship, loyalty, the desire for*
> *Democracy, equality, freedom and peace.*
> Remembering how hard fellow feeling is to summon
> When Wealth is what we do not have in Common,
> May every individual
> And all the peoples in each nation
> Work and hope and
> Strive for true communication –
> Only by a shift and sharing is there any chance
> For the Welfare of all our people and Good Governance.
>
> Such words can sound like flagged-up slogans, true.
> What we merely say says nothing –
> All that matters is what we do.[10]

This ability of Lochhead to go to the heart of the matter is a very important part of her appeal as Scots Makar. She was asked to write a poem for the launch of a recruitment drive for the Children's Panel, the informal juvenile court in Scotland, and the result was a touching poem from a child's point of view:

> Trouble is not my middle name.

It is not what I am.
I was not born for this.
Trouble is not a place
though I am in it deeper than the deepest wood
and I'd get out of it (who wouldn't?) if I could [. . .][11]

The speaking voice, the performing voice, remains vital to her art. It is, nevertheless, deeply personal as well as 'official': there is an integrity here that engages people, and a patent generosity.

She was asked by the new Scottish Partnership for Palliative Care to say a few words at their launch, and the heartfelt way in which she spoke of her own husband's treatment, before his death of pancreatic cancer less than a year previously, attracted not only newspaper headlines but also a rush of emails and letters from people who deeply appreciated her speaking out. This was not a poem, but using the position of Makar to make a plea for – among other things – the right words to be delivered with care and dignity.

At the time of writing, her most recent published commission also looks back to her married life and loss, in a way that will touch a chord with many. Scottish Book Trust asked people to write about their favourite places, and Lochhead chose Glen Uig, where she and her husband, Tom Logan, have had a caravan for many years.[12] The description of the drive from Glasgow is a Scottish road poem, full of the lovely particulars this painter-poet is so keen to note: 'the slow, untidy flapping of the flight of the heron, / the oil-black cormorant's disappear-and-dive [. . .] the / amazing coconut smell of the gorse', recognising the ups and downs of marriage: 'all the bickering over the packing [. . .] becoming *our good mood* / the more miles we put / between our freed and weekend selves and Glasgow'. Articulating our difficulties and pains was not what the Parliament asked for, but they appointed someone who could glory in the yellow on the broom and the 'moonscape Rannoch Moor', and also speak out of the heart of loss, very directly, to her readers and listeners.

Thanks to Liz
Andrew Greig

I first met Liz Lochhead minutes before my first reading, at John Schofield's Poem '71 festival, attended by nearly a thousand people, headlined by MacCaig, Sorley MacLean, MacDiarmid, Edwin Morgan, Robert Garioch. Down among the leprechauns were people like myself, who had published three or four poems. Liz already had her *Memo for Spring* booklet out and thus was an old hand.

My first thought was that she looked nothing like the dark-haired, dreamy and slightly fey woman on the cover. She was loud, lively, direct, wide-awake and funny.

Waiting to go into the hall, I was white with nerves. I had never read my poems out loud to anyone, not my mother, girlfriend or dog. The scabby typed pages shook in my hand. Liz's response was 'Jist enjoy yerself, Andy. You're being paid to show off – it's easy! Enjoy it!'

I had never looked at it that way. I often still remind myself, and poets new to reading, of her words. Whether writing, hearing or delivering a poem, never lose sight of the understanding it is *enjoyable*. The combination of warmth, encouragement, humour and the rasp of the sardonic 'paid to show off', was and remains exactly her.

At the tail-end of the 1970s, Ron Butlin, Brian McCabe, myself and Liz called ourselves the Lost Poets (tongue in cheek, I think, some kind of referencing of the *Last Poets*), and decided to put on a series of poetry and music evenings at the Theatre Workshop in Stockbridge, Edinburgh. This was partly to have an outlet for our own work, and partly to have the opportunity to invite and hear some of our favourite writers.

We soon discovered she could be relied upon for two things. She would nearly always arrive at the last minute (and on some occasions, long after the last minute) in a whirlwind of distraction, apology, explanation, hilarity. And she always delivered. She delivered her poems, she delivered her inimitable self.

Eddie Morgan's 1992 translation of *Cyrano de Bergerac* was staggeringly good, and the Communicado production was joyous, lyrical, comic, tragic and moving. It was visual, it was verbal, it was everything theatre should be.

I came out of the Traverse and bumped into Liz. She, like me, was blown away. As a practitioner of full-length plays in Scots, she knew just how wonderful that script was.

'That was so good, the rest of us might as well just give up,' I said.

She stared at me, then laughed.

'It means we're all just going to have try harder!' she responded vehemently.

She was right, of course. What a wonderful response to something wondrous. To be lifted up by it. To have the bar set higher.

At Rory Watson's leaving do at Stirling University in the new century we came to honour and celebrate some forty years of his energising, honourable engagement with our literature. It was as always great to see Liz there. Though she moved awkwardly, in much discomfort, and was openly desolated by her husband Tom's death, she talked well and movingly.

As soon as we moved on to drinks, she seized my arm. 'Come and see some amazing paintings!' she said. 'You've got to see these, they're wonderful!'

And she took me through to the gallery, and we encountered the paintings one by one, and she talked with passion and joy and insight about what we looked at. I was reminded that she had been to art college, and of how her acute visual sensibility informs her plays and poetry. I was reminded of her gift of enthusiasm and pleasure at good work, the essential generosity of art, her own capacity to pass on human experience even at times of great difficulty.

I have seen Liz read and perform many, many times over forty years. She always connects. The poems connect. She wants to enjoy herself, and she wants the audience to enjoy themselves. She talks and reads from a position of assumed equality that is profoundly democratic.

I also love it that, however much she wants people to enjoy and respond to her poems, she never oversells them or cheapens them (the poems, and the audience). We enjoy her presence, her delivery, that warm gust of humanity, wit and perceptiveness, but it remains clear that the poems themselves are what counts. The ease and casualness of the delivery can obscure just how much craft and content is going on.

This handful of encounters now seems like teachings, little encouragements and nudges – the kind the Lost Poets received from their elders, and the kind we need from our peers and pals as we live the curious writing life, and try to add some more chuckie stones to the cairn of our culture's literature. Liz has added more than most, and as friend, peer, mentor, role model, she has influenced more of us than she probably imagines.

It is good to state here my appreciation, respect and affection for herself and her work.

On 'Something I'm Not'
Robert Crawford

All poets face a challenge in balancing within language the most private impulses and an awareness that words are a social medium. What I like about Liz Lochhead's best poems is the way they communicate such a wonderful ear for language at the same time as being able to reveal subtle and often shifting currents of thought and feeling at work under the surface. Her work has gusto and wit; but there is also sometimes a bleak wariness. Her poems and plays ask their audiences to listen very attentively; they reward this listening not just with entertainment, but with challenge. For Lochhead at her most intensely communicative, listening becomes a moral act.

To show this, I've chosen to focus on a single short piece. There are many Scottish poems about emigration and exile, but not nearly so many about immigration. Perhaps the most distinguished twentieth-century poem to deal with immigration into Scotland is Liz Lochhead's 'Something I'm Not'. Its distinction comes not least from the way it registers prejudice in the speaker's voice, at the same time as a degree of admiration and openness. If there is a mid-point between the casual racism articulated by the speaker near the start of Hugh MacDiarmid's *A Drunk Man Looks at the Thistle* and the enthusiastic welcoming of the other in Kathleen Jamie's 'The Queen of Sheba', then this is it:

Something I'm Not

familiar with, the tune
of their talking, comes tumbling before them
down the stairs which (oh I forgot) it was my turn
to do again this week.
My neighbour and my neighbour's child. I nod, we're not
on speaking terms exactly.

I don't know much about her. Her dinners smell
different. Her husband's a busdriver,
so I believe.
She carries home her groceries in Grandfare bags
though I've seen her once or twice around the corner
At Shastri's for spices and such.
(I always shop there – he's open till all hours
making good). How does she feel?
Her children grow up with foreign accents,
swearing in fluent Glaswegian. Her face
is sullen. Her coat is drab plaid, hides
but for a hint at the hem, her sari's
gold embroidered gorgeousness. She has
a jewel in her nostril.
The golden hands with the almond nails
that push the pram turn blue
in the city's cold climate.[13]

Lochhead's title announces irreducible difference. Yet the way the title flows into the first line qualifies that sense of absolutism, implying that familiarity might reduce it to something more manageable. In its use of the word 'tune' (rather than, say, 'noise' or 'sound') the first line of the poem also introduces a hint of potential attraction, even as the pronouns 'their' and 'them' maintain an honestly registered sense of difference. There's something odd in the use of the phrase 'comes tumbling before them / down the stairs'. It's as if the momentarily guilty speaker of the poem, who remembers having forgotten to clean those stairs, might have a subliminal guilt that this forgetfulness could cause an actual fall, rather than just some sort of falling out. The phrase 'not / on speaking terms' backs up this last possibility, though its primary meaning is to signal an uncertain engagement. This is a poem about neighbourliness, about 'My neighbour and my neighbour's child', but we have to wait until the fifth line to discover that, by which time the neighbours already seem at a distance. The speaker does nod to them but has revealed already that she herself (if we can assume a female speaker) has also fallen short of neighbourliness. In a poem that seems to be set in a traditional Glasgow tenement community, she has forgotten to take her turn in cleaning the common stairs.

Several Lochhead poems are about neighbourliness, its small successes and failures and the implications this can have on a much larger scale. The second verse paragraph of 'Something I'm Not' acknowledges that neighbourliness involves a measure of wariness and suspicion as well as curiosity and interaction:

> I don't know much about her. Her dinners smell
> different. Her husband's a busdriver,
> so I believe.

The line-break before the word 'different' is beautifully judged. The tiny pause makes the word 'different' apparently neutral, yet signals perhaps the withholding of a stronger, more judgmentally negative adjective, as if the speaker is almost but not quite overcoming an element of prejudice. 'So I believe' has a similar effect in the next line. This is a speaker balanced between interaction and wary distance, but intrigued and observant. On rereading, if not necessarily on first reading, there's a nicely balanced distinction between the immigrant to whom Glasgow accents are 'foreign' and who shops at the mass-market supermarket 'Grandfare', and the poem's speaker, who seems at home with 'fluent Glaswegian' and yet who 'always' shops at the local, spice-selling 'Shastri's' and admires that shop's owner's commitment to 'making good'. When this poem was first published (in Lochhead's first, 1972 collection where it had the cruder title 'Local Colour'), the name 'Shastri' in Scotland was likely to signal someone who was an immigrant. If the poem's speaker is not an immigrant, nevertheless it is she who uses Shastri's shop most; the immigrant neighbour goes there much less often.

This is a poem that centres around an encounter between two women. Again, this is (or was in the early 1970s) relatively unusual in Scottish poetry. Lochhead doesn't stress that point; more subtly, but also assertively, she takes it for granted. In such taking for granted, surely, lies some of her importance for poets of a younger generation for whom Lochhead has been to a greater or lesser degree either a role model or, at the very least, a telling example of writing from a perspective and with a subject matter whose centre of gravity lay in the day-to-day experience of women, as well as of men. Her writing this way was liberating, and not only for women. It encouraged and was part of a climate where such different poets as Carol Ann Duffy, Kathleen Jamie and Jackie Kay made their work; it also gave support to Scottish poets of older and younger generations, such as Edwin Morgan and David Kinloch, who wanted to explore gender, sexuality and otherness in their work. Several of my poems in *A Scottish Assembly* and *Masculinity* were part of that climate.

'How does she feel?' asks the poem's speaker in 'Something I'm Not'. Most immediately Lochhead's poem may be about a tentative interaction between a speaker whose implied gender is female and a mother and child, but beyond that the poem is about experiences being shared (but seldom in those days expressed in literature) by a whole society. In 'Something I'm Not' the question isn't addressed directly to the other woman. Instead, the speaker imagines the woman's situation simply from observation, rather than dialogue. Implied is the separation of first-generation immigrants from their children who grow up in the host community, taking on its 'foreign accents'. The woman's outer coat of 'drab plaid' reveals only a hint of what is seen as a much more exotic identity underneath: 'her sari's / gold embroidered gorgeousness.' The richness of such words as 'gold', 'jewel', 'golden' and 'almond nails' mark a contrast with 'the city's cold climate' which causes the woman's hands to 'turn blue' as she pushes her child in a pram. The richness is admired, it would seem, but the final suggestion, surely, is that this woman may be greeted with a coolness that is not merely meteorological. The poem acknowledges the difficulty felt by the native community and by the incomer. It is sympathetic and empathetic, but only to a degree. It hints at a willing-ness on the part of the speaker to understand, but also indicates an impulse to maintain a certain distance, and simply to observe with a minimum of direct interaction. It is this last aspect of the poem that gives it its peculiar honesty, stopping it becoming a sermon on what it means to be a good neighbour (though that remains implicitly present), and instead doing the harder work of registering an unsettling but profoundly human wariness. Such wariness may not be the most beguiling aspect of Scottish or other societies, but it certainly exists, and the exacting honesty of Lochhead's poem both registers and articulates it, while also capturing perhaps more appealing notes. This ability, not just to see and hear, but most of all to sound so subtly multiple aspects of a complex encounter is what makes this poem such a fine example of the work of an unflinching poet.

Lochhead's Radio Drama
Marilyn Imrie

I have been working with Liz Lochhead to bring adaptations of several of her key works for stage to radio for over thirty years now, and in that time I have also worked on two new plays written by her specifically for the medium.

Radio is the perfect medium for Liz's work because she is a poet first, last and all the time, and so her dialogue just sings out in its rhythm and its subtle nuances; her poetry is a delight spoken aloud; her dialogue in drama carries the same musicality. Radio adaptations of her stage plays all offer a closer, more intimate encounter with the characters and the text. We always get a very strong and positive appreciative response from listeners to all Liz's work on radio. The radio audience is formed from a wider age range than theatre audiences often are, and many students of her work respond very appreciatively to the opportunity to hear her work performed on radio. Both *Cuba* and *Dracula* were broadcast on the BBC World Service to reach an international audience.

The first of my new commissions from Liz for radio was 'Fancy You Minding That' in which a grandmother and her granddaughter share and reveal memories during a visit to Glasgow's restored Tenement House. The play was commissioned for BBC Radio Scotland in 1983. The second was *The Mortal Memories* for the Stanley Baxter Playhouse on BBC Radio 4. I knew Liz, like me, had from childhood admired the comic genius of Stanley Baxter, and I wanted to put the two of them together, both playing to their strengths. I suggested to Liz that a play where Stanley played both the male and female characters would celebrate his gift for doing this. And of course his comic timing, and her ability to write unfailingly funny, moving and true dialogue, together with her passion for the poetry of Burns, meant that we had a winning combination. The real collaboration on *Mortal Memories* happened, as it often does, in studio where we rehearsed and recorded the play. Liz was with us for the whole production, and Stanley and she discussed the characters, the dialogue and the intentions behind the writing of both, and then he began to shape the performances as she and I listened and supported that process.

I have also produced five of Liz's stage plays for radio. The process of bringing a new play from Liz for radio to life, and adapting a Lochhead stage play share the same challenges. Liz writes dialogue with an unfailingly accurate ear; so whether it originates on stage or in front of a microphone, the dialogue always works and it is Lochhead's essential and highly individual tool in the telling of her stories. The first challenge lies in editing the dialogue so that all the elements that communicate character, plot and humour are retained. The second challenge is finding and directing the cast to take on the roles Liz has created. Her voice is unmistakable and unique; the actors need to be able to understand, tune into and revel in the way in which Liz phrases a line, how she uses punctuation, and to interpret accurately and deftly the wonderfully vivid richness of the words she chooses with such care and relish. Among the actors with whom I have worked on Liz Lochhead plays who have achieved this triumphantly are Siobhan Redmond, John Kazek, Anne Scott Jones, Myra MacFadyen, Stanley Baxter and of course Liz herself, whose solo performance as Verena in *Quelques Fleurs* for Radio 4 was memorably moving and technically superb.

Liz is a writer of great precision and she is a perfectionist in her craft. She always wants to rewrite, reshape and enhance her writing for every new production of it; so each time we have taken a stage play of hers to radio, Liz has given me a new script that enhances the story and the dialogue for an audience who are listening rather than watching. I have never had to make significant changes to any of her plays for radio; they always work in both media, because she is a sublime wordsmith, and radio drama is all about words and the images they convey; Liz is always completely at home in that medium.

Latin for a Dark Room
Joe Ahearne

I met Liz in 1990 at a screenwriting course where we read each other's scripts and clicked. After she saw my first short film at the Edinburgh Film Festival in 1993, we began to discuss doing something together. Liz introduced me to the amazing architecture of the city and brought me to the camera obscura where *Latin for a Dark Room* occurred to her. She wanted to make a film constructed around images and their juxtaposition rather than dialogue. As a Hitchcock fan, that chimed with my interest in photographing people thinking, not talking. She was taken by the crowd-pleasing routine the camera obscura guide performed, capturing an unsuspecting figure outside – oblivious at being observed – from the projected screen by lifting a white card. That moment became a pivotal part of the story. She knew my love for suspense thrillers and I remember asking for sex and murder. I got both but not in the way I expected.

Liz settled on the character of Maria Short, who opened Edinburgh's original camera obscura on Calton Hill in 1835 and used her as a starting point for a tale of twisted romance. The location of Calton Hill overlooking Edinburgh presented great opportunities for voyeurism and visual poetry. The imposing, half-finished Acropolis, 'Edinburgh's Folly', was one of a number of key images echoed through the script, from the ancient Greek scene in the print made by her lover, representing her camera obscura or own 'private scientific folly', to the Greek goddess costume in which he photographs her. The opening incantatory lines of the film, in darkness, before our camera's eyes open, situate us in 'The Athens of the North'.

Liz took the central location of the camera obscura and developed it not just in a linear narrative sense – 'what kinds of story can we use this device for?' – but in a poetic and thematic sense – 'what kinds of seeing can we use this story for?' *Latin for a Dark Room* used photography, lenses, print-making, her camera lingered on eyes, glass eyes, grapes, soor plums. The belladonna poison she drips into her lover's eye for an examination, the poison she swirls into his tea. The pennies her lover wears on his eyes as a joke, to the pennies he throws to a prostitute, to the insult she receives from her husband: 'I'm making a richt penny-geggie o'masel' which she explains to her lover means 'spectacle', to the pennies he wears on his eyes after she murders him, like copper spectacles.

Her script was so visually dense, it was a dream to direct. There was no striving for effect as the action was already laden with possibilities. She had explored in her writing and selection of events how related and contrasting objects and ideas play off each another. One needed only to film the actions she described simply and clearly, uninflected. This is the opposite of common TV and film practice where it is incumbent upon the director to find a unique and distinctive way of filming two actors in a kitchen arguing about their relationship. Close-ups are often described as inserts – a detail to explain further a mundane action. The close-ups in Liz's design were never detail or explanatory, they were like her choice of words in a poem.

Liz's dialogue had a different quality from most character interchange I have encountered. I have never worked on a script where the concentration of ideas in the spoken word was so great, the sexual undercurrent so potent, even in the opening exposition of Maria's demonstration of the camera obscura: 'Passing through the locked treasure room of the pinhole, the images were cast the right way up by a concave mirror onto a white sheet.' The dialogue was full of puns and alive just with the musicality and joy of language.

Liz provided a number of central sequences in which the story unfolded entirely without words, like a silent movie. Love scenes are a nightmare for any director but she imagined one on the screen of the camera obscura itself, so that her camera could linger on the lovers' bodies which themselves became the screen for projected images of lovers and children walking outside. Our own voyeurism projected onto the scene itself. The final third of the film plays almost without dialogue as Maria uncovers her lover's betrayal. Nor is the betrayal a simple infidelity, but a richer confusion of how he sees her against how he sees other women.

Liz created opportunities for montage that rarely occur in more naturalistic scripts. The early sequence of Maria dislodging a glass eye during her lover's examination, which rolls along a shelf and drops onto her lover, staring from his crotch until he picks it up, flips it up and pretends to swallow it, is a sequence that can only be constructed and exist in the film space. It relies on a proper classical interrogation and manipulation of elements, not by filming an action from many angles and deciding later. The film was storyboarded and over 90 per cent of the camera decisions were made at that stage.

The cast came through Liz's contacts in the Scottish theatre and film world. The film was written with Siobhan Redmond in mind and the part of her lover was filled by Neil Pearson, her then co-star in BBC series *Between the Lines*. The film was technically ambitious as Liz had properly ignored any budget guidelines on length or production design. Instead of a ten-minute contemporary drama she wrote a twenty-five-minute period drama with a very complex central location. There is not enough light to film in a real camera obscura, so all the projected scenes had to be filmed and vertically projected in a studio set which we had no money to build. We were able to construct half the set and rotate the action for reverse shots.

I've not managed to learn how Liz wrote that script, otherwise I would have had a much more rewarding time as a writer/director in the years since. In all my other work, it is evident where I am fully engaged, which is never for the entire length of the story. There are sequences of concentrated imagery separated by the 'necessary' explanation. Only in *Latin for a Dark Room* was I able to work on a story where every scene and moment was working to maximum effect with no intermissions. Perhaps to write a script like that you need to be a poet.

[*Latin for a Dark Room* was broadcast on BBC Scotland on 4 January 1995, directed by Joe Ahearne, and performed by Siobhan Redmond and Neil Pearson]

With Theatre Babel
Graham McLaren

[speaking to Anne Varty,16 August 2012]
I have worked with Liz on the Greek dramas and for these plays in particular she brings linguistic fireworks to the theatre that I simply cannot find anywhere else. Her translation of *Medea* contains her best writing, her most complete writing for the stage, though some of *Thebans* is linguistically even better. Audiences have never experienced this before, even though they may have seen translations by better-known poets. Liz's poetic skills make the potential of her dialogue special for actors too: she is simply unrivalled by anyone living today.

I have a clear memory of getting the first draft of *Medea*. I'd spent about three months trying to persuade Liz to translate it; she insisted that there were plenty of speakable translations already available. But I was sure they all had something missing, and eventually, because she was a fan of the company I was running at the time (Theatre Babel), and we knew each other socially, she agreed to take it up and to write a scene. She wrote the scene, about twelve pages, in which Jason and Medea have a go at each other. What's published now is still that first draft; it didn't change at all. 'Is that the kind of thing?' she asked. 'It's brilliant, this argument, it's brilliant.' I remember printing it out on my little printer and thinking 'This is unbelievable.' About two, or maybe four, weeks later the whole thing came in. During that time we'd been talking on the phone, mid-week late-evening conversations, and agreed that Aigeus did need to be changed. It had always worried me that *Medea* goes into magic to provide the catalyst. We talked about what else could be the catalyst. Liz thought of the idea of the other woman, and I asked her what she would be like. 'Young, pert, sexy . . .' Liz replied. 'So what would she say to her?' I asked. 'I'll write that,' she said. And the Aigeus piece arrived, in bits, the next day.

Liz's linguistic talent was evident from the start. There's no punctuation in that text, for instance. My view of the gold standard for translations of the old Greeks used to be Ted Hughes's adaptation of *Oedipus*, produced by Peter Brook in the 1960s. That text is the gold standard because Hughes understood the pacing of the language. Liz understands that too. Her text has 'mouthfuls'. The gaps between phrases on the page represent the pacing; each phrase is an actor's mouthful. The rhythm is given to the actors and it just flows out of her. I always think of Liz's rhythm here as being like the sound of a bag of hammers falling down the stairs. Our first public reading of *Medea* was with drama students, in the Traverse Theatre, Edinburgh. There was one rather pompous fellow who remarked that it was fascinating that Liz had chosen to translate this into blank verse. I pointed out that it was not blank verse at all. Once you recognise her unique rhythm, hammers falling down the stairs, it frees the self from feeling that there's a strict metre, and then that liberates the actor. For these plays her job was a linguistic one; the dramaturgical structure was of course already there and there was no need to change something that was already good.

I talked with Liz about a new project. I wanted to do *The Mandrake/La Mandragola* by Machiavelli, or some weird, lesser-known Roman comedy. And she said a brilliant thing: 'I don't understand the in.' What she meant was, 'How is a modern audience going to see themselves reflected in this?' And she's good at telling me when 'it's rubbish, no one's going to get it'. So we settled on Molière [*Educating Agnes*], because when a horny old guy fancies a young girl and convinces himself that it's a good idea . . . the audience gets the in. In *Medea* the first scene is crucial, Jason fucking another woman. That's the start. We've played it all over the world, and everyone gets it.

We played *Medea* in Manchester on 11 September. We'd watched the planes come in during the day. We were young, all in our twenties, and we were debating what we should do. We were all very worried about the wife of the actor playing Jason; she was an air hostess and actually in New York at the time, and we hadn't been able to contact her. I said, 'I don't think we should go on tonight. The thought of doing something as trivial as a play today, it doesn't seem right.' Finlay Welsh, who was playing the King, insisted, 'This is the very night we *have* to go on.'

The audience did come, to our huge surprise. It was something about needing a sense of congregation. In the play there is a monologue, spoken by the guard, explaining how Glauke the Princess is burned alive. It takes the actor exactly nine minutes to deliver that speech. We all know the academic thing about catharsis, Aristotle's idea that catharsis allows us to see suffering through someone else's eyes, and to understand that man is not the measure of all things. I have been in search of this, and *Medea* is not a tragedy in the strict Aristotelian sense. That night something happened. We understood. We understood catharsis as if for the first time, during that speech. Liz's ability to describe a young girl burning alive, her language is so evocative, with words like 'shrivel', 'suck', 'strangling', 'blebbed and burning', 'melting'. There was not a breath in the auditorium for nine minutes. That is one of my all time favourite moments in the theatre.

I called Liz the next day to tell her. I felt I wanted to call people I knew and loved, to check in with them. As we talked on the phone I said, 'I think it's time for us to make another show about this. The Theban story.' A couple of weeks later Liz sent me the Chorus from *Thebans*, the speech that begins, 'Fear, that's the god that rules us now.' She is writing from the perspective of people waiting to be shelled, waiting for the bombs to fall out of the sky. *Medea* won accolades, but her best writing is in *Thebans*.

The 'in' was there: our helplessness. That gave a genuine sense of our potential for catharsis. I messed up in the production, we ran out of money and I did not do it justice at the end. There's some unfinished business between us in that. But her writing was never better. She brings great poetry to an already extant great play. Of course, she has written other plays, *Perfect Days* for example, where she shows her dramaturgical understanding of how to bring a play together. When the structure does the necessary then she just flies linguistically. I've not always had an easy working relationship with Liz. She is very demanding and wants instant brilliance from everyone. That is a challenge. But it's well worth the challenge. She often says to me, 'I don't think I'm going to bother writing another play.' She is a great dramatist, a world-class poet. Because her language ranges from Standard English to broad Scots, people don't engage with her poetry as much in the UK as they do in Europe. The Greek plays have been translated back into modern Greek. That's like selling sand to Arabs, it's the ultimate accolade.

CHAPTER TWO

Choices: Poems 1972–2011

Dorothy McMillan

Liz Lochhead's *A Choosing: Selected Poems* appeared in the autumn of 2011;[1] nearly forty years earlier when she was twenty-five, her first collection, *Memo for Spring*,[2] had won a Scottish Arts Council Book Award and had been well, if a little condescendingly received.[3] According to Alison (Ali) Smith, the title (an adaptation of the final poem in the volume, 'Memo to Myself for Spring') was chosen by the publisher, Gordon Wright, and Lochhead was not very fond of it, 'feeling it was too "pretty"'.[4] It is an irony that has pursued Lochhead that, combative, outspoken and innovative as she is, she has been in danger of having her teeth pulled by the very liking and admiration she has attracted. The Foreword to *A Choosing* is by Lochhead's friend Carol Ann Duffy, the current Poet Laureate. *Memo for Spring*, she says, 'blossomed out into the very male landscape of Scottish poetry and somehow managed to make that landscape female'. This is incontrovertible but worth repeating. Duffy remarks Lochhead's wit, her 'zeitgeisty energy', her feminist aesthetic, her liberating influence on a generation of women writers. She has become, she goes on, 'a National Treasure' as well as Scottish Makar, and although Lochhead modestly says that it is poetry not poets that should be garlanded, 'she *is* garlanded, justly so, and is well loved for her generous, life-enhancing poetry'.[5]

Who can argue with such generosity, such love? Yet, might not a poet also value the identification of something less comfortably accepted, something dangerous, something even unintelligible in their poems? It is discomfort with the potential slackness of the well-meaning that provoked Michael Schmidt in his STANZA lecture in 2006: 'Poetry's mere cheerleaders do the art more harm than good. They are in a way the real censors because they discourage engagement, shrouding the poem in good will.'[6] Carol Ann Duffy in paying a tribute to a fellow poet is not cheer-leading, but Liz Lochhead, and she is not alone in this respect, will in the end suffer if her whole audience, its withers unwrung, loves her uncritically. It is the curse of accessible art that it makes life too easy for the reader and, therefore, possibly for the writer. But it is the curse of difficulty that readers feel shut out, refused the key

that gets them into the club. In the Author's Note to *A Choosing* Lochhead
refuses to offer any key to her audience: 'I don't want to say anything about
the poems in this book except here they are.' She continues with an allusion
to 'Revelation', not the first poem that she wrote but the one she chose to
lead her first collection *Memo for Spring*:

> A boy in a school once said to me, 'See when you wrote that poem about the
> bull, what were you *really* trying to say?' – a question that both struck me dumb
> and made me sad for him; his teaching had made him feel that a poem was a
> coded way of saying something else. A tedious code, too, that he had to crack,
> and prove he'd cracked it in an essay, and pass an exam. 'Well, *that* really, was
> all I could, eventually manage.'[7]

Poor lad, but this is chastening too for a critic about to embark on a journey
from the beginning to the end of Lochhead's poetry. It is all very well to insist
that reading shouldn't be easy but be careful how you respond to its difficulty.
For it is part of the power of 'Revelation' that '*that* really' is not '*it*' really – in
some sense the boy is right to worry. The poem is a remarkable entrée and
it retains its mystery, its unspoken and unspeakable darkness. The poet as a
child sent to the farm for milk and eggs is allowed a glimpse of the black bull,
a 'monster', unreduced by his name, Bob. The immense darkness that the
bull is and represents is fearful and the pig-tailed girl flees from its threat to
her integrity and her purity: 'scared of the eggs shattering – / only my small
and shaking hand on the jug's rim / in case the milk should spill'.[8] But it is
a darkness that attracts, even compels the child and a darkness that neither
the poet nor the poem can do without. The distinct indistinctness, yet the
developing, enveloping clarity, of the 'Black Mass' of the bull, the unholy
sacrament invoked by these capitals, and the perfection, yet vulnerability of
the eggs and the milk, show us a young poet who goes as close to the tethered
'black devil' as she can, knowing that she needs the thrill and fear that prox-
imity to him provides. Yet to be subsumed by him is to lose the special, even
sacred, attributes of the eggs and milk.

Where does this half-knowing terror come from? Where did an unprivi-
leged lower-middle/upper-working-class girl from Scotland in the second
half of the 1960s go, when she discovered that her desire to write was more
powerful than her talent for art: where did she go for models for her writing?
On the one hand, Liz Lochhead attended the extra-mural class run by Philip
Hobsbaum and was encouraged, even 'discovered' by him; but she was never
so closely a disciple of Hobsbaum that she was pressured by his suspicion
of Modernism and foreign influence.[9] On the other hand, she was cautious
about embracing Scottishness and the vernacular uncritically because of the
overwhelming maleness of Scottish Modernism, insofar as it was dominated

by MacDiarmid. Yet Scottish writers, like Lochhead, seeking to engage with how people around them actually spoke, had to take account of MacDiarmid's practice and his undoubted stature.

Looking back on these early days, admittedly from nearly thirty years' distance in 1992, Lochhead refers to the 'implicit, incredible sexism' of *The Drunk Man Looks at the Thistle* and to MacDiarmid as the 'big black devil' she and others had to struggle with:

> Most of the young writers certainly in Glasgow that I knew at the time, we all agreed very much with MacDiarmid about the oppressive power of English English, but instead of being attracted towards the things that he had done I think at that time there was an enormous attraction towards American Poetry. You know it was all William Carlos Williams, Creeley and the breath, the voice – things that are actually there in MacDiarmid as well. But perhaps it was too close, you know, perhaps it was the devil that we knew in so many ways or the devil that we thought we knew. There was a feeling – once again, it's not MacDiarmid's fault at all – but there was a feeling that he was a kind of prison and, you know, such a giant oppressive figure – that the thing to do about it was to ignore it and do something quite different.[10]

In the light of these remarks, it is hard not to feel that 'Revelation', even as it offers a girl intimidated yet thrilled by the male oppressiveness of adult sexuality, also suggests the young writer's awareness of the danger and attraction of the male poetic traditions available to her.

But in truth, taking a good look at the dangerous darkness, even merely as a prelude to running away, is what serious poets must do, whatever their models. That 'big black devil' in one form or formlessness or another remains in Lochhead's work to be approached and fled from over and over again. It is there in the darker myths and fairy stories of *The Grimm Sisters*, in the monsters within and without *Dreaming Frankenstein*, in the 'fin-/de-siècle gloom' and 'slimy reptilian turds' of the Berlin aquarium in *Bagpipe Muzak* ('aquarium 1', 'aquarium 2').[11] The desire for the 'devil' is even there in the on-the-surface light-hearted 'Hell for Poets' from *The Colour of Black and White*, for the great poets are 'so delic- / iously dangerous to know'[12] and it's there too in the tortured flesh of the homage to Lys Hansen, 'Warpaint and Womanflesh',[13] for only by facing and representing the dark can the suppressed rages and terrors we live with be admitted.

But 'Revelation' is far from the whole story of *Memo for Spring*: it is a much more various, even miscellaneous collection than I have suggested so far. In its concluding poem, 'Memo to Myself for Spring', with its opening glance at *The Waste Land* ('April/April first you must fool me'),[14] the young poet celebrates the tantalising possibilities of life and art and concludes that she probably will be fooled into more experience, however painful, and more kinds and styles of art – new lipsticks and 'a new dress'. The poet fooled into exploring art's inexhaustible wares is, in this concluding poem, offering both a summation of the collection and a promise for the future.

Recently Liz Lochhead recalled some early reading that helps to explain the nature of these early poems and even her subsequent strategies. In 2011 Laureate Education announced a new project, 'Anthologise', which aims 'to encourage the wider reading, appreciation and enjoyment of poetry by pupils in schools'.[15] To that end school groups are asked to come together to create an anthology of poetry of their choice. The project is 'spearheaded' by Carol Ann Duffy, and Liz Lochhead as one of the project's judges of the products spoke about what anthologies had meant to her. It's worth quoting a good bit of this – it does the work of a number of interviews:

> My personal favourite anthology ever, though? I've just taken down from my shelves (and spent a whole afternoon reading, when I was supposed to be working!) *Voices, the First Book* and *Voices, the Third Book*, two anthologies edited by a man called Geoffrey Summerfield, who changed my life.
>
> These were books I found in the English Department cupboard in the comprehensive school I first taught in when I was twenty-three years old. (I bought copies for myself, though they were officially school books for teenagers and I was supposed to be grown up.) I was beginning to write things – I had been doing so since I was eighteen – and I was beginning to read, and read over again, poems I loved.
>
> So in *Voices* I recognised poems by Roger McGough, Philip Larkin, MacCaig, Morgan, Heaney, Hughes, Plath. Loved them all over again. But I did not know the poems by Denise Levertov, Carl Sandburg, Charles Causley, Robert Lowell, Tony Connor; nor, though I'd *heard of the poets*, of course, even read some of their work, *these* poems by Robert Frost, Gerard Manley Hopkins, *that* Blake, *this* D. H. Lawrence poem called 'A *Sane Revolution*' that proved poetry *can do* politics. There were some great new poems by Anon. (She's just the best ever. Always will be.)
>
> I don't think I'd have kept writing poems if I'd never come across this anthology. The one volume introduced me to small, perfect, Chinese poems translated by Arthur Waley and, on the other hand, to an American poet called John Logan and his long poem that is *nearly* prose, *almost* a story, a wonderful poem that starts 'It is the picnic with Ruth in the Spring [. . .]' This book taught me that I needed all these voices as I searched for my own. And it made me hungry to write.[16]

The praise of these anthologies is not excessive. I did not know them but I do now and am most grateful for the experience: any teenager, any pensioner, who has read all the poems in them will be pretty well educated. Their eclecticism is intelligent and seductive, and the poems are interspersed with black and white photographs, and reproductions of paintings, drawings and cartoons. *Voices 1* begins with 'Seven Anglo-Saxon Riddles', which is followed by two delightful pieces by May Swenson, riddles in a fashion, 'Was Worm' celebrating the transition from worm to butterfly, and 'By Morning' charting the transformations of a fall of snow. A little later traditional children's rhymes rub shoulders with translations of Roethke, Ch'èn Tsu-lung, Miroslav Holub; Denise Levertov's 'Melody Grundy' and Emily Dickinson's 'I'm Nobody! Who Are You?' are within a stone's throw of Edward Thomas and John Clare. In *Voices 2* two poems by Villon usher in Andrei Voznesensky's 'The Nose' and later two Leonard Cohen verses frame Lady Heguri, an anonymous Japanese poet and Robert Graves's 'Cat-Goddesses': every page turn is an adventure in surprising connections.[17]

Lochhead's devotion to these anthologies clarifies both her eclecticism and her desire to be understood. Her poetry is characterised by pieties and loyalties that she refuses to betray or relinquish, but at the same time, as 'Revelation' shows, she is aware that poets cannot merely accept what is comfortable. These anthologies, then, showed Lochhead how what is known and familiar, safe and loved, can be transformed by being put beside what is strange and new; and how the experimental can be made less rebarbative by juxtaposing it with the traditional. In *Memo for Spring* she begins what was to become the central practice of her art: she allows the popular to rub shoulders with the difficult, the challenging with the charming, in a manner that enhances both.

The anthologies also offer specific traditional kinds which Lochhead can appropriate and force to perform more radical tasks. Riddles, ancient and modern, are one such surprising kind: the popular cliché that femininity is itself a riddle can be seized and deconstructed. Poetic riddles provide ways of seeing things differently that revivify – reshaping clichés, 'putting new twists on old stories'. A good deal has been written about Lochhead's way with clichés: certainly Lochhead is peculiarly adept at exposing the lazy and prejudiced thinking that lurks in the cliché – and so she reveals how clichéd habits of speech and thought may offer consolation in a hostile world, then ruthlessly removes the props, or as in 'Phoenix' exposes the cliché's self-serving tricks – 'I'll think of burnt-out romances / as being my old flames'.[18]

The *Voices* anthologies, then, provided Lochhead with a precedent for taking what is known and familiar and putting in the danger. Composing and arranging her poems in this manner Lochhead exploits and revivifies what has become clichéd, on the one hand, and on the other, introduces the strange, the unexpected. The strategy is to seduce the readers before felling them with the outré, the shocking, a strategy which conditions the structure of *The Grimm Sisters* (1981) and *Dreaming Frankenstein* (1984), as well as shaping a number of individual poems within these collections, including the much quoted 'What The Pool Said, On Midsummer's Day'.[19]

Criticism of these collections has tended, however, to look rather for organising themes or issues. Discussion commonly clusters round Feminism or Being a Woman, Nationalism or Being a Scot. I took these as my own default discussion positions in 'The Ungentle Art of Clyping' in 1993.[20] But poets are getting rather fed up with these ways of characterising their work. Here is Kathleen Jamie, for example, trying to escape from the 'issues' that she admits have engaged her:

> In the past I've had to address 'issues' in my work, of gender and national and personal identity, just in order to clear space. 'Do you consider yourself a woman writer or a Scottish writer?' is a question I can no longer answer politely.[21]

Liz Lochhead is more equivocal about the shibboleths of feminism and nationalism. At the Edinburgh Book Festival in 2011 she delivered the already much quoted quip: 'Feminism's like hoovering: every five years you have to do it again.' And since she has been Scotland's Makar she can hardly ignore the question of the nation; with a new production of *Mary Queen of Scots Got Her Head Chopped Off* in 2011 she could hardly want to.[22] There is no doubt that if Lochhead's poems are read against a timeline of women's history, including women's fashion, and the history of the women's movement, they will show how deftly her eye for telling detail memorialises the best and the worst. From the Amami perms, kisscurls and Persianelle of 'The Grim Sisters'[23] to the ambiguous 'frank and free' 'crack' and 'strictly Sapphic' 'gals' of 'Song for a Dirty Diva'[24] Liz Lochhead has the times pinned down. And Scotland is equally traced through time, in language and incident, from 'the steel clang, the clash of creeds of 70s Motherwell' in 'On Midsummer Common'[25] to the spurious dawn of Glasgow's Year of Culture,[26] to the somewhat admonitory celebration of the opening of the Scottish Parliament in her first year as Makar.[27]

On national questions Lochhead is careful to avoid party politics, to say that she is not a member of the SNP, although she has recently come out for independence. She is not at all confined by national borders: at the beginning, in 'Memo for Spring', transatlantic political and social life inform her poetry. In 'Letter from New England' she admits her discomfort with being a spectator rather than a participant in 'rioting on a campus & / striking matches / for people burning draft cards';[28] years later *Five Berlin Poems* complement the local Glasgow poems of *Bagpipe Muzak*. Thus the defining events of the second half of the twentieth century inform both Lochhead's national and her personal poetry. And on gender questions, although Christopher White accuses her of essentialism in some of her poems,[29] generally she seems to me not to have turned her back on the desire expressed in 'Inner' in 1978 for 'an art that could somehow marry / the washed-up manmade / and the wholly natural'.[30] The tactful pun in 'manmade', along with the attention to rendering the natural in art suggests more complex concerns, more complicated intermingling of genders, of art and experience than can be subsumed under political banners. I want to try, therefore, not to make these 'issues' of gender and nation the default positions of my discussion, although I don't deny them as a constant in everything else I say.

Unignorable in any reading of Lochhead's work is the method of revisionary story-telling, a prominent characteristic of the middle period collections, *The Grimm Sisters* (1981) and *Dreaming Frankenstein* (1984). The method is consonant with the anthology strategies of challenge and surprise. Liz Lochhead gave a talk at the Scottish Poetry Library as part of the Scottish International Storytelling Festival 2011 on 'Retelling Myth'; no contemporary poet has more right to give such a talk – not even Carol Ann Duffy or Dilys Rose. For Lochhead was in the van of this practice. Of course, the manipulation of myth and legend is a technique as old as the hills or Shakespeare or the Augustans, or the Romantics, or the Victorians, or Hardy, or the oral and ballad tradition, although it was T. S. Eliot, I think, who made it seem avant-garde, part of a modern bag of tricks rather than a manifestation of atavistic longing. Yet that special kind of re-visioning of myth, legend, fairy story that we have come to take for granted from such popular versions as Roald Dahl's *Revolting Rhymes* (1982) to Carol Ann Duffy's *The World's Wife* (1999) was far from commonplace in 1981 when Lochhead published *The Grimm Sisters*.[31] H. D. had followed Helen of Troy into Egypt and Angela Carter's *The Bloody Chamber and Other Stories* came out in 1979,[32] but before Liz Lochhead only Anne Sexton in *Transformations* (1972)[33] had tried to do in poetry anything like the stories, monologues and tales that cluster under the subheadings of *The Grimm Sisters*: *The Storyteller Poems*, *The Beltane Bride* and *Hags and Maidens*.

Lochhead has always been fascinated by the nature of story and of storytellers. She understands and approves its function of clarifying and explaining the world, of making sense of what we experience. At the same time she is suspicious of any story that is too confident of its explanations, any version of the world that is too neat. For stories are both necessary and deceptive, comforting, yet potentially self-serving and duplicitous. As early as the first version of her play *Blood and Ice* in 1982 Lochhead has Mary Shelley put down her husband's celebrated aphorism: 'Oh yes, Shelley, I know "True love differs from gold and clay. To divide is not to take away . . ." I'm not sixteen years old any longer! I've learned to suspect any sentiment which rhymes that easily.'[34] In this suspicious attitude to story-telling Lochhead shares the wariness of one of the writers she most admires, Alice Munro. Alice Munro, like Emily Dickinson in her genre, always 'tells it slant': her short stories never follow a simple forward trajectory; she weaves in and out of different perspectives, moves backward and forward in time and seldom reaches a clear conclusion; the human truths she reveals are always caught out of the corner of the eye. Lochhead's poetry works in similar ways – she refuses the satisfactions of conclusion and solution, yet in her most serious story poems (which are often very funny) she never leaves without offering some kind of epiphany, even if she at once shrouds the light in doubts and hesitations.

'Storyteller' establishes the socially useful function of organising and enchanting, as the listeners wait for 'the ending we knew by heart',[35] but the poems that follow expose how often endings have been engineered to favour views of the world that endanger the vulnerable, who are often women – but not always, for the duplicitous tale-tellers may themselves be women, like 'The Mother' who sends 'a little child on a foolish errand in the forest / with a basket jammed full of goodies / and wolf-bait'[36] or the mother in 'My Rival's House' who prepares to fight her potential daughter-in-law with 'capped tooth, polished nail' and 'salt tears'.[37] These two poems are typical of the story-group's sophisticated deployment of the conventions of traditional story to examine complicated relationships between the generations, in which protective and destructive impulses are inextricably and upsettingly intertwined. Certainly, a number of the disentangled tales have female victims, but they are never passive – Mad Meg (Dulle Griet) in one of the ekphrastic poems that are seeded through Lochhead's work is a maddened embarrassing slut ('Harridan'),[38] the Bawd becomes a 'bad lot' to disguise her secret fearful self ('Bawd'),[39] the three witches hideously feast on the disgusting soup of their discarded lovers ('Last Supper').[40] Endings are sometimes brave or defiant but other poems close with a smell of fear ('Song of Solomon'),[41] a smile of rage ('Stooge Song'),[42] or as in 'Rapunzstiltskin' a satisfying ending is achieved only by self-destruction: 'I love you?' he came up with / as finally she tore herself in two',[43] although blessedly in 'Midsummer Night' there is a momentary conjunction of 'good and strange' – the sweet, earned consolation of pain and struggle.[44]

Dreaming Frankenstein develops the love/hate relationship with danger and darkness, introducing the more radical proposition that there is no safety in fleeing the monster because the monster, the creature of darkness, is within. The opening poem 'What The Pool Said, On Midsummer's Day' in a reversal of 'Revelation' figures the darkness in various sexual allusions as female, sucking in the fearfully desirous male. In 'An Abortion', often paired with 'Revelation', the poet obliquely compares a cow's refusal to abandon the deformed, dead foetus of her calf, to her own guilty and desperate creativity.[45] But the tale that provides the central metaphor for the darkness within is Mary Shelley's *Frankenstein*, the monstrous birth of which novel has spawned so many retellings in every possible medium. Among these Liz Lochhead's version can hold its head up as an imagining of female creativity itself, as simultaneously a monstrous and rational art: 'Dreaming Frankenstein' brilliantly invokes multiple legends, all converging on the monster who has found his way inside Shelley, so that in a cathartic and terrible struggle, she must rid herself of the darkness by transforming it into art: 'Eyes on those high peaks / in the reasonable sun of the morning, / she dressed in damped muslin and sat down to quill and ink / and icy paper.'[46] All three poems, without fuss, draw on a hinterland of allusion which provides a wider context for art and experience: 'garrulous banks, babbling' pull in Tennyson; the 'flash' of the 'kingfisher's flightpath' invokes Hopkins; the cow's 'Guernica of distress' calls on Picasso's great painting and the hideous event it commemorates; the love charms of 'Dreaming Frankenstein', the egg filled with salt, the 'seven swallowed apple pips', democratise the processes of art. These are all shorthand ways of extending the significance of short poems.

The collection has considerable range; and it remains faithful to those strategies of anthologising: miscellaneousness, surprising juxtaposition, familiarity and danger. Several poems cross the Atlantic: 'Fourth of July Fireworks', 'The Carnival Horses', 'Ontario October Going West', 'Near Qu'Appelle', 'In Alberta'. These evocations of over there allow investigation of love, distance, partings, reunions and farewells in a number of moving personal poems which are in turn supported by bittersweet recollections of childhood – 'In the Dreamschool', 'The Teachers', 'The Prize', 'The Offering'. The past offers no simple release from the claims of the now: a number of poems explore the icons and the shibboleths of the times – 'Legendary' a brilliant manipulation of fairy-tale and legend deals with the tragic union of Sylvia Plath and Ted Hughes, the haunting ballad-like verse more fitted to the purpose than anything else I have read on the famous pair.[47] In the final poem, 'Mirror's Song', the image in the mirror, an incoherent jumble of 'whalebone', 'lycra', 'Valium', 'Coty', 'Tangee' 'Greenham' and other junk, demands her own destruction: only once this prefabricated mess of tat and belief is smashed will a new woman give 'birth to herself'.[48]

Although *Bagpipe Muzak* comes seven years after *Dreaming Frankenstein*, seven years largely devoted to theatre (to both plays and reviews), structurally it is not all that different from the collections that preceded it: it follows the principle of the anthology, its miscellaneousness guaranteeing its freedom from ideological design, yet there is an overall coherence, signalled indeed by the paradoxes of its title, the zeugma of the familiar, the homely even, and the brashly new. The title and title poem are satiric but the overall tone of the collection is more complicated than this. 'Bagpipe Muzak' is, of course, an appropriation of Louis MacNeice's 'Bagpipe Music', which famously attacks what is spurious and anti-intellectual in the culture of its day. But both 'Bagpipe Music' and 'Bagpipe Muzak', like many satires, including others of Liz Lochhead, are more than half in love with the muddle of things that try to oust high culture. The bagpipe is both authentic and ersatz, embedded on the one hand in the real traditions of the country, yet on the other appropriated for sentimentalising versions of Scotland at weddings, funerals and so on. But what could be more real than weddings and funerals? And the notion of 'muzak' both vulgarises and vitalises the traditional. It is this mixed, impure quality of experience that the collection celebrates.

Like the revisionary poems of *Grimm Sisters* and *Dreaming Frankenstein* the poems of the last section of *Bagpipe Muzak* try to make sense of this mixed nature of experience: 'Papermaker' considers the beautiful and seemingly pure end-product of the rubbish that goes into the making of paper, emblematic of the 'mulch of memory',[49] the *Five Berlin Poems* chart different ways of trying to make sense of the mess of post-war Europe without falsification or sentimentality: in '5th April 1990' the poet asks what sense can be made of the souvenirs of the post-wall Berlin visit: 'three painted Polish Easter eggs, / Hungarian opera duets, Romanian symphonies, / an uncopyrighted East German Mickey Mouse / painted the wrong colours': the care taken with the detail of description is itself an answer to the question.[50]

That loving attention to detail is memorably caught in the poems in *The Colour of Black and White* (2003), a number of which pay tribute to the past of the poet's family, especially her aunties from whom she learned 'that everything was in the detail' as 'their mouths made rosebuds / to recall *rows of toty-wee covered buttons*'.[51] This seems charming, but as usual Lochhead's poems are not as nice as the delightful 'toty-wee covered buttons' make them sound – the darkness and the danger are not simply in the past, the story of Lochhead's poetry has not decided to have a straightforwardly happy ending. The aunties after all argue about the past, which, employing the metaphors of dressmaking, is of an undetermined colour, 'that might or might not have been / sprigged with tiny flowers'.

The need to revisit and memorialise the past is an imperative in *The Colour of Black and White* which Colin Nicholson characterises as including poems 'where personal and familial memories carry the rhythms of West of Scotland working-class experience into a form of social history'.[52] 'Your Aunties', 'Clothes' and 'Social History' all invoke the past, its particularity and its refusal to break down into mere ideograms of experience. To be rooted in a past is a blessing that is not available to the 'Unknown Citizen' of the opening poem or to 'The Man in the Comic Strip' who lives in an inescapable and often terrifying now.[53] The terrifying 'now' is crude and unnuanced – real things are never as we represent them: real things are not 'ideograms of roasted chickens / and iced buns like maidens' breasts' or red hearts for love. Real things are never the same twice and so it is unsurprising that the poetic practice of a middle-aged poet involves a revisionary return to what has mattered in the past – yes, Lochhead in her poetry as well as her drama does make new excursions, does go out on the tiles again, but there is a constant return to domestic duties and old loyalties.

Nevertheless, even those late poems that appear to come to some conclusion about the trajectory of her own writing turn out to be more complicated or more duplicitous than they seem at first. 'Kidspoem/Bairnsang' would appear to be a clear declaration of linguistic preferences with its juxtaposition of felt Scots and learned English, and its conclusion: 'the way it had to be said / was as if you were posh, grown-up, male, English and dead'.[54] But the poem comes after a lifetime of poems in a version of English and is placed among a number of poems in a kind of English that is far from dead. The poem is much quoted as if it represented Liz Lochhead's last word and real position on the use of English in her poetry: of course, the poem is making a polemical point and the drive towards the last line is seductive. But the poem is neither a manifesto nor a summing up; such a reading is limited and many poems in the collection confirm this. Certainly some of the equivalents are not that in any case – 'kid' in verse is not an English equivalent for 'bairn', an old word, rooted in oral and print tradition, a 'pixie' is not a 'bobble-hat' and so on. But this is the point. Liz Lochhead cannot *feel* what an English mother would have said to her child and so she cannot articulate it. Thus in the case of a poet, now middle-aged, for whom access to childhood is vital, if she is to understand what she has become, it cannot be accessed in a language that was not the feeling language of her early years. But her potential audience is larger than her family; she must, as she has done before, write in that 'dead' language and so she must, as she has done before, bring it to life. And so in *The Colour of Black and White* Lochhead's linguistic terrain remains mixed, if a little more sloped towards the Scots of her childhood, since it is that childhood that a number of the poems reach back to, but 'Kidspoem/Bairnsang' makes its readers understand just how difficult it has been to achieve the sense of ease that governs Lochhead's linguistic practices.

And after all the loving details, after the revisiting of the past, the praising and the reappraising, there is in some of these later poems the sense that marks Lochhead out in Paul Celan's terms as a real poet, the sense that there is something beyond words that poetry seeks but cannot quite reach: 'not to include the resistance of the incommunicable in the poem is not to write a poem at all'.[55] This sense, which is redemptive, not helpless, is there especially in the poems that strive to comprehend and celebrate the other arts, particularly the arts of the painter and sculptor, of George Wylie and Lys Hansen and Paul Cézanne. In all these poems the struggle with words is unending but the poet seeks also to understand what is beyond words, to understand the body and with the body as a painter must.

In 'The Beekeper' the poet risks her own body to achieve a connection with the natural world that is at once dangerous and loving:

I flip my net back
and go bare-armed on and out to them
wishing only to trust my own good husbandry
and do nothing
nothing but feel them
crawl and trawl the follicles, stamens
and pistils of my unpollened arms.

The poem looks back to the rather sinister bee poems of Sylvia Plath[56] but Lochhead movingly and courageously avoids the alienation of Plath's poems not by triumphing over the natural world but by becoming part of it. The poem is dedicated to Carol Ann Duffy and in this way looks forward to Duffy's 2011 collection, *The Bees*, in which the bee figures what is most precious, most endangered and most mysterious.[57]

I should like to end where I began, with *A Choosing*. Liz Lochhead says she called the 'selected poems' A and not *The Choosing* because 'another day, another year, I might have come out with a quite different selection' (and I hope she does – several times) but its title also invokes the poem 'The Choosing' from *Memo for Spring* in which the poet compares her choice of life with that of an equally clever girl from her earlier school days whom she sees pregnant and much-loved by her young husband, as the poet herself emerges alone from the library carrying books: 'I think of the prizes that were ours for the taking / and wonder when the choices got made / we don't remember making.' The poet's reflection is a little rueful, yet the unconsciousness of her choice makes it an inescapable destiny – she has to be a poet whether she likes it or not.

If you have to be a poet then that means you must respond even to the most unspeakable event of your life – for Liz Lochhead the death of her husband – as a poet. I will finish with Liz Lochhead's incomparable elegy for Tom Logan within the short compass of which so many of her characteristics as a poet are shown.[58] The poem is named for a drawing of persimmons by her husband and thus marries language and visual art in the permanence given to the persimmons in his drawing and her account of it; it pulls in and gently pushes out religious meaning as consolation in its refusal to call the persimmons 'sharon fruit'; in the same refusal of the 'rose of their other name' it lightly glances at the doomed lovers, Romeo and Juliet; it even has the effrontery to gesture to the dark in its allusion to 'strange fruit', before moving at last to the open-ended story played with in 'still life'. It is not the 'still life' of illusory hope for the 'still life' is of 'what's eaten and done with', after all, but drawing permits the operation of loving memory, the underpinning emotion of many of the later poems of Lochhead's career: 'now looking I can taste again'.

CHAPTER THREE

The Colour of Black and White and Scottish Identity

Laura Severin

he'd found that Gaelic words for colours
weren't colours as he thought he knew them.[1]

In her essay on postcolonialism and Scotland, '"Scotland, Whit Like?":
Coloured Voices in Historical Territories', Carla Rodriguez Gonzalez adopts
Cairns Craig's notion of Scottish difference as located in language, rather
than skin colour. As Craig claims, '[i]t is not by our colour, of course, that we
have stood to be recognised as incomplete within the British context, it is by
the colour of our vowels.'[2] Gonzalez warns, however, that past definitions of
Scottish identity have often ignored Scotland's entire spectrum of linguistic
colours, including those of women and people of colour. She argues that Liz
Lochhead's *Mary Queen of Scots Got Her Head Chopped Off*, with its 'use of
different registers, dialects and languages', is an important corrective to this
tendency, a reminder of 'the dangers caused by the transmission of essential-
ist assumptions from past to present'.[3] She points out that Lochhead was one
of the first female writers to argue for the 'inclusion of difference within the
national discourse'.[4] For Gonzalez and many others, Lochhead has served as a
key voice in complicating notions of Scottish identity.

Lochhead's 2003 collection of poetry, *The Colour of Black and White*,
continues this work, but the volume is less a critique and more a celebration
of the role that art, not only writing but also the visual arts and music, play
in 'colourising' Scotland, or pluralising its identity. The volume traces an
evolving Scotland from the anglicised black and white world of World War
Two and the postwar to a more vibrant, contemporary Scotland, transformed
by art. Illustrated with wood and linocuts by Willie Rodger that also link
past and present worlds, the volume looks forward, with joyous expectation,
to Scotland's post-devolution future. It marks a tonal change in Lochhead's
work, not as one reviewer remarks from 'sassy' to 'bitter-sweet', but rather
from ironic cynicism to measured optimism.[5] Influenced by historic events
such as the fall of the Berlin Wall and the opening of the Scottish Parliament,
Lochhead rejoices in *The Colour of Black and White* at the dawning of a new,

more vibrantly colourful century, the product, at least in part, of the radicalising power of art.

A number of the poems in *The Colour of Black and White* are reprinted from earlier volumes, *Bagpipe Muzak* (1991) and *Penguin Modern Poets* (1995), but the volume is nevertheless a new artistic product. What distinguishes it from those earlier volumes is Lochhead's re-visioning of past poems into a historic understanding of Scotland, developed and expanded upon by the addition of new poems. The volume is divided into eight groupings of poems, each with a frontispiece illustration by Rodger, which form distinct sections or 'chapters'. Unlike Lochhead's earlier volumes, which are thematically organised, these groupings are organised historically, and present a trajectory from a Scotland past to a Scotland present. But this history is one that encompasses the voices of many other nationalities and times, moving backward as often as forward. Hers is no simple, linear vision.

The first set provides an overview of the book in its mixture of poems from different time periods, some representing the rigidity of the past and others suggestive of the hope that art promises for the future. 'In the Black and White Era' is particularly significant in that it introduces the reader to Lochhead's interpretation of the 1950s. The poem suggests that the decade's black and white nature is the product of a mental landscape, characterised by dualism, rigid hierarchies and policed boundaries. Divided by class and custom, the characters in this narrative poem are suspicious and afraid of anyone who is different, or acts in unaccustomed ways.

'In the Black and White Era' tells the story of a tramp who tricks a middle-class family into letting him inside their home, so that he can rest and give his dog a drink. However, once it is figured out that he is not an old army buddy, but an intruder of the poor on the middle class, the woman of the family chastises him for interrupting:

> 'A fine time of night this is to come to folk's door –
> and here they're away on their holidays tomorrow too!
> You with your shaggydog stories of walking to Hamilton
> And needing a bowl of water for your dog.
> The doorstep wasn't good enough for you, was it?'[6]

Although the stranger is not menacing, he poses a threat in that he has insinuated his way into the house, across class boundaries, when he should have recognised his place and stayed outside.

His story is connected in the poem to the Hitchcock film *Lifeboat*, which the son of the family and his father were watching as the intruder knocked at the door. Released in the US in 1944, and considered war propaganda, the film depicts an 'us v. them' mentality, in which a German survivor, saved by a lifeboat of Allied civilians, eventually kills one of them and tries to turn them over to the Germans.[7] The film-narrative pairing connects the 'black and white era' not only to rigid class boundaries but to rigid national boundaries as well, the antithesis of the post-Berlin Wall world that Lochhead presents in later poems.

Nevertheless, the film performs a subversive function in that it portrays the German survivor as intelligent and resourceful. Finler points out that 'Lifeboat caused some controversy at the time it was released, since the Nazi came across as the most resourceful of the group.'[8] It is this aspect of the film, the beginning of the film, that is the poem's focus. The son of the family, who narrates the poem, states that he never sees the end of the film, because of the homeless man's intrusion, and therefore his experience of the film has been of its potentially subversive opening, and not of its nationalistic ending. Life, in the form of the homeless man, and art, in the form of the misviewed Hitchcock film, come together to set the son on a different trajectory. The poem ends with the son commenting that the film 'has never been repeated',[9] which suggests that he and his generation have moved away from the dualisms it presented. However, the poem lingers only for a moment in this future; largely it remains rooted in 'the black and white era', represented by the family's black and white television.

The volume's second set of poems, seemingly more personal, and less cultural in that they focus on the intimate details of Lochhead's childhood, also depict a history of Scotland during and after World War Two. In Lochhead's remembrances, this period is a bleak time that only can be recalled in the colours of black, white and grey. The weather is dark and dreary, as in 'Kidspoem/Bairnsang'. In 'The Metal Raw', the urban landscape is ugly, desolate and menacing, characterised by mud, corrugated iron, black cold fires and a black dog that threatens the narrator. Even the inhabitants of this world are colourless. In '1953', the men are associated with the exterior of their dwellings and the black dirt of their gardens, while the women stay inside, hidden by the white of their curtains. Here, there is no escape from the black, white and grey, even in pleasure. The single form of entertainment is the 'tiny grey T.V. screens',[10] which feature Cold War scenes and the threat of death from nuclear war.

In 'Kidspoem/Bairnsang', the child goes to school only to have her world of colours, represented by her 'navy-blue napp coat' and 'rid tartan hood',[11] transformed into the black and white world of the English. She recalls her day in Scots dialect but knows that it cannot remain a memory in that form. It must be translated:

Oh saying it was one thing
But when it came to writing it

in black and white
the way it had to be said
was as if you were posh, grown-up, male, English and dead.[12]

Here, outer landscapes of black and white become inner landscapes of
repression. Scotland in the 1940s and 1950s, as Lochhead represents it, is an
occupied nation – occupied by anglicised thought structures.

'Social History', another poem from this section, reveals that dualistic
gender categories were policed in much the same way as ethnic designations.
The poem is told from the point of view of a daughter relating her mother's
experiences during World War Two. The mother is proud that she remained
faithful to the narrator's father during the war, rejecting all proposals from
other soldiers visiting on leave. However, the narrator does not interpret her
mother's behaviour in the same way:

my mother never
had sex with anyone else
except my father, which was a source
of pride to her, being of her generation
as it would be a source
of shame to me, being of mine.[13]

Unlike her mother, the narrator feels the loss of love and pleasure, and is
angered by the behaviour exacted of women, but not men. That her mother
did not question these social roles is a disappointment, rather than a source of
pride, for the narrator. She notes, with a sense of regret, 'The sex my mother
could've had / but didn't / sounded fantastic [. . .].'[14] As part of a younger
generation, she cannot identify with her mother's sense of sacrifice and duty,
and its connection to traditional definitions of femininity.

In these poems of Lochhead's childhood, there are only a few vivid
colours, mostly remembrances of repressed feelings. One of the few colours
that occasionally flashes out is red, symbol of Scotland, but that too is often
muted. It is associated with the 'crude red (rid)'[15] gravel of the road leading
from a housing development, or the 'maroon' counterpane that characterises
the fading love of a marriage.[16] The only true red is the tartan hood that the
narrator wears in 'Kidspoem'. As a young person, the red of childhood feel-
ings has not yet been transformed by the black and white world of adulthood.

Another repressed colour language depicted in these poems is that of
women, who when they get together speak in a shared language, based on
colour. In 'Clothes', they recall their favourite dresses with a passion that is
lacking elsewhere:

Something had never been 'blue' but
saxe or *duck-egg* or a 'shade somewhere
between *peacock* and a *light royal*
almost an *electric blue* – but no as gaudy' [. . .][17]

In their language is a remembrance of joy and pleasure, and the melting of boundaries between individuals, who all share similar experiences. Like children, they have a place or territory 'outside'. It is so memorable that the daughter of 'Sorting Through' recalls these 'imagined' colours even after her mother dies and she must dispose of her mother's clothes.[18] But these colours rarely surface in the postwar poems. Mostly Lochhead depicts a world of black and white, bleached of life and vitality.

Willie Rodger's wood and linocuts, in black and white, underscore this postwar world. They are a reminder of the past, since the woodcut is one of the oldest forms of book illustration.[19] In the thick, almost crude, lines of Rodger's illustrations, people are defined by their social roles; it is their clothes and their posture that stand out, not their features. The baker in the poem by the same name is a stereotypical working-class man, hunched over and wearing a baker's apron.[20] In 'Social History', the three couples on the dance floor are distinguishable only by the pattern of the women's dresses.[21] But the illustrations can also be whimsical and therefore act as a reminder of the deconstructive potential of art, which leads to new ways of seeing. In this way, Rodger is able to make use of the 'association of linocuts with children's work'.[22] His sometimes fanciful characters, surrounded by blank, white space, might be anywhere; they are not limited by present realities. Thus, the illustrations for *The Colour of Black and White* both document history and look forward to new worlds, as do the poems. They serve as a reminder of the transformative potential of art, and its ability to move society in new directions. Their ancient craft is also a reminder of persistence, in this case the persistence of the Scottish art world.

As the volume progresses, the poems focus more and more frequently on the contributions of art in recreating society. Lochhead dedicates section VI to memories of the Scottish poet Edwin Morgan, an early voice of literary nationalism. Reprinted almost exactly from her earlier collection *Bagpipe Muzak* (1991), the poems take on a new meaning in the context of this volume. They trace a history of hope from the failed devolution referendum of 1979, referred to in Edwin Morgan's *Sonnets from Scotland*, to the successful referendum of 1997 and the opening of the Scottish Parliament in 1999. Lochhead's Morgan poems take place in Berlin, shortly after the fall of the Wall, on 9 November 1989. This historic event becomes a harbinger of hope and a sign of art's radical powers, represented through the graffiti that even now adorns the remains of the Wall. Given the odd coincidence between the

Wall's fall and Margaret Thatcher's fall, in the same month, this event acts as a transitional moment for the poet. The joy of the Berliners at regaining a unified Germany prefigures the Scottish road to renewed nationhood.

The first poem in the section, 'The 5th of April 1990', opens as the narrator returns from a poetry conference in Berlin, shortly after the Wall has fallen, and reminds the reader that art, in all its forms, has always been a breaker of boundaries. The narrator lists, somewhat facetiously, what she has gained from her journey – actual, material souvenirs, but also a historic understanding:

> Smithereens of history, the brittle confetti
> of chiselled-off graffiti,
> trickle on to the brave blue dogeared cover
> of my signed copy of *Sonnets of Scotland* [23]

This image, of Edwin Morgan's poems mixed with bits of the Berlin Wall, almost seems to suggest that his poems caused the Wall to fall. His rhythms of hope, written in response to the failed 1979 Scottish referendum, create an earthquake-like shock that radiates out, in the poet's mind, to other cultures. Though this image is a flight of fancy, Morgan's poems inspire the poet to document her historic moment just as he documented his. The poet concludes the poem with the lines, 'I think who could make sense of it? / Morgan could, yes Eddie could, he would. / And that makes me want to try.'[24] The poet identifies with those other writers of Morgan's collection, Gerard Manley Hopkins and de Quincey, who, rather accidentally, ended up being pulled into another place in history, in their case Glasgow, in hers, Berlin. Her poem, in turn, creates a chain of hope that starts with Morgan, continues with the fall of the Berlin Wall, and becomes a harbinger of what will come for Scotland – the successful referendum in 1997. As Morgan writes in 'A Golden Age', 'a strengthened seed outlives the hardest blasts'.[25]

'Almost Christmas at the Writers' House', the concluding poem of the section, again focuses on Morgan's ability to inspire change, here through the optimism he radiates to Scotland's next generation of poets. The poem portrays him as a forceful, directive figure who orders the other writers into their place in his photograph, recalling his *Instamatic Poems* (1972) and his photographic poetic techniques:

> Behind Morgan,
> Withers, Mulrine, McNaughtan, Lochhead
> well-clad, scarved and booted
> stamp and laugh
> (impatient for Gulaschsuppe and Berliner Weisse
> at the restaurant by Wannsee S. Bahnhof)

then breathe, stilled
as his shutter falls, stopped
by this one moment's
crystalline unbroken vision
of the dreaming order in the
purring electric heart of the house of our hosts.[26]

Though the younger poets are distracted by their anticipation of dinner, he makes them stop for a moment to take a photograph, and it is this photograph that captures his hopes for the new year – the 'dreaming order' that represents a new Scotland. Just as in 'The 5th of April 1990', the poet finds herself 'whirled [through] space' and time into the future.[27] She, and the other writers, become the continuation of Morgan's dream.

Robert Crawford's criticism of this set of poems, in *Bagpipe Muzak*, as 'an act of homage' that 'becomes too apologetically deferential', has some truth in that context.[28] But in this volume, Morgan is only one link in a chain of Scottish poetics that leads from him to Lochhead and then to the younger generation of Jackie Kay and Carol Ann Duffy, referenced so often in the volume. As Amy Houston argues, Morgan's purpose in *Sonnets from Scotland* is to 'actively celebrate the power of the imagination in establishing the past, current, and future identity of his country', and this becomes Lochhead's purpose as well.[29] In *The Colour of Black and White*, Lochhead becomes his co-conspirator, not his acolyte, in forging the chain of Scottish poetics and history.

Though the volume is most preoccupied with poetic legacy, and specifically the poetic legacy of Scotland, Lochhead also focuses on the power of the visual arts in shaping new worlds, particularly in section VII. 'The Journeyman Paul Cézanne on Mont Saint Victoire' celebrates Cézanne not as a painter but as a builder, a journeyman. His work does not just depict mountains, it makes mountains:

The cylinder, the cone, the sphere,
this mountain.
In the light of perfect logic
this mountain built of paint more permanent than stone:
constructed.[30]

Left alone on its own line, the word 'constructed' underscores the artist's powers of transformation. The poem concludes with the line that is reflective of the entire volume: 'Colour can move, can make, mountains.'[31] That is, the artist can reshape the reality that exists – move mountains – or start over, and create new realities – make mountains. With her focus on Cézanne, Lochhead pays homage to the Post-Impressionist influence on early twentieth-century

Scottish visual art.[32] Through this reference, she invokes the old connections between Scotland and France, instead of the wounds of the Scottish/English past. Cézanne, who paints mountains that recall Scottish landscape, with its own mountainous terrain, becomes a Scottish ally, a fellow traveller. As with *Sonnets from Scotland*, Lochhead pulls other artists from distant times and places into her history, suggesting that historic advancement is not a simple trajectory, but an intersection of the like-minded across centuries.

This power of art, Lochhead's collection claims, is largely responsible for changing Scotland, for breaking down the rigidities of the past and opening the nation to new possibilities, in which old distinctions of the past dissolve. The last section of the volume, section VIII, focuses largely on new-world poems. In this world of the future, the colours of black and white become not the symbols of division but actual colours in their own right – colours that no longer have the power to divide.

'Black and White Allsorts', dedicated to the Scottish poet Jackie Kay, documents this process. Born of a Highland mother and a Nigerian father, Kay, as a person and an artist, represents the coming together of black and white, and the triumph over rigid boundaries. The poem begins as a recitation of all the most beautiful black and white objects that the poet can envision:

> coconut, caviar, a wee pet lamb
> a jar of home-made blackcurrant jam
> spilt salt, wet tar, black ointment, the Broons
> a box of Black Magic and an old black-and-white
> on a Sunday afternoon
> a white dove
> a long black glove
> a scoosh of mousse, the full moon
> a soot crust, a snowball, a Lee's macaroon
> a meringue, a mascara, a dollop of Nivea
> talc on a black lino
> the (shuttered) dark
> a dropped domino
> a white angora bolero[33]

Suddenly, black and white are composed of many colours, from the greenish black of caviar to the purple-black of blackcurrant jam and from the cream colour of a lamb to the pure white of a snowball. All kinds of textures are mixed together, soft and hard, smooth and rough. The black and white images of this poem, with all their sensuality, no longer belong to the black and white world of the earlier poems, though they are intimately connected to earlier expressions of women's clothing language. This focus on variety and variation creates a kind of movement in the poem, as it begins by describing

static objects but then transitions to objects in motion: 'the (shuttered) dark /
a dropped domino / a white angora bolero'. The motion becomes increasingly
frenetic, moving from the clicking of a shutter to the sexual movement of a
bolero dance, in a play on the word 'bolero'.

The poem ends with even more frenetic movement as it focuses on an
image of black and white coming together, across the colour divide: 'two daft
dalmatians in the snow / in Kelvingro- / ve park'.[34] These dalmatians repre-
sent the power of the artist in her creative joy. They are 'daft', that is, refusing
to accept the white world of the snow. But their daftness is also brilliance.
They end up changing the reality of the park, through the breaking up of the
word 'Kelvingrove', so that it is seen anew. This point is further reinforced
by the illustration at the bottom of the page, wherein Rodger presents us
with a small, smiling dog, one of the most spectacular and enjoyable images
in the book. Given that dogs do not usually smile, he is obviously a fantastic
representation – in this case, perhaps of the artist, who invites the reader into
his world of reality remade. Lochhead thus pays homage to Kay, who almost
single-handedly 'coloured' Scotland, making her audience see the colours of
black and white in a new way.

This poem and others suggest that Scotland has changed from the drab rigid-
ity of the 1950s into a place transformed by new and more hopeful possibilities.
Another poem in this last section is 'Year 2K email epistle', which celebrates
the poet's friendship with Carol Ann Duffy and casts her daughter Ella as the
emblem of Scotland's future: '– While into each new moment, day, millenium
/ Your Ella skips'.[35] 'Year 2K' looks backward in the collection to another New
Year's poem, 'View of Scotland/A Love Poem', reprinted from *Bagpipe Muzak*.
Like the Berlin poems, it ties together the beginning of the 1990s, and the hope
they provided, with the turn of the century, and the opening of the Scottish
Parliament. It focuses on the generational change from Lochhead's mother to
Lochhead herself, and thus prefigures the movement forward from Duffy to
Duffy's daughter, Ella. In the process, it celebrates women, and women artists,
as makers of history, not mere passive recipients of history.

As 'View of Scotland/A Love Poem' opens, a woman and her mother, most
likely modelled after Lochhead and her mother, are getting ready to bring in
the New Year, one that marks new hope for Scotland. Gone are the tensions
between mother and daughter reflected in the earlier poems. The daughter
understands why the mother works so hard to prepare for Hogmanay, or the
New Year: 'If we're to even hope to prosper / this midnight must find us / how
we would like to be.'[36] The mother in this poem is a conservator of tradi-
tions – she represents a history of preparation that has led to this moment.
As in Lochhead's earlier poem, 'Storyteller', from *Grimm Sisters*, it is women
who provide cultural continuity, passing the nation's heritage to the next
generation: 'To tell the stories was her work.'[37]

While the mother represents the past, the daughter represents the future. She is focused on the calendar and the change it represents:

A new view of Scotland
with a dangling calendar
is propped under last year's,
ready to take its place.[38]

It is not clear what is coming in Lochhead's poem, but all await it with anticipation, sure of better times. The colour of the future is golden ('golden crusts on steak pies'),[39] no longer black and white. Just as Lochhead's own history merges with Scotland in early poems, so it does here too, with personal joy over a new love co-mingling with joy for the nation: 'And this is where we live / There is no time like the / present for a kiss.'[40] As Lochhead writes in 'Epithalamium', '[w]hen at our lover's feet our opened selves we've laid / We find ourselves, and all the world, remade.'[41] Personal and social histories intersect throughout the volume, suggesting that each prefigures the other.

The volume does not end on a New Year poem, though, but on Lochhead's exuberant, 'My Way', a parody of the Sinatra song, in which a seemingly feminine voice delights in her achievements of disruption. It recalls the performance poetry of *True Confessions*, as well as *Bagpipe Muzak*, and binds Lochhead's past to her present, to what Robert Crawford has described as her 'reliance on the orality of poetry', derived from 'older music hall and ballad traditions'.[42] The speaker's confidence, as in those past poems, is also drawn from traditions of African-American music, where the speaker's arrogance is a mechanism for inserting the marginal persona into the cultural mainstream.[43] She boasts that she has reconfigured love ('I did it to piss on his chips and put his gas at peep')[44] and society ('I did it to go out in a blaze of glory / I did it to make them listen to my side of the story').[45] There is nothing, apparently, that her poetry cannot achieve. Her poem resounds with the refrain of the Professor in *My Fair Lady* and claims the voice of male triumph for the female poet:

But I did it
I did it
I did it
Yes I did[46]

As in *My Fair Lady*, it is really a woman who has done the work. The poem and the collection ends with a Rodger woodcut of the male Sisyphus rolling his stone up the mountain, but it is the female poet who has done the heavy lifting. The poem represents not only Lochhead as an individual, but women artists as a group, who through their persistence and bravery, have forced society to change. Though the collection as a whole focuses on the general legacies of art and artists, here she chooses to end on women's voice and women's achievement in reconfiguring history through art.

It is fitting that *The Colour of Black and White* is an artistic collaboration between two artists, one a visual artist, the other a poet, since the book is really about collaboration in a larger sense. As a collection that so often celebrates the creative triumphs of others, it pays homage to art in all its forms. Together, the poems represent the way in which the world of art changes both the personal and the political. To the author, it brings freedom and love. To the world, it brings hope and creative possibilities. This is perhaps the most optimistic of all Lochhead's volumes in that it represents her vision of a transformed Scotland, colourful ('rid') once again. Leaving behind her white and black volumes of the past, *Dreaming Frankenstein* and *True Confessions*, Lochhead creates a volume that is both black and white, but, most importantly, red. The cover of *The Colour of Black and White* features Rodger's image of Adam and Eve, with Eve holding a bright red apple, symbol of women's transgression. Always the visual artist, Lochhead maps her career through colour. But like Morgan's *Sonnets from Scotland*, and the three-hundred-year-old attempt to restart the Scottish nation, still not yet over, her optimism is hard won. The collection is not without its notes of dissonance and darkness, which serve as reminders of historic complexity and the limits of poetic imagination. As Lochhead's Lucy says, in a play on one of Stevie Smith's most famous lines, 'I'd like to swim far out, not drown.'[47] Imagination is a consequential force, to be reckoned with, but Lochhead recognises that it is not all-powerful, and must interact with the forces of history.

CHAPTER FOUR

Liz Lochhead, Shakespeare and the Invention of Language

Nancy K. Gish

1.

Interview with Liz Lochhead and Margery Palmer McCulloch
[This interview is excerpted from a longer conversation, conducted on 20 April 2009 in Glasgow, with Scotland's new Makar, Liz Lochhead, and Margery Palmer McCulloch. The following chapter is indebted to their insights.]

NG: I'm interested in asking, before we see the play, about 'inventing a whole language' when you wrote *Mary Queen of Scots Got Her Head Chopped Off*.[1] Would you think it was possible to translate *Mary Queen of Scots*?
LL: Oh yeah.
NG: Into English? What would happen to it then?
LL: Oh, into English? No. Well, it is in English; it's English and Scots English,[2] but you could translate it into German with particular different German dialects, or Italian, definitely Italian. I think somebody has done something with it in Italian. But sure, you could translate it. I mean, you might lose some things. Probably English is the only one you couldn't really translate it into. I mean, you could do a straight Italian or a straight German version or a straight American.
NG: Oh, you could do American?
LL: Yeah, I mean there was a great American production once; they just used it as the language, just like they would do with Shakespeare, find out what the word means and say it. So someone would be saying something like 'oxter', you know, in American, why not? But English people couldn't do that really. But, no, there have been English productions and very good, but they tend to put on a Scots accent for the Scottish characters.
NG: Isn't it central to the play that those different voices are there?
LL: Oh yeah, yeah. But something would maybe get through. I mean, it may be a good enough story to get through at least partially in English. I mean, you could translate it, it would just lose all oomph, but, there's no need to

translate it for English people, because English people would understand every bit of it. Every single bit.

NG: Well, that interests me, because my thought, in advance, was that any Scot would know all of it, but that it would be harder for people from, say, south-east England, to follow it all.

LL: No, because it's said by actors who know what they're talking about, and because they know what they're talking about, you know, you would understand it. It'd be hard for them to read it. It would be hard from the page; it's written to be done out loud, so, you know, it's a bit hard for some of the actors as well [. . .] A poem is more difficult [. . .] I wouldn't probably have found [Hugh] MacDiarmid's poetry so difficult, if I'd been listening to him do them out loud. I'm sure I wouldn't have found them as difficult as I did on the page. It just didn't attract me.

You know, Scots is not a really discrete thing, not for a Scottish person. There are various different degrees of dialect and language. I'm furious whenever actors don't understand what they're saying. Even the right pronunciation doesn't matter; they've got to know what it is. They've got to occasionally teach people what something means, but the key to that is what the person wants. Mostly, in *Mary Queen of Scots*, I've got – it's the technique that I was reading about later, a technique of Shakespeare's that Ted Hughes writes about in that wonderful wacky book on Shakespeare that he's done. Do you remember it? Oh it's fascinating. It's about the triple god, the goddess of being. I think it's called *Shakespeare and the Goddess of Something Being*,[3] and it is quite a wacky take on it [. . .] But he was talking about Shakespeare's linguistic technique, which is, you know, he was the greatest one at that kind of stuff, and was literally inventing language. A lot of those words were new-coined. A lot of the words didn't catch on and have fallen out of use. None of us knows what this 'mobled queen' is, you know,[4] and all that. So he often, according to Hughes, wrote in Latinate for the people high up and Germanic Anglo-Saxon things for the groundlings. So you would get something like 'the multitudinous seas incarnadine / Making the green one red'. It's said twice, and, when I read that, I thought, 'I used that technique all the time in *Mary Queen of Scots*', just instinctively. I would write something like 'this old tod fox'; now nobody who was actually just writing in Scots would bother to translate it, you know. They would just call it a tod and expect you to know that was a fox, but I didn't expect people to know it was a fox, but I found it rhythmically quite interesting to say 'tod fox' or 'wud mad', which means the same thing. You know 'wud' is a word for 'mad,' and 'mad' is the English, but I used the Scots almost in an adjectival way in those cases. But, yes, I was aware that I wanted people to understand it, but they wouldn't necessarily be able to do a vocabulary test on it if they were taken out of context, but I think that's the same with a Shakespeare play. You know, if somebody said, 'What does x, y, zed mean?' I wouldn't know, but in context I do know. It's just like when my nephews come in and use a new bit of slang. I never have to ask them what it means. You know, the user of a language teaches you.

[Marjory McCulloch arrives and joins the conversation]

NG: My question – and I'm sort of reiterating a question I gave to Liz earlier, but I would be interested in both responses – is, not whether you were influenced by MacDiarmid or you liked him or used him directly but whether you think the development of Scottish use of Scots, even though it's moved more towards many dialects and using your own voices, could have happened if MacDiarmid hadn't made that incredible shift from the Kailyard School?

LL: I don't know. I just don't know. I don't have any theory about that. I tend to think it would have happened anyway, because I don't think that the people who went along in MacDiarmid's method in Scots really cut it, most of them.

MM: Well, I'm a MacDiarmid fan.

LL: I am now! I wasn't.

MM: I don't think this could have happened without MacDiarmid because I think what he did was so different. I mean, he really changed the whole way you could use Scots, and it was such a huge change that even although I think people did not always follow him, later on, I think he changed the whole way we looked at that language. It was no longer a language stuck in the kailyards; it was a modern language. And Edwin Muir wrote – I think it was an article on literature in Scotland, and he said the outstanding thing about MacDiarmid was that he uses Scots the way a Frenchman would use French or an Englishman would use English or anyone would use their main language. He used Scots in that way and, therefore, he just transformed what you could do.

LL: No, I'm sure you're right. I'm just meaning that personally, for, say, [Tom] Leonard or me, maybe the fact that he existed, you know, helped, but we didn't read him. Not early on, because [. . .] he wasn't taught in schools the way that Burns was taught in schools, and Burns was taught not as a contemporary but one of those strings to your bow [. . .] It's the lyrics that do it for me. But I think I like them because of my enjoyment of Burns's lyrical side. I enjoyed them in the same kind of lyrics. I mean it was the song, but, and this is not anything I'm proud of, but I was saying to Nancy that I didn't even read A Drunk Man Looks at the Thistle until the late 1980s.

MM: Well, I didn't read it till the early 1980s. I knew his name, but I didn't know anything about him, and I went away and bought John Manson and David Craig's Penguin Selected Poems and read A Drunk Man Looks at the Thistle and that was it. That's why I came into Scottish studies, and I've always loved MacDiarmid really.

NG: So do I. And also because of reading *Drunk Man*.

MM: I would love to do a book, sort of on the theme of Burns, MacDiarmid and beyond, kind of bards and radicals, and I would like to do Burns, MacDiarmid, Morgan, obviously. But, when I came into the modern period, what I would like to do then is to pick up your writing and Jackie Kay's after you, because it seems to me that all of you have this kind of 'bardic voice' in the sense that you speak out for the tribe, and you obviously do this very much with feminism as well as other things and women.

LL: Well, I think there's an element of that. I did feel, when I was looking at *Mary Queen*, because I was watching it again recently, because I was editing a film, whatever, and getting quite close to it. I did feel, and this may sound conceited, but I thought, 'This is in the tradition of something like the *Drunk Man Looks at the Thistle.*'

MM: Yes, it is.

LL: It is, though it's a play, and in a certain sense, a big bawdy poem. You know?

MM: It is a poem.

LL: And where with MacDiarmid and the *Drunk Man* you would get these different lyrics and the different bits, it's like that with these scenes that are quite different: different voices coming through and different registers and different [. . .] it was that patchwork element, and I had – I don't know if I had – no, I hadn't read the full *Drunk Man Looks at the Thistle* until after I'd worked on *Mary*. But when I was looking at it, I thought, I can see the connection between [them], a sort of confidence with the language.

MM: And the vitality of the language.

LL: You see, this is what MacDiarmid did too I think. He moved from Scots to English of course, even though he was insisting we should do it in Scots, but I think he gave people the confidence to say, 'We can use any language we want.' We don't need to copy the English, you know; we can use anything.

NG: Kathleen Jamie called it the 'Scots polyphony', and I think that's probably not just her term, but that is really what I see in your writing, more than almost anywhere else.

LL: I like that word. That's a nice word. But yeah, you know, I'm Scottish, and I speak Scots and English and I write in them all and I, I don't actually think 'I'll write this play in Scots, or this poem.' It's a voice that has to come out to write anything. I don't think of anything. People talk about a poem for the page. That means nothing to me. The page is only a score for the voice. I mean, I think it's for the page too, but I don't think of it as a page poem. I think that's just silences and spaces and that's what the page is to me.

NG: I want to ask one more question about the language in *Mary Queen of Scots* because you were saying you could translate it into German, and I could imagine it in American, and like Flannery O' Connor's characters. On the other hand, it is so steeped in a specific Scottish history that I wonder how that would carry over.

LL: I don't know; that's none of my business really. It's a good story. I mean, I could watch a German story. You know, I could go and watch a Wagner story and I don't know that mythology, but if it's a good story, it will get across [. . .] It wouldn't mean the same thing to people, but you know, it will mean something more basic.

NG: I wonder whether you have a sense that Scotland's oral tradition has always been here in the singing and the talking and so on, and whether that has been part of what has produced a 'confident voice'?

LL: Totally.

MM: I think that's a very important thing to say. It's a confident voice because I think that's what, at least to me, as a critic or scholar looking on, I think that's what in fact Scottish poets and Scottish writers have learned in the twentieth century: how to have a confident voice. Not to be trying to put on somebody else's voice or be apologetic about the voice you use, but actually to go ahead with your voice.

LL: It's just the sound. If a voice comes into being, you know, you go, 'Oh good!' And of course there are political or cultural annoyances about the lack of dominant culture squashing these things down, but you can't really do anything about that except keep singing your song.

2.

Liz Lochhead's play, *Mary Queen of Scots Got Her Head Chopped Off*, opens with an authorial direction, 'An eldritch tune on an auld fiddle, wild and sad'. For readers, this takes us immediately into another world with a single figure in 'cold spotlight': La Corbie, the crow/woman chorus speaking in a Scots both defamiliarised and accessible. Whether one recognises 'eldritch' or not, it is framed by 'wild and sad' and the 'ragged ambiguous creature' it accompanies. Audiences also hear it at the end of scene five: Bessie, Mary's lady-in-waiting, says it when Mary asks if Bothwell is a warlock because 'he frichtens me.' 'Ah dinna think', Bessie responds, 'there is anythin eldritch or extraordinar in tha [. . .]'[5] We need not know a dictionary definition of 'eldritch': the context reveals it. In Lochhead's words, 'the user of the language teaches you'.[6] And La Corbie, once revealed and musically framed, 'teaches' us language distinctly Scottish, whether we catch every word or not. Scots words evoke place, weather, culture, history. In context, with framing, new lexical combinations, and play with sound, rhythm and multiple meaning, they reach a broad audience.

This linguistic diversity includes English as well as Scots vocabulary, and, though Scots speakers will all understand the English, the reverse is not the case. As Anne Varty notes in her account of the play's early productions, the initial Communicado performance in both Scotland and England, and the Contact performance in Manchester, evoked the 'universal cry that the language of the play was difficult for English ears to understand'.[7] 'Lochhead,' she added, 'had anticipated such criticism in 1987: "This can't be made into Mary Queen of Surbiton. If people can't hear what's being said, I suggest that they're not listening."'[8] As she points out in our interview, words that may be difficult on the page are understood when spoken in dramatic context. Few speakers of English could pass a vocabulary test on Shakespeare, yet they understand all or nearly all at performances; so too with Scots. What some see as 'difficulty' is better understood as invention and renewal of confidence in Scots writing.

Combining the familiar and, for non-Scots and some Scots, unfamiliar, La Corbie describes herself in words that estrange, shimmer, create an uncanny identity both harsh and compelling, and play with wit in its early sense of acumen or mental quickness:

> How me? Eh? Eh? Eh? Voice like a choked laugh. Ragbag o a burd in my black duds, aw angles and elbows and broken oxter feathers, black beady een in my executioner's hood. No braw, but Ah think Ah hae a sort of black glamour.[9]

This opening monologue demonstrates what Lochhead calls 'inventing language'. Other than easily recognised cognates with different spelling and pronunciation, like 'burd', 'aw', 'een', 'ma' and 'hae' ('bird', 'all', 'eyes', 'my', 'have'), only three words are specifically Scots: 'oxter' (the underpart of the upper arm; armpit) 'braw' (English 'brave' but with more and different meanings, including 'handsome', 'worthy', 'fine',' of fine physique', 'splendid', 'gaily dressed') and 'glamour' (retaining in Scots its early meaning of 'enchantment',' witchcraft', 'magic'). Both readers and audience are thus plunged into a rich, many-layered language, knowable in varying levels. For all, it carries the overarching presence of the weird, ambiguous bird/woman chorus whose sounds and rhythms amplify her strangeness, with the gleam of beady eyes and iridescent feathers linked by sound with 'burd', 'braw' and 'black'.

Like La Corbie's opening monologue, the play as a whole mixes many forms of Scots; it incorporates English as well as words and lines in French and Italian, archaic words and innovative combinations that twist or intensify seemingly familiar terms like 'glamour'. Like Hugh MacDiarmid, Lochhead aims for a language available for all modern purposes and draws on whatever Scots words will work. Unlike MacDiarmid's conception of a return to one national language, hers is linguistic play across the vast range now present in a country with three languages,[10] one of which is Scots English in varying degrees of mixed vocabulary and accent. Like Shakespeare's English, contemporary Scots is not codified; lexicon and, to a lesser extent, grammar and syntax provide meanings not available in any single form. It has often been noted that Lochhead uses an extensive range of registers, styles, levels of diction and markers of identity.[11] When Lochhead was named Scotland's Makar, Joyce McMillan in the *Guardian Books Blog* said 'She uses poetry, and the fluid energy of a changing language, to shape new theatrical worlds in a way that seems almost Shakespearean.'[12] It seems so because it is – Shakespearean, not 'almost'; her many voices are available because of the currently vast range of her resources and her ability to hear and create the full possibilities of those resources.

While Scots and English share most words despite differences in accent and rhythm, a great many words only in Scots or of different meanings in Scots retain an immediacy, physicality and differentiation less available in modern English, for which meanings have, to a much greater extent, been established or limited in usage. Scots writers thus have a lexicon allowing for radical experimentation at the level of the word. This was a key claim of MacDiarmid, who called *Jamieson's Dictionary* 'an inexhaustible quarry of subtle and significant sound'[13] and took words directly from it for their sounds and specific cultural references. He thus opened up the language to a long period of poetic development. Although the methods have changed, the sense that Scots can be used in any way authors choose derives in large part from that rejection of English as the only medium for serious literature.

In *Mary Queen of Scots* Lochhead uses that lexical potential to create her many styles and registers. 'Oxter', for example, is both the armpit and the upper inside of the arm or 'the corresponding part of an animal'.[14] Unlike any English equivalent, it points to La Corbie's ragged wings in a way 'armpit' could not. The combination of 'braw' and 'glamour' is, for English speakers, unusual and slightly unnerving, since 'braw' as 'brave' immediately evokes its primary meaning of courageous or perhaps making a fine show, while in English 'glamour' is almost exclusively linked to romantic attractiveness and elegance. For Scots speakers, La Corbie has already denied attractiveness when she says 'no braw', and the retained sense of magic or witchcraft remains, bringing all these mixed and contradictory meanings to the surface.

Lochhead thus uses common, uncommon and foreign words to evoke a particular world embracing centuries of Scottish and English history, culture and attitudes. The lines following La Corbie's monologue frame this world in images: the famous Scottish painting of 'The Skating Minister', the crude and harsh nest of the crow, and the crow as Anglo-Saxon beast of battle. La Corbie's words in context demonstrate what Lochhead calls an 'invented' and 'theatrical'[15] language for Scotland both in the sixteenth century and now.

What does it mean to invent a language? In Lochhead's words, for me it's always about inventing a whole language [. . .] you start a new play, or a new poem, it's just this new world that you've got to find. But for some people they just have to find the world and the language is already there. I didn't feel that.[16]

No language, in fact, could be already there for the world of *Mary Queen of Scots*, with its multiple registers of Scots and English and its speakers in many languages across centuries: nor could any one language approach the richness of this mix. 'Inventing a whole language', Lochhead realises she also 'instinctively' uses a Shakespearean technique in saying something twice, in Scots and then in English, as in 'tod fox'. But the similarities go far beyond doubling words: Lochhead uses a broad range of other linguistic techniques that parallel Shakespeare's 'inventions': her lexical experimentation often creates similar effects, most fully in *Mary Queen of Scots*.

In *The Stories of English*, David Crystal notes, 'It is only to be expected that an age when linguistic resources are increasing so much in richness would be immensely stimulating to creative writers.'[17] Describing Shakespeare's use of this language in the Introduction to the Arden Shakespeare's *Complete Works*, the editors point to its range and flexibility: 'The fluidity of English in the late sixteenth century was a gift to a linguistically inventive generation of writers. Shakespeare did as much as any to exploit and extend the wide range of literary styles and linguistic registers available to him. His characters speak in all styles.'[18] Today, the increasing use in poetry of many versions of Scots has produced what Derrick McClure calls an 'efflorescence of Scots as a poetic medium',[19] including many different vernacular forms, such as Janet Paisley's 'contemporary urban colloquial',[20] the transcribed Glaswegian of Tom Leonard, or the north-east Doric of Sheena Blackhall. The many dialects of Scots joined with English allow for a similar wide range of literary styles. Liz Lochhead's many voices – her great store of registers, idioms, dialects, diction and mixtures of colloquial, clichéd, formal, pompous, or vulgar – draw on the still fluid and uncodified forms of Scots and Scots English. In *Mary Queen of Scots* she moves beyond her earlier work to create a distinctive, experimental mixture capable of finding a 'new world'.

Though now consistently labelled a classic, the play remains radically innovative and modern in both Modernist and contemporary senses. For despite Lochhead's early sense of reacting against MacDiarmid's difficult and dense Modernism, it is, as she also acknowledges, in the tradition of *A Drunk Man Looks at the Thistle*, not only in what she calls its 'patchwork' of styles and scenes but in language that probably could not have developed had not the Scottish Renaissance occurred. Yet unlike MacDiarmid's 'synthetic Scots', Lochhead's mix of many Scots and English dialects and her focus on local vernaculars and spoken voice place her 1987 play in a very current linguistic environment of differentiation, polyglottery and new forms of wordplay not framed by the twentieth-century conflict over Scots and English.[21] For Lochhead, as for many younger Scottish writers, that conflict is either obsolete or irrelevant: they write in their own local voices or use any available voice. Lochhead deploys differentiation and interconnection between and within English and Scots to articulate the long, complicated relationship of the two countries. Her solution to the once-perceived dilemma of writing in Scots or in English is neither medieval nor contemporary; if it is to be defined by period, it is more like the 'changing language' of the Renaissance.

Like Shakespeare, Lochhead invents by finding, using, combining and contrasting all her available lexical sources for a story both particular and – 'mair or less' – translatable. Two great political women wanting both to rule and to love, and at odds with each other, is itself a powerful tale. In other languages, 'something would get through'. The particulars of Scotland's linguistic and cultural history embedded in the language itself as well as allusions, ballads, actual historic figures and events could be recreated only in part. For the play is also, in Lochhead's words, 'a big, bawdy poem' structured in many varied scenes and from many perspectives. And the poetry is inseparable from the interplay of languages. It may seem ironic that Lochhead says English is the only language into which it could not be translated, but much of it is, of course, already English or easily recognisable cognates. When asked why she used such a mixture of languages, Lochhead replied, 'It's about Scotland and England, so, obviously [. . .] Everybody in Scotland at that time, even the nobles, spoke Scots.'[22] The use of both along with their shared vocabulary takes identity beyond gender, class and nationality to the difficult relations of England and Scotland and their two queens. To a large extent, it is through the interaction of Scots, Scots-accented English and Standard English that Lochhead 'invents' a language for the whole world of the play.

Although, in 'Think on My Words': Exploring Shakespeare's Language, David Crystal calls the belief in Shakespeare's 'invention' of language a myth, what he means by this is the claim that Shakespeare created thousands of new words; Lochhead's 'invention', however, is not coining words but what Crystal calls 'introducing a word to the language'.[23] What she often does, in fact, is reintroduce words and/or use them in strikingly new ways so, in the words of the Guardian reviewer, they 'glitter and smoke on the page'.[24] Unlike English and American modernisms, focused on breaking syntax to alter and twist standardised, conventional words, Scottish modernism focused predominantly on words themselves, the immense lexicon MacDiarmid found in the storehouse of Jamieson's Etymological Dictionary of the Scottish Language and combined into haunting lyrics. This lexical experimentation takes many new forms in Lochhead because she incorporates contemporary usage of nonliterary and even nonstandard spoken Scots.

Crystal identifies a series of ways Shakespeare used words, of which coining is only one. In addition to creating words, he used afresh many already available, including 'easy words', 'difficult words', 'false friends', 'old' and 'new' words, 'clusters', 'repetitions' and 'collocations'. Lochhead employs the same or parallel techniques, significant linguistic strategies because they demonstrate the great potential for using Scotland's distinctive mix of language, particularly in drama where voice and gesture aid in 'teaching' the audience meanings. According to Crystal, only relatively few words in Shakespeare are 'difficult' in the sense that, like 'mobled', they are no longer in use. Similarly, in Lochhead, only a limited number of words are 'difficult' in the sense that they do not exist in English.

Using Crystal's categories for *Mary Queen of Scots*, 'difficult' words would be those few that English speakers could not define out of context, such as 'eldritch', 'kittocky', 'oxter'. 'Easy words' are variant spellings and pronunciation needing little context, such as 'twa', 'ony', 'stane', 'aulder' ('two', 'any', 'stone', 'older'). False friends are words that exist in both languages but with different meanings, such as 'glamour' or 'greet' ('weep'). 'Old words' appear in both languages, such as 'poltroon' and 'knave' in English or 'lusome' ('lovable') and 'put to the horn' ('to outlaw') in Scots. Words in French and Italian (in scenes with the suitors or with Riccio) also turn up, sometimes also 'old', as in 'junket' ('a cream dish; a delicacy') from Old Northern French. By 'collocation' in Shakespeare, Crystal means a series of coinages creating a densely difficult passage; a passage with a string of 'difficult' Scots words creates similar obscurity, though, even here, context and action clarify. Repetitions – the use of two words together denoting the same thing in both languages, as in 'tod fox' or 'wud mad' – appear in many places, as in 'kittocky kitlin-cat' (a kitten-cat or cat-cat of loose morals) and a series of words for a woman of bad character that mixes English and Scots, like Bothwell's description of Alison Craik as a 'tail, brass nail, hure (whore), daw (slattern), penny-jo (penny-lover)'.

Lochhead's Scottish characters also employ Scots grammar and syntax such as '-it' rather than '-ed', as in 'forcit' and 'commandit'; omission of 'g' in the present participle, as in 'chitterin' or 'slaiverin'; elision such as 'o' rather than 'of' or 'a' rather than 'all'; compounded words such as 'shouldnae', 'canna', or 'isnae'; or the use of 'no' rather than 'not,' as in 'she better no', or 'do I no put ye in mind'. Syntactical patterns like 'Whit like is it?' or 'Here's mines' appear, especially in La Corbie's lines. Though none of these variations in pattern prevents understanding, they assert identity and shift rhythm and tone to distinguish characters as well as nationality. Elizabeth, for example, does not use them, nor does Marian or Darnley. That is, the play is in both languages and varying degrees of each: Elizabeth says 'forced'; Knox says 'forcit'. Elizabeth says 'We do not'; Mary says 'Ah dinna'. Interestingly,

Knox, whose speech – as Margery Palmer McCulloch points out in her
'Scotnotes' – is 'very anglified', retains Scots grammar, as in 'commandit',
'corruptit', 'o', 'fechtin', 'glisterin'. Moreover, he slips into Scots when con-
fronted by Leezie and Mairn and drops the elevated tone of his exchanges
with Mary or Bothwell for coarse, sexual terms, revealing a mean character
beneath his religiosity.

That the play could not be translated into English is thus in part because
much of it already is, and nearly all is comprehensible on stage. Yet it is often
the 'difficult words', 'false friends,' 'old words' and 'foreign' words that give
the play its 'glitter and smoke'. These are the words that, like 'eldritch' and
'glamour', demand attention, startle us into awareness, or complicate easy
assumptions about the story. The contrast of what Lochhead calls Elizabeth's
'almost parodic version of slightly antique (think forties black-and-white
films), very patrician RP' and Mary's 'totally fluently' spoken Braid Scots
'with a French accent'[25] frames the many conflicts of nationality, power,
religion and culture, but it is in the Scots that we are more consistently chal-
lenged to reimagine language. A key example can be made by comparing
the two sections of scene five, 'Repressed Loves', divided into a section with
Elizabeth and Marian speaking in English and another with Mary, Bothwell
and Bessie in Scots. La Corbie is, as always, hovering in both. In the first she
speaks only an opening four-line comment; in the second she remarks on the
dialogue throughout. The scene is revealing because the frequent point about
Lochhead's many registers applies to both languages: in 'Repressed Loves
(The First)', Elizabeth's English, emotionally charged because of her anguish
over Leicester, varies from childlike dream-memory, to royal assertiveness in
formal syntax and diction, to colloquial and even crude words like 'bloody'
and 'piss', to the poignant echo of Biblical phrasing and poetic rhythm in
her weeping collapse: 'What shall it profit a woman if she can rule a whole
kingdom but cannot quell her own rebellious heart?'[26]

In 'Repressed Loves (The Second)'; all the characters speak Scots: Mary,
Bothwell, Bessie, La Corbie. In her opening comment this time, La Corbie
uses 'difficult' words like 'eldritch', 'hurdies' (buttocks; hips), 'thon' (a
demonstrative adjective in Scots that lies beyond 'that' in the sequence:
'this', 'that', 'thon'; roughly equivalent to English 'yonder'), 'quine' (an
ummarried woman, also a bold, impudent woman; slut); and cognates that
are not obvious, like 'wud' (in this context 'would' not 'mad') and 'funns'
(finds); false friends, like 'chancy' (not simply unpredictable but 'unfortu-
nate', 'unlucky'), 'greet' ('weep'), or – punning – 'caw' (as both the crow's
cry and 'call'); repetitions are more frequent, as in 'greet' used with 'weep',
'kitlin-cat', 'gloamin daurk' – this last used, in Lochhead's words, adjectivally,
adding connotations while retaining denotation, since 'gloamin' is specifi-
cally the darkening of twilight at evening or morning. Similarly, 'tod fox,'

denotes 'fox fox' but adds connotations of an untrustworthy person to the 'crafty' and 'cunning' associated with foxes; and 'wud mad' denotes 'mad mad' but 'wud' adds extreme connotations including 'violent', 'wild', 'demented'. The Germanic words 'ken' and 'gang' ('know' and 'go') remain in modern Scots though not in English, as does the German cognate 'Kirk' for 'Kirche' (church). 'Old' words like 'hind' for a female deer or 'put to the horn' for 'to outlaw' along with 'collocations' of 'difficult' words like Bothwell's string of epithets for Alison Craik complicate this much more linguistically dense section of the play. But they are contextualised in ways that reveal meaning to anyone attending to the context and action, and they call for attention to language, meaning, cultural differentiation and the power of words. As with any form of defamiliarisation, this lexical mixture has the power to evoke new imaginative combinations.

While linguistic range, fluidity and diversity characterise all of Lochhead's work, *Mary Queen of Scots* may be her greatest achievement, and that value may be attributed to her extension of Scots, in combination with English, to a 'bardic' voice that combines 'invention', 'difficulty' and 'confidence in the language' with techniques like Shakespeare's: the multiple implications retained in 'difficult' words, the forging of identity in 'easy' words and Scots grammar, the complications and revelations of 'false friends', the adjectival expansions and accessibility of 'repetitions', the intensity of 'collocations'. It is a language that speaks neither to Scots alone nor to an audience artificially expanded by erasing the sensuality, immediacy and culturally distinct vocabulary of Scots, but to any speaker of Scots and/or English who is listening.

My argument that recent writing in Scotland has moved beyond the early twentieth-century binary opposition of Scots or English is neither new nor only mine: Maurice Lindsay and Lesley Duncan make the point eloquently in their Introduction to *The Edinburgh Book of Twentieth-Century Scottish Poetry*: 'the old agonising over the actual nature of the language used by Scottish poets has ceased. Poets – whether employing standard English, classical Scots, Lallans, regional dialects, city patois, or any permutation or combination of these – are linguistically relaxed. No place now for the fierce debates of the Muir–MacDiarmid era.'[27] My thesis here is that it makes possible a strikingly inventive language, comparable to the fluidity of the early modern English Shakespeare could use, and a model for future cultural development within and beyond Scotland. The single, national language that MacDiarmid wished to restore with his 'synthetic Scots' has thus, in breaking up and diversifying, led to an extraordinary capacity for experimentation and linguistic range. Rather than placing Scots outside what T. S. Eliot considered 'tradition', it expands and enriches the linguistic range in Britain to retain its Germanic and Celtic along with its Romance sources. There is, in other words, a larger, more expressive tradition that is as valuable and no less accessible than Shakespeare. Like Ezra Pound's 'make it new', William Carlos Williams's 'invent', or the 'quite new rhythm' Eliot attributed to Marianne Moore, Lochhead's techniques of reclaiming words, using many Scots and English dialects both separately and together, and creating a confident voice, make what was long imagined to be provincial into an international classic.

CHAPTER FIVE

Lochhead Translated

Susanne Hagemann

Translation of works by Liz Lochhead started as early as 1983, when Angus Ogilvy's anthology *Trees*, which includes 'Churchyard Song' and 'Good Wood', was translated into German by Hein Verstegen.[1] To date, ninety of her poems, performance pieces and plays have been translated into eighteen languages and published in twenty countries on three continents: Austria, Brazil, Bulgaria, China, Croatia, the Czech Republic, Finland, France, Germany, Hungary, Israel, Italy, Luxembourg (in French), Macedonia, Mexico, the Netherlands, Poland, Romania, Slovakia and Sweden (in German and Swedish). Yet Lochhead scholarship, while interested enough in Lochhead as a translator, has maintained a deafening silence on her as a subject of translation.[2] Why this should be so is a matter for speculation. It would be facile to blame the silence in this area on indifference or ignorance. Exploring other possible causes of the widespread lack of awareness raises further issues, such as into whose purview the study of these translations could fall and what kind of research problems could be addressed here. The present chapter will examine these issues within the framework of descriptive translation studies, a branch of translation studies which focuses on the status and role of translated texts in the target culture.

To begin with, does a translation belong to the source culture or the target culture, to the original author's oeuvre or the translator's? There is obviously no single or simple answer to these questions. While it is easy to see why Lochhead's own translations have been appropriated by Scottish Studies to form part of the Lochhead canon (a play such as *Miseryguts* is unmistakably by her as well as by Molière) translations of her works into other languages may or may not be similarly appropriated by the target culture; this will depend on a variety of factors including the translator's literary profile, translation strategies, publishing decisions and the patterns of literary critical discourse within the target culture. Irrespective of the situation in the various target cultures, however, Scot. Lit. so far has not laid claim to (single or joint) ownership of these translations. This may be partly due to the sheer difficulty of bibliographical research. The *Bibliography of Scottish Literature in Translation*

(BOSLIT) is far from complete, and other resources go only a little way towards filling the gaps.[3] Another, weightier reason may be the problem of what questions a Scotticist could ask of translations many of which he or she will not be able to read and some of which will not be physically accessible. The mere fact that translations exist says nothing about Lochhead's impact and reception abroad, which can only be judged from within the cultures concerned. But what, then, is there left to discuss, apart from statistics? It is perhaps not by chance that research on Scottish literature in translation has mostly been either of the broad-lines or of the language-pair variety, and that publications on translations of an individual writer's work into different languages are scarce.[4]

Referring to research on Scottish literature in translation begs the question of whether 'Scottish' is an appropriate label to apply to Lochhead. Many Lochhead experts would answer this in the affirmative, and some might even wonder why the question should have been asked. However, contextualisation is not quite as simple as that, even for the original texts. For instance, while poems by Lochhead have been included in numerous volumes with a Scottish focus, they have also appeared in anthologies of British poetry, English-language poetry, women's poetry, socialist poetry and childhood poetry, to name but a few. The same is true of Lochhead translations, which have been classified not only as Scottish poetry, but also as British, English-language, women's and love poetry. And at the risk of stating the obvious, since translating will always change the language of a text, poems by Lochhead which, irrespective of setting etc., come across as Scottish on the strength of their language alone may well be perceived differently when translated. As will be shown below, the various ways of translating Scottish linguistic features may point readers in directions other than Scottish identity, and may in the process open up new ways of interpreting Lochhead's texts.

As far as statistics are concerned, the most translated of Lochhead's works is *Perfect Days*, which has been translated eight times (into Czech, Finnish, French, German, Hebrew, Italian, Polish and Slovak). With one exception, all of these translations have been for performance rather than publication. The same applies to the extant translations of *Good Things* (into Finnish and Polish) and *Dracula* (into Finnish). By contrast, translations of *Mary Queen of Scots Got Her Head Chopped Off* have been published in drama anthologies (in Croatian and Italian), and *Blood and Ice* on its own (in Italian). In poetry, the front-runners, with five translations each, are 'Dreaming Frankenstein' (one each into Czech, French and Italian, and two into German), 'Poem for my Sister' (one each into Italian, Polish and Swedish, and two into Chinese), and 'What The Pool Said, On Midsummer's Day' (one each into Chinese, French and German, and two into Italian), followed by 'My Rival's House' (into Finnish, German, Hungarian and Italian)[5] and 'Song of Solomon' (into Dutch, Macedonian, Polish and Spanish). Five other poems have been translated three times, seventeen twice and fifty-eight poems and performance pieces once.

What can such a list tell us? As far as the source culture is concerned, the texts selected tend to be formally conservative: in drama, romantic comedy is the preferred genre; in poetry and prose, performance pieces are somewhat underrepresented. However, this reveals little about the translations, not only because a translation never simply reproduces the original but also because even features that are kept more or less invariant may have an entirely different function in the target literary system. For instance, techniques and topics that form part of the standard repertoire of contemporary Scottish literature may be highly innovative elsewhere, and vice versa. It does seem safe to assume, though, that in the majority of target cultures formal innovation was not the primary selection criterion, simply because this criterion would not explain the conservative bias of the source texts. Personal communications from translators and editors show that, in some cases at least, selection has been governed not by target-cultural considerations but by responses to the source texts alone, with criteria ranging from personal preference to representativeness in terms of creative periods, forms and strengths. Translatability can be a further criterion, though it is rarely mentioned, and strongly depends on what the translator is aiming to do. Thus, Adele D'Arcangelo states that 'After the War' was excluded from her and Margaret Rose's 2005 Lochhead collection, *Poesie – Och!*, because it is too 'culture-bound';[6] but the poem's numerous references to the source culture (which in this case is British, not Scottish) have not prevented it from being translated into Dutch, Polish and Brazilian Portuguese.

The two target languages in which the largest number of Lochhead texts have appeared are Italian and German, the former with fifty-nine translations (the majority in *Poesie – Och!*, compiled from six Lochhead collections), and the latter with twenty-three. However, once again, quick conclusions should be eschewed. The figures alone do not necessarily imply that Lochhead is known in Italian and German-speaking literary circles, since, as mentioned above, the existence of translations does not per se indicate any significant awareness of that existence. Reception must be judged by different means.

The internet can provide a first, albeit crude indicator of reception. A Google search for 'Liz Lochhead' on Italian (.it) websites in August 2010 yielded 134 hits; fifty-seven remained after elimination of multiple similar hits. Two-thirds of these fifty-seven pages were in Italian, and one-third (nineteen) included references to Italian translations. This may not seem much, but if Lochhead's internet presence in Italian is marginal, in German it is almost non-existent. Within the .de domain, there were 196 hits (eighty-four after elimination of multiple similar hits), but the vast majority of these pages were written in English, and all of them, with one single exception, referred to Lochhead's original texts rather than the German translations. Austrian (.at) websites did slightly better, despite a lower number of hits (fifty-eight/thirty-two): two pages of the Graz periodical *Lichtungen* included mention of translations. The difference between Germany and Austria, and between these two and Italy, may be partly due to the fact that the majority of translations into German were published between 1983 and 1991, that is before the expansion of the internet, and two of the few more recent ones appeared in *Lichtungen*, whereas translation into Italian did not start until 1991, and intensified from 1999. Another reason, as will be shown in the following, may lie in the profiles of the German-language publishers and periodicals.

Where a translation is published will affect its initial position in the target literary system and its chances of reaching a mainstream audience. A text may be available without being widely read, and arguably this is what has happened with Lochhead translations in the German-speaking area. 'Widely' is of course a relative term, since poetry in general is a niche interest in contemporary German and Austrian culture. But this niche has an internal structure, and Lochhead translations tend to be situated on the periphery rather than in the centre. Since the case of German translations is illustrative, it will be discussed in some detail. Translations have appeared in books from the following publishers:

- Bert Schlender: a small West German publishing house that was founded in the 1970s and is now defunct. Its programme was mainly literary, with an emphasis on little-known authors and an esoteric strain (a volume on an alleged Celtic tree oracle was a good seller);
- Mariannenpresse: a (West) German art and literature publisher (1979–2008) that specialised in limited bibliophile editions;
- Folio: a publisher founded in 1994 and based in Vienna, Austria and Bolzano, Italy (South Tyrol). Folio specialises in contemporary literature from Austria, Italy, eastern and south-eastern Europe, and English-speaking countries, as well as contemporary art and regional (mainly South Tyrolean) non-fiction;
- Nimrod, based in Hörby, Sweden, under its small German-language imprint, Edition Rugerup: Nimrod was founded in 1994; Rugerup, in 2005. Rugerup focuses on poetry.

Furthermore, the following periodicals have carried Lochhead translations:

- *Forum – mainzer texte*: a short-lived West German literary magazine;

- *Nachtcafé*: a West German magazine that originated in the 1970s alternative scene and was published at irregular intervals until the late 1980s;
- *Litfass: Berliner Zeitschrift für Literatur*: a (West) German magazine whose Bulgarian founder aimed at bringing together West and East German, and more generally West and East European literature, as well as literature and art (1976–95);
- *Lichtungen*: an Austrian magazine founded in 1979 and aimed at promoting young Austrian, and in particular Styrian, writers and artists.

The major names in German literary publishing, from journals such as *Akzente* and *Sprache im technischen Zeitalter* to publishing houses such as Hanser and Suhrkamp, are conspicuous by their absence. Since the publication of poetry is governed by severe market constraints, personal connections can play a key role in the choice of publisher. This was the case for instance with the three anthologies that Iain Galbraith edited for *Forum – mainzer texte*, Folio and Nimrod/Rugerup.[7] The fact that the two latest volumes were published outside Germany and that, apart from grey literature, the last Lochhead translation to appear in Germany itself dates from 1991, probably has no wider cultural significance but simply reflects the degree to which such translations depend on the initiative of individuals.

The situation in Italy is somewhat more propitious. Italian is the only foreign language in which, as mentioned above, an entire collection of Lochhead's poems has appeared (not counting a Polish booklet which comprises a mere nine poems by her). Other things being equal, this is of course a better way of bringing an author to the public's notice than an anthology where her name will remain hidden in the main body of the text. While the Italian collection, like some anthologies which include poems by Lochhead, comes from a rather small literary publisher, other translations have been issued by well-known periodicals or publishing houses such as *Poesia* (a leading international poetry magazine founded in 1988), *Linea d'Ombra* (a rather short-lived but widely appreciated cultural magazine, 1983–99), *Panta* (a literary review founded in 1990 by Bompiani, one of the major Italian literary publishers), or Le Lettere (a literature and humanities publisher with a substantial poetry list). One translation is accessible online in a literary e-zine. In Italy, Lochhead translations are thus not only better publicised on the internet but also more frequently available in high-profile publications than in Germany. However, the fact that in some cases the Italian translators themselves seem unaware of the work others have done in the same target language can be taken to indicate that even in that country Lochhead has not yet entered the public consciousness.

Those of Lochhead's plays that have been translated for performance are usually not available in published form. In these cases, the degree to which target audiences are familiar with Lochhead will depend on factors such as the venue, the number of performances and the number of tickets sold. This is not relevant to either Germany or Italy, however. The published Italian translations of *Blood and Ice* and *Mary Queen of Scots Got Her Head Chopped Off* do not seem to have been performed, and neither has the translation of *Perfect Days*, which is part of an unpublished degree thesis. The German translation of *Perfect Days*, by contrast, was commissioned by the stage publisher Hartmann & Stauffacher and produced for performance, but is still awaiting its German première.

Another aspect of Lochhead translations concerns the translators' and editors' profiles. These are quite varied, but the majority of translators have experience both in literary translation and in another relevant area: they are either poets, playwrights and so on in their own right, or academics who specialise in Scottish and/or English literature, drama, or translation.[8] Editors of anthologies that include poems or plays by Lochhead usually have similar profiles to the translators'; in fact, editors are often also translators. The varying backgrounds once again reflect the importance of individual initiative for Lochhead translations. In Italy, for instance, there is a strong predominance of academics over literary writers, whereas in France and Germany – two countries with an academic tradition in Scottish Studies – research and teaching do not yet seem to have generated much translation activity, at least as far as Lochhead is concerned, though one as yet unpublished German translation has arisen out of a course in poetry translation at Mainz University. In the case of academics with a relevant specialisation, it seems reasonable to assume that the translators themselves will often be the decision makers who select the texts and arrange for publication. When the translators are poets, they may either have been instrumental in choosing the texts, or have been commissioned to translate them by an editor. An affinity between their own work and Lochhead's may or may not exist. The small number of full-time translators is probably linked to the fact that in many cultures poetry translation is a non-remunerative activity. Translators of plays tend to be somewhat better placed, particularly if they are entitled to a share of box-office revenue for each performance; but in general, there is a much stronger market for professional translations of technical rather than literary texts.

It would be tempting to hypothesise that differences in presentation and translation strategies relate to differences in the translators' or editors' profiles, but in actual fact there seems to be no such correlation. For instance, translations in both periodicals and anthologies are frequently accompanied by academic material, but this is irrespective of whether the translator is a poet or an academic. Thus, Brazilian poet Virna Teixeira's 2007 anthology of Scottish twentieth-century poetry, *Ovelha negra*, includes an introduction which sets the poems in context, as does *Poeti della Scozia contemporanea*, a 1992 anthology by Italian academics Carla Sassi and Marco Fazzini; and *Färdväg*, a 1990 anthology of contemporary English-language poems edited and translated by Swedish poets Göran Printz-Påhlson and Jan Östergren, concludes with a lengthy essay on poetry in general and the poems translated in particular.

What is striking about the academic material, whether produced by academics or poets, is that it is quite often devoted exclusively, or almost exclusively, to the original texts and authors. Scottish poetry, Scottish drama, British poetry, or English-language poetry are the most frequent con-textualisations for Lochhead's translated works. This reflects a general trend in a number of cultures: introductions or afterwords to literary translations, even when written by the translators themselves, will more often than not gloss over translation as process and product. The pervasive silence may be partly due to the strong 'alternative' pressure of having to explain aspects of a foreign literature with which the target audience cannot be expected to be familiar (and even in countries such as Italy and Germany, the existing awareness of Scotland will not necessarily extend to its poetry and drama), but partly perhaps also to the cultural norms which govern translation. If, for instance, translation is predominantly regarded as a secondary, reproductive act, there may be little felt need to accord it any discursive prominence. Adele D'Arcangelo and Margaret Rose's Lochhead collection *Poesie – Och!* stands as a notable exception to this widespread trend, including as it does an eighteen-page afterword by D'Arcangelo which is exclusively concerned with translation issues (as opposed to Rose's eight-page introduction on Lochhead). Aspects covered in the afterword range from general questions such as the translatability of poetry to the translation process and the translation strategies chosen. Another editor who needs to be mentioned in this context is Iain Galbraith, whose German-language anthologies include both discussions of translation issues and bio-bibliographical notes on the translators.

Translators' footnotes are another way of making translation visible. In contrast to introductions, afterwords and so on, notes are usually avoided by the Lochhead translators. There are some exceptions, however: for instance *Ovelha negra*, where Teixeira uses notes to explain culture-specific references left in English in her translations, such as 'The Black Country' and 'REME' in 'After the War/Após a Guerra', as well as other terms which she evidently assumes her target audience will find difficult, such as 'ampersand' and 'sigrune' in 'The Unknown Citizen/O Cidadão Desconhecido'. Interestingly, some of these explanations refer to the English rather than the Portuguese text in this bilingual anthology. Thus, 'ampersand' occurs in the source text only; it is translated as '"e" comercial' in the target text, and a footnote in

Portuguese explains that the 'ampersand' is the & sign and used to be a letter of the English alphabet.[9] All footnotes, including those that relate to the English text, appear at the bottom of the Portuguese pages. This approach is worth noting not so much for its own sake but because it raises the question of how bilingual editions can be read.[10]

Financial constraints militate against bilingual publications because these require twice the amount of space that a monolingual edition does, incurring a higher manufacturing cost (unless the publication appears in electronic form). Yet most translations of Lochhead poems are in fact juxtaposed with the originals. This is true of the vast majority of translations published in anthologies, but also of a number of those published in print periodicals. The editors' or publishers' reasons for choosing this form of publication are varied. Some translations are presumably intended to help learners understand the source text: thus, the way footnotes are presented in *Ovelha negra* only makes sense if the source and target texts are read in parallel, with frequent back-and-forth movement between the two; and a few notes are clearly geared towards filling presumed gaps in readers' general cultural knowledge. However, it would be dangerous to generalise. Iain Galbraith's description of his own editorial stance in his bilingual anthologies is illuminating here:

> It isn't up to me to lay down rules about what kind of translation somebody is or is not allowed to publish! There are very many routes into and through a translation, and I am open to any and all of them. I do not see translation as an ancillary project necessarily, but am certainly not haughty if a translator chooses that role, or that guise. I am, however, interested in individual encounters, and prefer to convene a certain polymorphic or polyphonic gathering of translations than to lay down a law or establish an orthodoxy [. . .] The philological translation, the Lesehilfe [reading aid], the transliteration, these constitute a form of transaction which may be useful under certain circumstances, which does not necessarily lead to the original however, indeed often enough leads away from it.[11]

Even in a bilingual edition, then, translators can be free to choose the approach they find most productive. Adele D'Arcangelo explains in her afterword to *Poesie – Och!* that she has used different translation strategies, corresponding to the variety of source texts, and that some poems have not been included because they would not have translated well.[12] This is a far cry from translation as a learning aid.

What a bilingual edition is intended to achieve is, of course, a different matter from how it can be, and is, read. Lance Hewson argues that, unlike other translations, those in a bilingual edition have no chance of being perceived as part of the target culture because the original printed alongside will serve as a constant reminder of translatedness and a permanent link with the source culture.[13] Whether it is a good or a bad thing for a translation to be immediately recognisable as such remains a moot question; but the fact is that a bilingual edition will situate the text outside the literary mainstream of the target culture unless that mainstream is itself translation-oriented.

Another point made by Hewson is that if no countermeasures are taken to make the translator's choices explicit, a bilingual edition will invite readers to consider the target text as *the* translation rather than one out of a number of possible translations.[14] Such countermeasures, however, are rare in Lochhead translations. A simple, though surprisingly effective, strategy can be found for instance in the Austrian magazine *Lichtungen*, where the target text is printed on the verso side; the source text, on the recto. By upsetting the usual chronological order, this form of presentation provokes questions about the nature of the relationship between the two texts. Another countermeasure is Adele D'Arcangelo and Margaret Rose's decision to translate 'Kidspoem/Bairnsang' twice for their Lochhead collection: in one translation the opposition between English and Scots is rendered by formal/distanced vs emotional/intimate language; in the other, by standard Italian vs a generalised central Italian dialect.[15] Thus, while 'a really dismal day' becomes *una giornata davvero tremenda* in both versions, 'a gey dreich day' is translated as *una brutta giornata davvero* in the first, and as *'na brutta giornata pe'davero viva* in the second.[16] This dual translation emphasises the fact that a translation rewrites rather than reproduces the original. It also draws attention to aspects of the poem which for some readers of the original may be obscured by an identification of Scottish linguistic features with national identity: the issue of human closeness and distance in the first version, and the variety of linguistic power structures in the second (in Italy, a national standard language did not develop until the nineteenth century, the period which also saw the emergence of the Italian nation-state – a very different historical constellation from the one familiar to Scots).

As far as translation strategies in the narrow sense of the term are concerned, one that occurs in a number of poetry translations into various languages is a prioritisation of semantics over form. In particular, sound effects such as alliteration, assonance, or rhyme are often more prominent in the originals than in the translations (even in target languages where such effects are in common use in poetry). While this is a legitimate choice, it does raise questions about the function of the translations in cases such as D'Arcangelo and Rose's Italian version of 'Epithalamium', where the sonnet form is dissolved by adding an extra verse and scrapping the rhymes, or Donny Correia and Frederico Barbosa's Portuguese version of 'My Way', where the absence of rhyme detracts from textual coherence. Translating 'I did it to settle an argument with a friend / I did it to drive our Hazel round the bend' as *Eu fiz para acabar com a discussão / Eu fiz para levar à loucura* obscures the fact that this combination of reasons makes sense not least because they rhyme.[17] The persona thus comes across as extremely idiosyncratic. This may be seen as emphasising either the autonomy of the translation (because it invites other interpretations than the original) or its subservience to the original (because it relies on readers noting the rhymes in the English version).

Another widespread tendency is for references to the source cultures (Scottish and British) to be preserved, often without explanations – from 'Byres Road' in the German translation of 'Obituary' to 'Stafford Cripps' in the Portuguese translation of 'After the War'. This seems at odds with the prioritisation of semantics, since names such as these will have no meaning at all in many target cultures. If divergent strategies co-occur in a single poem, the question will arise as to how the tension affects the workings of the translation as a whole; this, however, is a matter for individual text analysis. D'Arcangelo explains that in her and Rose's translation of 'Advice to Old Lovers' references to songs and films have been Italianised because the poem's topic is universal;[18] but this strategy is exceptional even in their own collection, and certainly among Lochhead translators in general.

Style, finally, is a thorny issue. Paul Barnaby deplores the fact that translation anthologies often transform the heteroglossia of Scottish poetry into a single undifferentiated register.[19] The opposite may happen when a single author such as Lochhead has several translators in one target language: she may acquire additional voices. On the one hand this is natural, since the translator's voice – the voice of the person who actually writes the target text – will obviously be heard alongside the original author's. On the other hand the proliferation of voices will further fragment what is already a fragile and fragmented profile. To take German as an example, the formal register into which Michael Donhauser translates 'My Rival's House' has little in common with the stylistic, syntactic and semantic incoherences of Mitch Cohen and Wolfgang Heyder's version of '5th April 1990', or with the spoken though not colloquial language of 'Lucy's Diary' as translated by Ursula Kimpel, and even less with the explicit merging of the translator's voice with the persona's in a prose text by Andreas F. Kelletat based on 'What The Pool Said, On Midsummer's Day'. For instance, Donhauser's detached, abstract tone in *Abdeckung wie / Verdunkelung verhindern, / daß sich sein Glanz vermindert* ('Dust / cover, drawn shade, / won't let the surface colour fade') is quite remote from Kelletat's vivid description in *Mit ihren glitschigen schlingpflanzen um seine kräftigen schenkel könnte der fisch in ihr zu fleisch ihn machen, übel könnte das ausgehen* ('What's fish / in me could make flesh of you, / my wet weeds against your thigh, it / could turn nasty').[20] There are various Lochheads in German, some closer to the voice(s) of the original author than others. To say so is not a value judgement: closeness to the style of the original is one among many possible priorities for poetry translation.

In conclusion, what can be said about Lochhead as a translated author? The picture that emerges from the descriptive analysis in this chapter is ambiguous. A fair number of translations do exist, but translations that have been printed or uploaded will not necessarily be read and responded to; and even when they are, the focus may well be on the context (Scottish poets, English-language poets, women writers, and so on) rather than on the individual writer. Moreover, since Lochhead translations can be quite difficult to find, readers in some cultures may only be aware of a small part of existing translations. In many cases, therefore, importing Lochhead into another culture will not result in an impact on that culture. And to return to the question of belonging raised at the beginning of this chapter, Scottish Studies would do well to appropriate these translations as a research object because – given their highly peripheral status in the target literatures – it seems unlikely that the target cultures will.

Thanks are due to Iain Galbraith and Carla Sassi for discussing their anthologies with me; to Adele D'Arcangelo and Virna Teixeira for making their translations available to me; to Loreta Georgievska-Jakovleva, for help with researching Macedonian translations; to Thomas Kempa, with Chinese; to Virna Teixeira, with Portuguese; to Zsuzsanna Varga, with Hungarian; to Carla Sassi, for alerting me to an overlooked translation into Italian; to Jan Baeke, Justyn Hunia, Dan H. Popescu, Andrea Sirotti and Zhang Jian for information concerning their own translations; also to the staff of Johann Christian Senckenberg University Library, Frankfurt am Main, for looking through several volumes of *Das Nachtcafé* in order to locate Lochhead translations; and finally, to Reiko Aiura-Vigers, Mustafa Al-Slaiman and Annett Jubara, for searching for translations into Japanese, Arabic and Russian respectively.

CHAPTER SIX

Liz Lochhead's Drama Adaptations

John Corbett

When asked about the inspiration for her work at public readings, Liz Lochhead likes to recall Sammy Cahn, the Tin Pan Alley songwriter's response to the question of which came to him first: the music or the lyrics? 'First,' he replied, 'the phone call.' As Lochhead indicates, it is a telling anecdote for those who are considering her own work. First, we do well to remember that much of her drama, particularly the drama adapted and translated from other sources,[1] is commissioned. Lochhead's major adaptations, *Tartuffe* (1986), *Medea* (2000), *Three Sisters* (2000), *Miseryguts* (*Le Misanthrope*, 2002), *Thebans* (2003) and *Educating Agnes* (*L'École des Femmes*, 2008), must be seen first of all in the light of their commission by the Royal Lyceum Company and Theatre Babel.[2] Each company collaborates with invited playwrights to produce work in line with its declared policy: the Royal Lyceum, who commissioned *Tartuffe*, *Three Sisters* and *Miseryguts*, aims to mix new dramatic writing with a staple diet of British and European classics.[3] The mission of Theatre Babel, who commissioned *Medea*, *Thebans and Educating Agnes* is stated on its website:

> We work with collaborators from different disciplines to liberate some of the world's greatest plays, igniting the imagination of artists to explore the truth and release the extraordinary in classic myths and dramas.[4]

Lochhead's collaboration with the Royal Lyceum and Theatre Babel has largely determined the nature of her adaptations, which cleave to the classical repertoire of Molière, Euripides, Sophocles, Aeschylus and Chekhov.

That Lochhead references Sammy Cahn when discussing the nature of her 'inspiration' is, secondly, an indication of her continuing love affair with the jazzy, syncopated rhythms of popular American songs, whose distinctive twentieth-century cadences combine with her native Scots and English to produce a rich dramatic idiom. Finally, although conjuring the shade of Cahn might suggest that Lochhead is the equivalent of a Tin Pan Alley drone, churning out popular commissions to order, there is a shared dexterity, wit and artistry to their work that belies their commercial nature. Lochhead, after all, accepts the commissions that attract her, and latterly she has taken the initiative in suggesting collaborations, for example prompting Graham McLaren, Theatre Babel's artistic director, to drop plans for a version of Wycherley's *The Country Wife* in favour of her proposed new version of Molière's *L'École des Femmes*.[5] Liz Lochhead's adapted drama therefore bears scrutiny as a characteristic and substantial part of her oeuvre as a whole.

And yet the collaborative nature of the translation and adaptation of drama confronts the critic with thorny problems; it is easy to see why the theorist and practitioner, Susan Bassnett, describes theatre translation as a 'labyrinth'.[6] The analysis of Lochhead's drama translations-adaptations necessarily sees her at the centre of a network of relationships – with the producer, director and actors branching off in one direction, and, in another direction, the source authors (Molière, Euripides, Sophocles and Chekhov), as well as the unnamed earlier translators whose work Lochhead likes to consult. The plays, too, sit in their own web of relationships: *Tartuffe*, *Miseryguts* and *Educating Agnes* most obviously corresponding not only with their French originals but also with the tradition of 'MacMolières' that have populated the Scottish stage since Robert Kemp's pioneering version of *L'École des Femmes* (1948) was performed at the Gateway Theatre in Edinburgh.[7] Kemp's *Let Wives Tak Tent* was influenced by visiting productions of Molière to the Edinburgh Festival, and – like his adaptation of Sir David Lyndsay of the Mount's *A Satire of the Three Estates* which was first performed at the Festival the following year – was a deliberate attempt to give a dramatic voice to the Scottish literary 'renaissance'. Lochhead has acknowledged that her desire to adapt the third of her versions of Molière in Scots verse was prompted by rereading Kemp's prose version when it was reprinted by the Association for Scottish Literary Studies. Lochhead's chosen title, *Educating Agnes*, of course, also alludes to Willy Russell's popular, contemporary drama of a young, working-class woman's relationship with an older, university-educated mentor. The intertextuality of adaptations, then, extends well beyond the relationship of a target text to its source.

The 'Greek' adaptations also fit into a discursive space shaped by their relationships with the source texts (more obviously mediated by English bridging translations) and with a less celebrated, but still lively, modern tradition of reworking Greek plays and classical themes for the Scottish stage.[8] Indeed, *Medea* was first performed as the climax of a trio of plays, entitled 'Greeks', that included David Greig's *Oedipus* and Tom McGrath's *Electra*. Lochhead's plays also resonate with each other, showing clear developments in Lochhead's use of adaptation of classic work to confront contemporary issues; and, finally, the adaptations resonate with Lochhead's 'original' drama and poetry, echoing and prefiguring themes and techniques to be found elsewhere in her work.

How, then, is the critic to address Lochhead's adaptations, other than by leaping on a horse and galloping off simultaneously in all directions? In the present chapter I consider her work under three general and slightly overlapping headings: startling familiarities; forging a natural idiom; and particular universals. If these headings contain internal contradictions, then they are true to the paradoxical nature both of the translation labyrinth and of Lochhead's use of adaptation in the service of her own artistic ends.

Startling Familiarities

A standard question when considering translations is whether the translated text 'domesticates' or 'foreignises' the source text. As Maier and Massardier-Kenney observe in their valuable discussion of translation theory and its usefulness, this dichotomy echoes earlier discussions of language by German thinkers such as Johann Gottfried von Herder (1744–1843).[9] Herder argued that thought and therefore meaning were inseparable from the words used in any language, and so it follows that the act of translation either transforms the host language, or substantially changes the meanings originally expressed in the source text. The logic of Herder's argument informs later perspectives on the options facing translators:

> Schleiermacher's famous distinction between bringing the writer to the reader (which he rejects) and bringing the reader to the writer – which has now been popularized and (overly) simplified as a distinction between 'domestication' (making the foreign text fit the norms of the target language) and 'foreignization' (bending the target language to allow the foreignness of the text to be visible) – is but the application of Herder's focus on word usage.[10]

In respect of this dichotomy, Lochhead's preference is, at first glance, to 'domesticate', or to bring the writer to the reader. Her working practice as a translator and adapter would seem to fit this mould: while she can take advantage of her knowledge of French to refer to editions of the source texts for the Molière translations, she also uses a bridging text, an earlier English translation, to supplement the original. For adaptations of plays in other languages, she relies solely on earlier translations – in her introduction to *Medea*, she notes her preference for a 'pedantic, not at all speakable Victorian translation, one that would elucidate without unduly influencing my language'.[11] Likewise, in her introduction to *Educating Agnes*, she recalls:

> We [Graham McLaren, the director] and I looked at all the other Molières in the form I always work from, the original (flowery 'f's for 's's, et al) on one side

of the double-page spread, with contemporary seventeenth-, or occasionally eighteenth-century literals on the other.[12]

Since she also acknowledges familiarity with other, more contemporary, translations and adaptations, Lochhead's own work draws not so much on a single source text as a layered historical tradition of translation and adaptation, which she reshapes into her own structure and re-presents through her own voice.

To introduce a newspaper interview, Lesley McDowell counterpoints Lochhead's eclectic practice against the purism of a group of young scholars from Eton, in a discussion that took place during a visit by Lochhead to the college:

> 'What do you know about Greek?' the young people at the famous public school said to her. 'How dare you translate it!' 'But I don't translate Greek,' the famous Scottish writer replied. 'I adapt it. All you need to be a poet,' she told them, 'is to be good at your own language.'[13]

The contrast between the female Glasgow writer and the privileged male scholars is good journalism, but it also indicates where Lochhead consistently presents herself on the cline between domestication and foreignisation: she takes the source work as a pretext for her own domesticating adaptations, making the strange familiar and bringing the writer to the reader in ways that might have horrified Schleiermacher, as it apparently scandalised the young classicists. And yet the broad categorisation of translations as 'domesticating' or otherwise is, as Maier and Massardier-Kenney observe in the quotation cited above, an over-simplification. Lochhead's translations do bring the source text to the reader, often using domesticating strategies, but they nevertheless result in works of startling freshness. How is this apparent paradox achieved?

The earliest of Lochhead's adaptations, *Tartuffe*, just pre-dates *Mary Queen of Scots Got Her Head Chopped Off* (1987) and marks the point at which Lochhead finds a sustained dramatic voice in Scots. Her earlier long plays, *Blood and Ice* and the adaptation of *Dracula*, were in English, although her sketches for a series of revues, beginning with *Sugar and Spite* (1978), co-written with Marcella Evaristi, experiment with a range of voices. Lochhead herself recounts the process of composition in the introduction to the joint edition of *Miseryguts and Tartuffe*:

> I thought it'd be in English for Scottish actors to perform in their own accents. The Scots it emerged in was a big surprise to me. Well, I'd set it at the end of the First World War, when small businessman Orgon could've made a lot of money and married a beautiful young widow; could still plausibly think he could

tell his daughter who to marry; could still be head of a household with a maid. This was exactly my grandmother's time and her guid Scots tongue was evidently inside me waiting to be tapped. Words I didn't know I knew just tumbled out as I got on with the enormously good fun of my first attempt at a whole play in rhyming couplets.[14]

Taken at face value, the rhyming couplets were the trigger to what Randall Stevenson has called her 'triumphant Tartuffication'.[15] Lochhead's *Tartuffe*, in setting and language, is both an extension and a break with the tradition of 'MacMolières' that preceded it. Lochhead's setting of the play at the end of World War One updates the usual locations of Scots adaptations in the late seventeenth or early eighteenth century, a time at which the 'braid Scots' of many Molière adaptations would still be available to all social classes in lowland Scotland. Lochhead's Orgon is upwardly mobile, self-made middle class rather than landed gentry or of the professional class. Crucially, the link to the varieties of Scots that Orgon, Tartuffe, Dorine and the other characters speak is framed as a personal connection, Lochhead channelling her grandmother, rather than a portrayal of an alternative linguistic topography, a 'golden age' in which Scots was used by the highest and lowest in the land.

The relocation of Molière is even more radical in *Miseryguts* (2002). Molière's seventeenth-century comedy of manners centres on Alceste, an aristocrat who refuses to conform to the conventions of polite Parisian society, and is undone by his passion for the fickle beauty, Célimène. Lochhead takes the basic characterisations and structure of *Le Misanthrope* as a starting-point for her satire on political and media culture in Edinburgh in the early days of the new Scottish Parliament. Alceste becomes 'Alex Frew', a media commentator who tells it like it is. In one sense this is an extreme example of domesticating adaptation; in another it represents a startling defamiliarisation of the genre for those in the audience who came to the Lyceum expecting yet another 'MacMolière' that was situated safely and nostalgically in a pantomimic past. By appropriating and updating *Le Misanthrope*, Lochhead presents a 'functional' as opposed to a 'formal' equivalent to Molière's swipe at his contemporaries:[16] the adaptation draws an ironic parallel between two sets of privileged cliques. Again, ingenious rhyming couplets, this time largely in colloquial and slangy present-day Scottish English, contribute to the energy of the play. Lochhead's final Molière adaptation to date returns to the origins of the Scottish adaptations, and serves as a verse bookend to Kemp's prose version of *L'École des Femmes*. Set this time in the more distant past, in a 'provincial town', *Educating Agnes* arguably forsakes the experimentalism of *Miseryguts*. However, instead of relocating the play to a time nearer the present, Lochhead destabilised traditional expectations of versions of the play by advocating the casting of the young actress, Anneika

Rose, as her Agnes: 'tiny, beautiful, black, Glaswegian'.[17] The exploitative sexual relationship between Arnolphe and Agnes thus suggests a broader, racial and colonial aspect too.

In different ways, then, Lochhead's riffing on Molière draws on the established popular, music-hall appeal of his adaptations for Scottish audiences, while subverting theatre-goers' comfortable expectations of those adaptations, through judicious updating of setting, surprising casting and, most of all, her inspired blending of Scots and English, a topic we return to in more detail below.

In adapting the Greek plays of Euripides and Sophocles, Lochhead does not have the advantage of playing variations on a lively native tradition of translations and adaptations that have embedded themselves so deeply into the popular consciousness. This is not to say that a Scottish tradition of domesticating the classics does not exist; quite the reverse. As Ian Brown demonstrates forcibly,[18] the appropriation of classical drama and its resetting in a local context and idiom has been a staple of post-war Scottish theatre. Early examples were Douglas Young's translations of Aristophanes's *The Frogs* (*The Puddocks*) and *The Birds* (*The Burdies*) in the late 1950s, and performances of Greek drama. More recent examples have been Bill Dunlop's adaptation of Aeschylus's *Oresteia* (*Klytemnestra's Bairns*, 1993), Ian Brown's version of *Antigone*, after Sophocles (1969), and different versions of Euripides's *The Bacchae* (Ian Brown's adaptation was toured throughout the UK in 1971, and revived in a revised form in the Cardiff Festival in 1991; David Greig's 2007 version was staged at the Royal Lyceum). Lochhead's *Medea*, as noted above, was originally commissioned by Theatre Babel as part of a trilogy of Greek plays, all by Scottish playwrights. While the modern tradition of Greek adaptations is clearly a distinctive thread of Scottish drama, the productions have generally been smaller in scale than the 'MacMolières', and less frequently revived in Scotland. When Greek adaptations have been given high-profile productions in Scotland, as in the cases of Young's *The Burdies* and Greig's *The Bacchae*, the performances have tended to be commissions for the Edinburgh International Festival, and so can be read, at least in part, as aligning Scotland with the founding tradition in European drama for the benefit of an audience that is as much external as internal. In this context of Scottish engagements with a classical tradition, Lochhead still seeks, instinctively, to unsettle. As she notes in her introduction to *Medea*:

> It was only after seeing the play in performance here in Glasgow this Spring [of 2000], that it struck me the conventional way of doing *Medea* in Scotland until very recently would have been to have Medea's own language Scots and the, to her, alien Corinthians she lived under speaking, as powerful, 'civilised' Greeks, patrician English. That it did not occur to me to do other than give the

dominant mainstream society a Scots tongue and Medea a foreigner-speaking-refugee voice must speak of a genuine in-the-bone increased cultural confidence here.[19]

As I have argued elsewhere,[20] the shift in 'cultural confidence' that Lochhead here discerns characterises much Scottish translated drama in the immediate aftermath of devolution. Whereas in the decades before devolution Scotland had easily assumed a place on the periphery, occupying the cultural role of a marginalised nation, the years after 1997 saw an increasing tendency to rethink Scotland as 'the centre', and problematise the issues arising from being more directly in control of one's national destiny. While this tendency to assume a cultural position at the centre rather than at the margins is apparent in post-devolution novels such as James Robertson's *Joseph Knight* (2003), it is perhaps in translations of classical drama that the new dispensation is most clearly evident: by transposing Scotland onto the position of Athens, the 'Doric' nation is urbanised and centralised. The first Scottish audiences watching *Medea* and *Thebans* would thus be in the unfamiliar position of identifying with the lightly Scotticised, yet mainstream and patrician forces on stage and having to reflect on their 'smug and conventional attitudes of unthinking superiority'.[21]

Forging a Natural Idiom

As observed above, Lochhead's groundbreaking *Tartuffe*, in its setting and language, is both an extension and a break with the tradition of 'MacMolières' that preceded her. The rustic, slightly archaic stage Scots of Robert Kemp, Victor Carin and others is rebooted for the late twentieth century. In embracing a more urban idiom for Molière, Lochhead was not alone amongst her contemporaries; for example, Hector MacMillan employed an urban Scots in his adaptation of *The Hypochondriack* (1987), another popular success for the Lyceum. However, much of the joy of Lochhead's adaptation is the release of energy afforded by the collision of half-forgotten Scots, urban demotic and Anglo-American colloquialisms. In an often-quoted characterisation from Lochhead's introduction to the 1985 edition of the play, she calls it:

> a totally invented [. . .] theatrical Scots, full of anachronisms, demotic speech from various eras and areas; it's proverbial, slangy, couthy, clichéd, catch-phrasey, and vulgar; it's based on Byron, Burns, Stanley Holloway, Ogden Nash and George Formby, as well as the sharp tongue of my granny.[22]

Stevenson points to this gallimaufry of styles as an energising factor: it is both ebullient in itself and a means of dramatising conflict in performance. He observes:

Subversive, carnivalesque energies of opposition as well as engagement with official culture and language are especially apparent in Lochhead's *Tartuffe*. It is fuller of gutsy Rabelaisian physicality than Molière's, and equipped with a language shaped more comprehensively by 'arguments' between styles and forms, and the social stratifications they imply. Lochhead even adds to the range of registers naturally offered by 'the Scots idiom'.[23]

It may be more accurate to argue that the intertextual hotchpotch that Lochhead appropriates for Scots in her introduction to the 1985 edition of *Tartuffe* is in fact closer than traditional 'stage Scots' to the full linguistic range that contemporary Scottish speakers utilise in their everyday speech. An urban Scot in the present day has access to a variety of English registers as well as a range of Scots registers inherited from family, friends, popular culture and whatever educational and literary exposure has bequeathed him or her. In her introduction to *Miseryguts*, Lochhead acknowledges the reality underlying her invented idiom:

> Do they speak Scots? Well, they speak the way these particular Scotsmen and women do right now. Some Scots, yes, some Americanisms, lots of clichés and buzz-words, much casual profanity, I'm afraid. Like life.[24]

In relation to *Tartuffe*, Stevenson argues that it is this linguistic heterogeneity that allows Lochhead's characters to engage dramatically in a range of dialogues in a way that recalls Bakhtinian concepts of the carnivalesque, insofar as each character's idiolect expressively represents a differently nuanced stratum in a richly imagined society. The social strata clash when their strict, hierarchical certitudes are thrown into disarray by the forces of lust and love. According to Stevenson, Lochhead demonstrates the rich potential that Scots-English possesses for dramatising class tensions that already exist in Molière's original text.[25] In *Miseryguts*, however, the domestication of the source is much more radical.

It is pleasant to imagine a conversation taking place in the early 2000s between a fictional Scottish writer with, let us say, an established reputation as both an original playwright and a translator, and an equally fictional producer of plays for a major, publicly-subsidised theatre. The playwright is trying to convince the producer that a bitter, comic satire about television broadcasters in the era of the new Scottish Parliament is worthy of a full-scale production, and that, moreover, the play will be in rhyming couplets. The producer is unconvinced, and, looking over the accountancy team's summarised graph of box office receipts for the past three decades, asks the playwright to consider adapting a Molière play instead: the formula is tried and trusted and an audience can be guaranteed. This is not, of course, how Lochhead came to transpose Molière's *Le Misanthrope* onto New Town

Edinburgh just after the turn of the century, but it serves to suggest how translations and adaptations of classic texts can in fact open up spaces for the presentation of aspects of contemporary Scottish life and manners. Few who saw and enjoyed *Tartuffe* will have expected that Lochhead's next major Molière commission would dramatise the story of a cynical, straight-talking current affairs broadcaster, sickened by the hypocrisy of Holyrood politicians and spin-doctors, and doomed to be in love with a woman who cannot be faithful to him.

The carnivalesque language of *Miseryguts* is not so densely Scots as that of *Tartuffe*, but the ingenuity of the rhymes and the recognisably Scottish turns of phrase – again often clichés – is a great part of the pleasure of the text. Indeed texting is literally crucial to the plot in a scene in which Celia tries to persuade Alex that a message that she had sent to one of her current lovers, Oscar, was actually a message she forwarded in relation to his new-found, gay partner, David:

CELIA   Last night's the big date, David comes in, regales
        the whole office with the intimate details.
        The full bhoona! Who put what, where, when,
        how many times, what next . . . And then
        total blow-by-blow account! We're all like: Woh,
        young Dave, more than we need to know!
        It was a scream! I texted Oscar on behalf
        of the entire office, for a laugh!
ALEX   Do you think I came up the Clyde on a fucking bike?[26]

The familiar clichés of office banter ('we're all like: Woh','it was a scream','for a laugh') mix with local colloquialisms, old and new. The relatively new expression, 'the full bhoona' (i.e. the maximum extent possible) alludes to Scotland's lively Asian community and the introduction of Indian dishes like *bhuna* to the local palate, while 'do you think I came up the Clyde on a bike/banana skin/etc' is a long-standing and widely-used expression of disbelief. In *Miseryguts* there is much less evidence of the 'broad Scots' of *Tartuffe*, which is full of overt Scotticisms such as 'fechtin' (fighting), 'haud' (hold), 'saut' (salt), keekin' (peeking) and 'heid' (head). Even so, the 'Scottish English' of *Miseryguts* has many of the same qualities that Stevenson observes in the earlier adaptation – it is still a rich medium for the satirical portrayal of a particular class of people.

Indeed, in the introduction to *Educating Agnes*, Lochhead comments again on the diverse idioms she uses in her Molière adaptations. Returning to something closer to a period adaptation, she limits her Scots palette now mainly to the comic characters of Georgette and Alain; though the lead character, Arnolphe, who has been grooming young and innocent Agnes to be his bride, shifts into Scots at moments of intensity. The character of Lochhead's dramatic medium here bears interesting comparison with Kemp's prose version, for example, in the final act when Arnolphe (or, in Kemp's version, 'Oliphant') confronts Agnes with the fact that she has been about to elope with her young lover, Horace (or 'Walter', in Kemp's version):

AGNES   (*Recognising him*) Oh!
OLIPHANT   Aye, ye limmer, this time my face puts the fear o death on you
             and it's wi an ill will you see me here. I brak in upon thae ploys
             o love that hae turn't your heid ! (AGNES *looks to see if she can*
             see WALTER.) Dinna think your een can cry back your gallant
             to your side, he's owre far awa to bring you aid . . . Ech me, sae
             young and yet to mell in sic ploys![27]

Kemp's medium is consistently 'broad Scots', with a dense patterning of Scots vocabulary like 'limmer' (scoundrel), 'cry' (call), 'sic' (such) and 'mell' (mix). His stage Scots is founded on older vernacular speech and writing, and part of his artistic project is to update the contexts in which such a vernacular can be used as a viable artistic medium. While Lochhead also draws on older vernacular as a resource, she is less committed to its wholesale revival. Lochhead's medium is comparatively lighter in the lexical density of its Scots, though it is still marked as Scottish by terms such as 'sleekit' (sly) and the ubiquitous 'wee' (small):

ARNOLPHE   No point in shouting, pet, he's gone!
           And left wee Agnes with the Big Bad Wolf here, all alone.
           Disappointing, intit? The end of all your hopes.
           Because: It's Over. Read my lips.
           Still so young, eh? And so full of tricks.
           As sleekit as anything, giving it big licks
           With treachery, and cunning and . . . plain badness
           That I'd never have expected from my wee Agnes.[28]

In her own discussion of the main difference between her own adaptation and Kemp's version, Lochhead points to the earlier dramatist's decision to render *Let Wives Tak Tent* in prose. Lochhead considers rhyme as one of the crucial comic ingredients of Molière's comedy, although she agrees that the French playwright's alexandrines need to be transformed into native verse, preferably with 'polysyllabic feminine lines or outrageous near-rhymes'.[29] Though the 'broad Scots' register is more muted in *Educating Agnes* than in *Tartuffe*, the heterogeneity of Lochhead's dramatic idiom is still evident in the colloquialisms, both English ('read my lips') and Scots ('giving it big licks').

By comparison, in the 'Greek' adaptations, Lochhead restricts herself to a linguistic palette that is much closer to Standard English, but with occasional Scottish colouring. Certain turns of phrase still characterise Lochhead's 'Greeks' as Scottish; thus Jokasta berates her sons, and especially Eteokles on his reckless actions:

> JOKASTA   sons   there is more to old age than aches and pains
> and grey hairs   experience
> grant me this at least if you won't go as far as
> credit me with wisdom
> (*To* ETEOKLES)
> don't pursue false gods
> blind ambition   that's the worst   the wildest
> wrecker of human hopes   has been the downfall
> of many a family
> but you   you're daft for it[30]

The rebuke that contains the contemptuous term 'daft', which for many will be a covert Scotticism, domesticates the intimate but critical relationship between mother and son, a domestication that is unsettling for any Scottish audience expecting classical tragedy to be rendered in a consistently high-style and therefore English voice. A peculiarly chilling moment in the performance of *Medea* turns on the lead character's echoing of Jason's accusation, couched in a banal, colloquial phrase, during an argument in which he accuses her of displeasing the king, Kreon:

> JASON   I've always done my best
> to calm him down   persuade him you should stay
> I could have crept back to you in secret   would have
> but you can't keep it zipped   you will talk treason
> court your own banishment
> MEDEA   I can't keep it zipped!
> who   what   could be worse than you?[31]

Though the effect here is much more restrained than in the Molière adaptations, particularly *Tartuffe*, in the Greek adaptations Lochhead is still unafraid of slipping out of the 'appropriate' idiom associated with a particular dramatic genre – whether that idiom is the 'broad Scots' of period comedy or the 'elevated standard' of classical tragedy – and introducing an expression whose very inappropriateness is startling.

The spacing of phrases in the published scripts of *Medea* and *Thebans* further attests to Lochhead's concern with the ear; her way into both her Molière and her classical adaptations is through the poetic nature of the drama, whether that form is rhyming couplet or free verse. Whatever the form, she uses the poetry to unsettle the audience, often to lull them into false expectations of her adherence to a set of dramatic conventions that are undercut by an irreverent archaism here, a jarring cliché there, and an unholy alliance of Glaswegian and American slang elsewhere. And yet the effect is that Lochhead's medium is that of an instinctive, 'natural' idiom, since, as she points out, everyday speech is also a heterogeneous mixture of allusions, prefabricated phrases and recycled banter – Lochhead's verse in her adaptations intensifies and heightens the heterogeneous quality of the everyday speech of contemporary Scots.

Particular Universals

Lochhead is explicit in discussion of her adaptations that she feels free to change her source material. Indeed, playwrights are generally obliged to adapt their texts to the constraints of particular productions. She also considers the adaptation of canonical texts as a licence to subvert expectations, since the reputation of the plays will survive her adaptations. For *Educating Agnes* she condensed and changed characters to fit the remit of writing for only six actors, and in her introduction to *Medea*, she observes that she 'simply used the Euripides *Medea* as a complete structural template [and then] let go'.[32] While the plays are commissioned and developed in collaboration with producers, directors and actors, the individual writer still sits at the centre of this network of relations, and shapes the final script. It is therefore still legitimate to ask how Lochhead's adaptations relate to her original work.

In the *Edinburgh Companion to Scottish Drama*, Ksenija Horvat gives a useful recent overview of Lochhead's still-developing work for theatre as a whole, drawing in part on earlier discussions, such as those collected in Crawford and Varty, particularly chapters by Alison Smith and Robert Crawford.[33] Horvat characterises Lochhead's work as a poet, playwright, adapter and translator in terms that resonate with themes raised in the present chapter: she has an instinctive ear for the polyphonic qualities of contemporary speech, and a disdain for the ideological straitjacket of linguistic purism, be it advanced by guardians of Standard English or 'braid Scots'. She sees writing and performed speech as political as well as verbal acts; she is drawn to plots that focus on gender, political, ethnic or national relationships, often blurring and subverting easy categories and such binary oppositions as male/female, master/servant, Scottish/English. Lochhead's adaptations focus on those aspects of the source material that correspond to her own interests and which she identifies as 'profound, universal and eternal'.[34] Lochhead's characterisation of her source material as 'universal and eternal' might at first glance lay her open to charges of conservative liberal humanism by those critics who challenge the 'transcendent significance traditionally accorded to the literary text'.[35] However, Lochhead's approach to adaptation has much in common with those theorists who marshal contemporary documents, political commitment and close textual analysis to 'recover' the hidden histories of canonical literature. Lochhead's methods differ in that in her attempts to find a functional equivalent to those aspects of the source material that interest her, she relocates, selects and reworks the canonical text into a form that estranges the familiar source material by updating and domesticating it. However, the results are similar: on the one hand, an occluded historical and political issue is recovered; on the other, the extraordinary in the original material, obscured by difference in language, distance in time, and the familiarity of conventional performances, is revitalised and released.

It is well-documented that among Lochhead's preferred 'universal' themes are political and private concerns that fall broadly into the arena of feminism. She is particularly interested in the dramatic potential, both comic and tragic, of 'inappropriate love', a trope that drives all of her Molière adaptations, and which can be seen in her own comic study of female passion and heartbreak, *Perfect Days* (1998). *Medea*'s tale of the tragic consequences of female desire was written at the same time as *Perfect Days*, and Lochhead herself suggests that the two plays can be seen as complementary explorations of a woman's emotional desperation.[36] Combined with this 'private' concern in *Medea*, however, is the more public issue of the treatment by an intolerant society of a female outsider from a persecuted minority. At the turn of the millennium, as the 'new Scotland' was finding its way under a new form of governance, the inequitable treatment of refugees and minorities provides a context that further illuminates the choices made in the writing and performance of the adaptation. The 'universal' concerns are anchored in identifiably Scottish contexts and voiced by national and local stereotypes: from 'nippy sweeties' (bad-tempered characters despite intermittent pleasant appearances) to the 'unco guid' (inflexibly self-righteous). Lochhead's adaptations proceed, as we have seen, by embedding the universal in the near-stereotypically familiar, and then, through linguistic extravagance, astute casting, restructuring, updating and reimagining, taking the audiences beyond their expectations of a night in the theatre with a 'classic text'.

What next, after Lochhead's Greeks, Molières and a single stab (thus far) at Chekhov? Much will depend on the commissioning strategy of Scottish theatres in hard times; but it would be good to see, for example, what Lochhead the translator might do with a contemporary European, South American or Asian playwright whose concerns coincide with her own fascinations with gender politics and social hypocrisy, as they are realised in intimate, bittersweet, domestic relationships. Despite her avowed preference for adapting 'undamageable' canonical texts, there is some evidence that

Lochhead herself would welcome such a commission. In an interview she remarks:

> I would like to actually translate some poems or things that hadn't existed in various other versions in English or Scots. That would be quite interesting for me, but I would feel much more a sense of responsibility than I have to feel with these particular texts [i.e. the Molières and Greek adaptations], because these particular texts are going to find another day without me.[37]

In other words, Lochhead sees the adaptation of classical plays as part of an ongoing dialogue, not only between source material and translator, but also between different generations of adapters and translators of classic texts. Embarking on the adaptation of a lesser-known contemporary would be different: the opportunity might arise to inject into the bloodstream of Scottish drama a new voice, as Martin Bowman and Bill Findlay introduced the Québecois playwright, Michel Tremblay, or successive Scottish translators championed Dario Fo. An extraordinary, as yet unknown energy might well be released. But first, as Lochhead reminds us, there would have to be a phone call.

CHAPTER SEVEN

Liz Lochhead and the Gothic

Benjamin Poore

Liz Lochhead's version of *Dracula* is now over a quarter of a century old. It has, since its première at the Royal Lyceum, Edinburgh, become something of a classic stage adaptation of the novel, with a new edition published in 2009 by Nick Hern to supersede the popular Penguin edition.[1] In a newly-written introduction to the latest edition, Lochhead places the genesis of the play in its institutional context, as the idea of Ian Wooldridge, artistic director at the Lyceum, but also in the context of Lochhead's interests at the time: the stories of Isak Dinesen, of Angela Carter and theories of the unconscious. Critical analysis of Lochhead's *Dracula* has tended to follow this lead, presenting the play as a feminist critique of patriarchal repression: Bram Stoker's nineteenth-century perspective 'is replaced by a twentieth-century female writer's view that Dracula liberated his victims from their sexual and psychological repressions induced by a patriarchal culture and its dominant religion, Christianity'.[2] However, this chapter will argue that Lochhead's *Dracula* offers another Freudian rereading of Stoker's novel, one that is in some ways antithetical to the popular, familiar themes of repression and liberation: the uncanny. Freud's celebrated essay, 'The Uncanny' (1919) draws on the literary example of E. T. A. Hoffmann's 'The Sandman' to explore experiences of otherness, déjà vu, doubles, trance states and being buried alive. It seems tailor-made as an analytical approach to Stoker's *Dracula* (1897), where the vampire is a creature both alive and dead ('un-dead', in Stoker's coinage), and who can transform his victims into ghoulish, murderous doubles of their living selves. The double, in a much-quoted gloss on Freud, 'is paradoxically both a promise of immortality [. . .] and a harbinger of death',[3] and this is what the vampire, too, offers. Furthermore, this chapter will demonstrate that Lochhead's adaptation, through its rearrangement of character patterns, creates new uncanny doubles. In the second half of the chapter, I will use this sense of the uncanny to explore what could be regarded as Gothic elements, which lurk even in Lochhead's more naturalistic recent writing for the theatre. First, however, it will be necessary to establish the relationship between Lochhead's adaptation and its source text, as mediated by the cultural context surrounding the vampire in mid-1980s British culture.

The Uncanny Art of Adaptation

As William Hughes notes in his recent guide to *Dracula* criticism, Stoker's novel has had every trend in theory and criticism over the last half-century brought to bear on it, meaning that it 'is now a text that can seemingly be approached only through subsequent times, a novel whose critically accepted meanings both preface it and condition its reception'.[4] As Leslie Klinger points out, the first psychoanalytical study of *Dracula* appeared as early as 1959, and Richard Wasson had proposed a political reading of the novel in 1966. Such analyses and assumptions were culturally widespread, even if Lochhead had not been familiar with the work of critics like Moretti, Auerbach and Alan Johnson.[5] Furthermore, fictional approaches to the vampire from a female perspective were well-established by the late 1970s, not least in Anne Rice's phenomenally successful *Interview with the Vampire* (1976). Angela Carter's short stories in *The Bloody Chamber* (1979), which draw on vampire and werewolf tales, are mentioned as inspirations in Lochhead's 2009 introduction to *Dracula*,[6] and it is notable that Carter's stories feature such uncanny elements as a clockwork automaton, a magic mirror and a duke with no reflection ('The Tiger's Bride', 'Wolf-Alice'). However, as will be explored later, what is perhaps surprising in Lochhead's approach to adapting *Dracula* is the extent to which she draws on the popular-culture vampires of the Universal and Hammer movies.

Adaptation can be seen as the production of a cultural double. In the case of such a well-known novel as Stoker's *Dracula*, an adaptation can never be simply of the source-text alone, but of the cultural memories and associations generated by that source-text and its intertexts.[7] So, in a sense, Lochhead could not *not* adapt the movie Draculas as well as the 1897 text. However, as with the uncanny double, the production of a new work that strongly resembles an earlier one, and which takes its name, can be perceived as threatening to the identity of the older work, especially when the adaptation is from one medium to another, and may be perceived as taking a cult success to a mainstream audience (witness the protracted negotiations surrounding the scripting, casting and filming of Rice's *Interview with the Vampire*). Nina Auerbach argues that it is from Bela Lugosi's performance in *Dracula* (1931) that the popular impression was gained that the Count represented Eros, the repressed erotic element;[8] in Stoker's novel, it may be noted, Dracula is initially white-haired and pungent. Moreover, Auerbach continues, it is only with the Universal Pictures adaptation that van Helsing becomes effectively Dracula's double, the only one who can kill him,[9] an impression that is confirmed by their elements of physical opposition (white hair/black hair, piercing eyes/thick glasses) and similarity (indistinguishable foreign accents and stillness of manner). In contrast to Lochhead and the movies, in Stoker's novel, it is only the 'band of brothers', the 'Crew of Light', whose combined energies and professional expertise are able to defeat Dracula.[10] It was the Hammer film *Horror of Dracula* (1958) that rewrote all the novel's relationships as essentially familial ones, a pattern that Lochhead develops when she makes Lucy and Mina sisters. In fact, the relationship of the two young women was a feature of the much-lauded Traverse Workshop Company 1969 version directed by Max Stafford-Clark. In this production, he was beginning to develop the collaborative rehearsal writing methods that marked his work with Joint Stock. The script of this flexibly-staged production, which was revived and taken to London in 1972, was by a collective of poets and dramatists comprising Stanley Eveling, Alan Jackson, David Mowat, Robert Nye, Bill Watson, Clarisse Erikson and John Downing. Further, John Badham's *Dracula* (1979), set in the 1920s, lends to Lochhead's version a Renfield who is the truth-telling victim of authority, and the family literally sharing space with Dr Seward's madhouse, which is a feature of the flexible staging of Lochhead's script.[11]

The Parodic Double

If an adaptation of a canonical or cult work can threaten to overwhelm public consciousness of the source text, then the mischievous doubling that is parody can, like a poor adaptation, threaten the reputation of the original, can make us question whether it should ever have been taken seriously. At the time of Lochhead's adaptation, Dracula had been widely parodied and absorbed into mainstream culture, not least by the increasingly self-parodic Hammer films (such as *Dracula A.D. 1972*) and their afterlives in the television schedules. Dracula was already available as joke-shop fangs, as the 'ace' in a pack of horror Top Trumps playing cards, as an ice-lolly made by Wall's, and in reruns of *The Munsters* on TV. The uncanny threat of Lugosi's Dracula – always in the opera cape and medals – had been successfully recuperated into mainstream kitsch by postwar consumer society. Referencing the Count, and rendering his threat laughable, was a favourite practice for British comedians from The Two Ronnies and Spike Milligan to Alexei Sayle and Kenny Everett.[12]

These parodic doubles did seem to be having an effect on how seriously audiences were able to take their stage Draculas in the 1970s. In the wake of the sexual revolution of the late 1960s, Freudian interpretations of the story were nothing new, but could end up seeming more ridiculous than the Victorian morality they were supposedly highlighting. In 1976, the

Royal Court hosted an adaptation of *Dracula* by the Pip Simmons Theatre Group.[13] Here, the *Sunday Telegraph*'s reviewer noted, 'the perception of this Gothic horror tale's anticipation of Freudian symbolism, leads to a good deal of nudity'.[14] Dracula himself, Milton Shulman observed, 'was no dapper fanged-toothed gentleman [but] [. . .] a bull-necked, bald-head Kojak character wearing beneath his swirling cape a black leather jock strap and fish net stockings'.[15] What had made it even harder to take this kind of Freudian deconstruction of the vampire seriously was the enormous cultural purchase of *The Rocky Horror Show*, musical brainchild of Richard O'Brien, which had been developed, again at London's Royal Court Theatre, in the early 1970s.[16] The show eventually relocated to the King's Road Theatre, where it played until 1979; meanwhile, the film version, *The Rocky Horror Picture Show*, began to develop a cult following across the Atlantic.[17] The play and film reference 1930s and 1950s horror and science fiction, given a 'liberated' 1970s twist: the characters Frank, Riff Raff and Magenta all come from the planet Transsexual, in the galaxy of Transylvania. Frank-N-Furter himself, memorably played in the film by Tim Curry, cuts an unforgettable figure with his Dracula-like prominent incisors and undead panstick makeup, complemented by a sparkling corset, suspenders and high heels. As Raymond Knapp argues, the film makes the genres' sexualised dimension 'explicit and dominant over other elements (such as science and politics) [. . .] making [the films] seem, in retrospect to have been mainly about weird sex in the first place'.[18]

I want to suggest a further example of parodic doubling which helped to set the conditions for the reception of Lochhead's *Dracula* in the mid-1980s. In 1978, two rival productions of *Dracula* opened in London's West End: *The Passion of Dracula* by Bob Hall and David Richmond, and starring George Chakiris as the Count, played at the Queen's Theatre, whilst *Dracula* starred Terence Stamp and revived the 1927 script by Hamilton Deane and John L. Balderston, and opened at the Shaftesbury Theatre. Both productions having originated in America, *The Times* reported conclusively on 12 November 1978 that *The Passion of Dracula* had won both the critical and commercial battle. The production starring Stamp 'got worse reviews and has had such poor houses that it will close at the end of next week' – this despite reportedly being 'one of the most expensive straight plays ever mounted in the West End' and making striking use of sets and costumes by Edward Gorey.[19] However, it is not altogether clear on what artistic basis *The Passion of Dracula* was considered more successful. The *Sunday Telegraph* complained that the Stamp production 'resolutely refuses to take the work seriously', and the *Financial Times* found that the 1927 text was 'played with self-conscious mockery'.[20] Milton Shulman, on the other hand, found the opposite: 'Whereas *The Passion of Dracula*, which opened a few weeks back, has gone red-handed for parody, this production assumes there is a public eager to get their horror relatively straight.'[21] What this contradiction seems to indicate is an increasing difficulty – perhaps even a generation gap – in reading the *tone* of adaptations of *Dracula* in a post-1960s, post-glam rock, post-punk, post-*Rocky Horror* culture.

The way that Lochhead's adaptation handles this is by incorporating audience expectations of comedy, and their cultural competence and narrative foreknowledge, into the texture of the play. This is especially noticeable in Harker's meeting with the Count at Castle Dracula, surely one of the most famous and most-parodied film moments of all time. Dracula's conversation is arch and double-edged; eyeing Jonathan, but supposedly discussing cookery, he professes a preference for simple things: 'I know what I like.'[22] He hurriedly talks his way out of being photographed, and performs his '*classic recoil*' from Harker's crucifix.[23] This is a Dracula whose obvious vampirism, and Harker's ignorance of it, is a source of amusement to an audience with the cultural competence to recognise a vampire. He even attempts a feeble joke, and ends the scene with a Freudian slip on destiny/destination.[24] This Dracula, at least, does not quite carry on as though Frank-N-Furter had never happened.

Moreover, crucially, Lochhead does not distance herself from the source text (and its intertexts) or mock it; her stage directions frequently borrow verbatim from Stoker, with notes of approval for the richness and suggestive perversity of the material: '*Now, this is more out of Bram Stoker and can't be beat for atmosphere or stage direction*'; '*As described in Stoker's book* [. . .]'.[25] In an essay on the theatre company Punchdrunk, Frances Babbage traces the stage history of *Dracula* and notes, with regard to Lochhead's play, how the novel's 'unstageable' elements have become more accessible due to audience 'familiarity with anti-illusionist stage conventions' and the use of physical theatre.[26] Nevertheless, what is striking about Lochhead's script is the way that, while characters are rearranged in new patterns, the staging challenges are often presented to us verbatim from Stoker, suggesting that however it is achieved, it is fidelity to the novel's atmosphere that is crucial in these moments. As she states, seemingly in wonder, in her introduction: '*Such scenes . . .*', as if they already existed as drama in Stoker, without her mediation.[27] No doubt Stoker's experience as a man of the theatre, as Henry Irving's long-time business manager at the Lyceum Theatre in London, sustained this aspect of his writing.

Goths: The Living Undead

Finally, before analysing the play in further detail, we may note a further type of vampiric double. Whilst Lochhead's vampires were performing at the Edinburgh Lyceum in the mid-1980s, Goths were becoming an increasingly visible presence in Britain's urban spaces, some taking their style cues from nineteenth-century vampires. Britain at that time was a country ill-at-ease with itself, reeling from the alienating ideological and industrial shifts of Thatcherism, which were particularly strongly felt in the north of England, in Scotland and in Wales. One response was the dark escapism of Gothic rock (initially groups such as The Cure, Siouxie and the Banshees and Bauhaus). Whether the movement is read as a critique of bourgeois culture and a resistance to gender and sexual norms,[28] or as a means of expressing discomfort with 'the realities of the late-capitalist, post-modern Western world',[29] Goth has proved a remarkably long-lived subculture. Nancy Gagnier argues that Goths 'are particularly drawn to the vampire because of his spiritual isolation and failure to assimilate', and yet, paradoxically, 'the ethos is that of the victims in Stoker's novel. That is, the fact that the Harkers and Dr Seward can't prove the authenticity of their experience of Dracula makes the whole of their young lives a private, underground affair'.[30] As a further paradox, the vampire-inspired Goth dresses to signify a perceived outsider status, to appear uncanny, where Dracula himself was desperate to blend in and go unnoticed in late-Victorian London. Nevertheless, Lochhead's adaptation, with its blurred stage boundaries between castle, home and asylum,[31] its identification with the vampire and his victims (as the next section will explain) and its exploration of the psychological limits of sanity and desire, could be seen as a version in tune with that generation of the subculture's interests.[32]

The contemporary significance of Goths as interpreters of vampire style adds a further dimension to Lochhead's descriptions of the vampire brides in the 1980s text of the play, where they appear to 'strange synthesised music', with swirling fog, in tattered bridal dresses 'like bad parodies of Mina's (later) . . . their hair all fluffed out and them painted up red-lipped, white-faced and hectic'.[33] In contrast to the Hammer female vampires, these brides have had a Goth make-over of back-combed hair, red lips and white faces. They are, to borrow Gagnier's terms, both vampires and potential victims (since they are played by the same actresses as Lucy, Mrs Manners and Florrie). They are both Victorian nightmares and 1980s street style, implying a modern relevance to the ideas of duality presented in the play. If, as Goodlad and Bibby note, Goth fashions proffer 'fetishized representations of past bourgeois social formations' which work uncannily,[34] then the Goth vampire brides in Lochhead worked uncannily because their dishevelled inversion of past bourgeois social formations would have appeared strangely contemporary to its audience.

The Two Freuds in Lochhead's *Dracula*

In their introduction to the uncanny, Nicholas Royle and Andrew Bennett postulate that there are two Freuds: the Freud of the popular imagination, spouting 'mechanically predictable theories' such as the Oedipus complex, and the Freud who is 'different from himself', the implications of whose work run counter to his stated themes and assumptions.[35] There is no doubt that Lochhead's adaptation of *Dracula* was influenced by, as she states in looking back, the staples of Freudian psychoanalysis such as the 'polymorphously perverse' and 'the unconscious'.[36] What is questioned here is whether the 'other Freud' is also present in the text, given the many uncanny 'scenes' and situations in Stoker's novel. Lochhead insists that 'Rule One' for becoming a vampire victim is, 'First of all you have to invite him in',[37] but what if he is already there inside us? Is not that the more terrifying prospect? Dracula boasts to Mina, having tricked her into letting him in by disguising his voice, in Act II: 'I can whisper in your ear in the voice of your own conscience', and he gains access to Lucy whilst she is sleepwalking around Whitby.[38] So while, on the one hand, Dracula is fond of grand entrances, his hypnotic and telepathic powers make an invitation something of an empty courtesy: he is already in us, and can coax us out to him.

The implication of this interpretation is that there is a discomfiting parallel reading available in the play, for all the comforting medicalised classifications of the hysteric and the anorexic,[39] and the feminist reading that Dracula's intrusion 'signals liberation, empowerment, which the women effect for themselves'[40] or that Mina in the play realises 'the hidden potential of her female gender'.[41] Nor is this simply a case of Lochhead's adaptation being swamped, or straitjacketed, by the (by some reckonings) rampant misogyny of Stoker's text. Lochhead counterbalances what we may call the feminist/therapeutic reading of the play – that Victorian sexual and gender repression can be thrown off by letting something of the night rub off on Lucy and Mina – with, at every turn, suggestions that we have an implacable, (self-)destructive, demonic side that Dracula is able to tap into.

So, on the one hand, in the play's opening pages, Lochhead puns about the girls being '*as buttoned up as each other*', while the seemingly happily unrepressed (but mad) Renfield takes a break from sexual and scatological talk to advise the buttoned-up Seward to 'get some life' as Seward reads about the proto-Jungian animus theory, and of being 'starved of spontaneity'.[42] On the other hand, there is Lucy singing into the mirror and kissing it, Mina mentioning her likeness in a locket and Seward greeting Harker by their old school names (Harker insists that this younger Seward was 'a monster').[43] Whilst the imagery of birds in cages, and the appearance of a servant called Mrs Manners who keeps Mina and Jonathan's sexuality in check, suggests a questioning of patriarchy and social mores, Lochhead adds a second Mina to Stoker's cast, Harker's secretary, the offstage character Miss Bell, who is alternatively 'A peach' (as Mina has already been described) and 'A dragon', depending on who is listening.[44]

In a similar way to the doubling of 'good' domestic female characters with Gothicised vampire brides, the characters of Nurse Grice and Nurse Nisbett (one a sadist, the other a masochist) are played by the same actress in the original production, so that Renfield and the audience are disorientated by the unpredictability of the double. Once Renfield is dead, they begin '*reconciling themselves into one whole person*' as they wash down the body, which makes for another uncanny moment in the theatre, when the production has to find a way of showing that two characters who inhabited one actress's body are now the same characters in two bodies. No sooner has this happened, however, than Florrie doubles as both herself and the Nurses for that scene, '*switching from one character to the other*'.[45]

Florrie: 'Very strange. Very ordinary'.

Florrie Hathersage is Lochhead's creation; there is no character named as such in the book, although the first name, suggestively, was that of Stoker's widow Florence, who had to defend her husband's creation against the rapacious glances of stage and screen moguls.[46] Apart from the moment quoted above, Florrie does not have a 'double' in the play, except for the vampire bride that Harker sees. In a psychoanalytical framework, this can be put down to her common-sense attitudes; she declares to Lucy that 'bogies is all kinds and sorts of things except bogies', although her refusal to countenance superstitious garlic and crucifixes actually does let the bogey in.[47] An alternative reading, however, might be that Florrie remains 'undoubled' because her soldier boyfriend Jem has made her pregnant: there are already two of her. If the double often figures in literature as reflecting a crisis of identity, or lack of identity,[48] then it is especially interesting that the down-to-earth Florrie does not have the same other-generating crises of self that the middle-class characters have. After Mina's brief experiment in 'equality' in scene ix of the first Act, Florrie says sardonically to herself, 'better pinch yourself, Florrie my girl, look in the mirror, pinch yourself to see if you're real'; she already knows that she is, despite the vacillations of Lucy and Mina.[49]

Lucy: Perfume and Poison

As indicated above, Lochhead does not alter the schema of Stoker's novel, which insists that the vampirised Lucy is now 'unclean', demonic and must die. The vampire's bite induces a Jekyll-and-Hyde state where, far from being liberated, 'sweet old' Lucy is engaged in a prolonged struggle with the evil side of herself, full of rage and clamping its teeth like a beast – or a machine.[50] This battle lasts for the first two-thirds of the play. Once Lucy dies for the first time, the Hyde side of her has won, and she is resurrected as pure evil, in

the same body. Her staking is not a symbolic rape or revenge for a promiscu-
ous appetite, as some feminist interpretations would have it;[51] Seward is not
punishing her but asks her forgiveness that he failed her.[52]

While she is sick, Lucy tells Florrie, recalling a childhood game, that the
same rose petals can be used to make perfume or poison; Florrie adds that it
is easier to make poison.[53] This image should inform our reading of the play's
final moments. It has been argued that Dracula in Lochhead's play is linked to
'the cyclical nature of the earth' and that the red petals under which Harker
and Mina embrace at the end of the play 'signify the end of one cycle and
the beginning of another'.[54] However, if the red petals signify blood when
they fall, and if rose petals turn from perfume to poison, then Jonathan and
Mina's erotic reconciliation, under petals turning from white, to pink to
red, suggest an absorption of this poisoned blood. Their pleasure is bought
at Dracula's expense – it is Dracula's cloak of darkness that they lie upon –
and indeed there is a certain sadomasochistic thrill in their caresses being
accompanied by the screams of the vampire brides. Love acquires a degree of
cruelty.

Much has been written of van Helsing's connection with Dracula in the
play, here and elsewhere,[55] and so little will be added here, except that the
characters' knowledge of each other as old enemies has been read by some
critics as a mirrored identity, of the type manifested in other fin-de-siècle
pairs such as Jekyll and Hyde, and Holmes and Moriarty.[56] Leslie Klinger's
New Annotated Edition of *Dracula* even mischievously entertains the pros-
pect that van Helsing is Dracula, by taking the novel's narrative entirely
literally, and drawing attention to van Helsing's inconsistencies and malprac-
tice.[57] Structurally, we may note that van Helsing's appearance in the play
at the beginning of the second Act heralds Dracula's withdrawal: the hunter
becomes the hunted and van Helsing arrives as a 'good parent' to tell the
young people: 'These are the rules.'[58] The rules involve forgiveness, but also
supposedly-decisive stakings.

Despite this, while Mina has lost the external mark of sin on her forehead,
she still '*shudders* [orgasmically?]' as if the hammer blows at the end were
going through her.[59] Lucy's staking was referred to as '*a consummation*' in
death,[60] but Mina's consummation requires others' deaths so that she might
take on their properties (in the theatrical sense – the cape, the petals – and,
we are invited to think, in the figurative sense, too). The novel ends with
Jonathan's hasty post-script assuring us that Godalming and Seward are now
happily married, and that Mina has safely delivered a (human) baby boy.[61]
The play, on the other hand, invites us to question Harker's assumed happy
ending. While Lochhead follows the book's logic that vampirism is some-
thing that must be destroyed and suppressed, it is not: it no longer resides out
there, but in Mina.

It is useful at this point to delineate the distinctiveness of Lochhead's choices by comparing her adaptation with that of Jane Thornton and John Godber, undertaken for Hull Truck Theatre Company ten years later. While there is some actor doubling in that version, it is far less prominent (Renfield and Dracula, Harker and Holmwood), and there is more emphasis on an ensemble storytelling approach, where the actors address narrative to the audience and observe all the action, occasionally interjecting like a classical chorus. Like Lochhead, Godber and Thornton choose to make Mina's return to 'purity' at the end questionable: she even cries out 'Oh my love . . .' almost exactly as Lochhead's Mina does when Dracula dies.[62] However, Godber and Thornton's focus is firmly on Dracula as a dominant-male seducer who gloats about his multiple conquests, his taunting bringing out an animalistic urge in Stoker's Crew of Light to punch, kick, stab and shoot this monstrous manifestation of their sexual inadequacies.[63] The vampire is an alien, external threat, an idea reinforced by the concentration on vampire lore, Dracula's plans to conquer London and the practicalities of pursuing him. By contrast, Lochhead's play concentrates on the confines of Bedlam, and the language keeps returning to incongruous juxtapositions – like van Helsing's King Laugh speech – and the familiar made disturbing, like Jonathan seeing Lucy in every serving girl in Transylvania.[64]

It may also be useful to think of the success of Lochhead's *Dracula*, as an adaptation of a Gothic text, alongside the theatre company Shared Experience's version of Charlotte Bronte's *Jane Eyre*, scripted and directed by Polly Teale. In the 2006 revival of this popular adaptation, a large, multi-functional set allowed Bertha Mason Rochester, the 'mad woman in the attic', to pace in an upper area that is always visible to the audience, rather as Renfield comments on the action in Lochhead's *Dracula*. Shared Experience's staging made clear the correspondences between Jane and Bertha, and in fact suggested that in some ways Bertha was Jane's suppressed, passionate, almost feral 'other'. Such an interpretation of the novel had already gained cultural traction through the feminist and postcolonial critiques of the 1970s and 1980s. Hence, Teale, like Lochhead, was presenting a theatrical interpretation of a classic text as read through contemporary criticism.

Theorising the Double

The concept of the duality of man – and woman – of course predates Freud's essay on the uncanny, and indeed, Freud draws on literary examples, from Hoffmann's *The Devil's Elixir* to Oscar Wilde's 'The Canterville Ghost', to make his observations. What this section aims to do is to bring out some further aspects of the double, which Freud took for granted when writing

'The Uncanny', but which are of particular use in commenting more widely on Lochhead's use of duality.

In his study, *Doubles* (1985), Karl Miller shows the double life to have been a particular preoccupation of nineteenth-century Scotland and its literature. Most famously, there was Stevenson's *Strange Case of Dr Jekyll and Mr Hyde* (1886), a novel which, while nominally set in London, is commonly agreed by critics to draw on Edinburgh's Old Town/New Town divide, and also aspects of the bohemian double life that Stevenson, the supposedly respectable law student, was living there.[65] Miller emphasises the background to Stevenson's tale, in the history of William Brodie, an eighteenth-century deacon of Edinburgh town council, who led a secret life as a burglar, and about whom Stevenson co-wrote a play.[66] There is also the important Scottish literary precedent of James Hogg's *Confessions of a Justified Sinner* (1824). In that novel, Robert Wringhim remarks, on meeting his evil double, Gil-Martin, that he feels 'a deliverance, but at the same time a certain consciousness that I was not thus to get free of him, but that he was like to be an acquaintance that was to stick to me for good or evil'.[67] As Linda Dryden explains, with reference to Henry Jekyll and to Victor Frankenstein, once these misguided protagonists have created their monsters, there is no escape: they are 'bound to them until death'.[68]

Indeed, the notion of Scottishness itself as providing grounds for a 'divided self' is worked out even more thoroughly by Stevenson in what is arguably his macabre masterpiece, *The Master of Ballantrae* (1889). Like *Strange Case* (1886) and the unfinished *Weir of Hermiston* (1894), *The Master of Ballantrae* features a persecutor-villain, a creature of infinite cunning and moral vacuity who hounds his victim – in each novel a taciturn and normally self-possessed man – until death parts them. The seeds of the animosity between the two brothers in *Ballantrae* are sown when James goes to support Bonnie Prince Charlie's rebellion while Henry stays in the ancestral home, making a familial display of loyalty to the crown. As in vampire stories, James Durie, the Master, is several times assumed to be dead, only to return years later to continue financially, and emotionally, bleeding the family dry. And, as in other Gothic tales, the climax centres on a live burial, after the tension is ratcheted up by a series of murders in a remote mountainous region. The appearance of 'Mister Bally' (one of James's many names, nicknames and titles) is similarly supernaturally-charged, carrying an impression of the spectral, of deformity – like Hyde – and appearing to grow both older and younger with the passage of time.[69] As a swaggering, disloyal and doomed model for Scottish heroism, it is interesting that in the second part of the novel James reappears with a silent and mysterious Indian servant, the suggestively named Secundra Dass (a 'second self'?). He carries out his spying work, but could also be taken as a metaphor for the Scots' own role in British imperialism.

Duality in Lochhead's Earlier Drama

These ideas of the second self also figure consistently in Lochhead's work, and critics of her drama and poetry have already noted her extensive use of doubles. McDonald and Harvie refer to Lochhead's 'favourite device' of doubling.[70] Robert Crawford has also spotted this interest in duality in Lochhead's poetry: she 'likes to define her works in terms of splits or binary oppositions – female/male, Scottish/English, Scot/Celt, working-class/ middle-class, performance/text [. . . but] [w]hat seems fixed in Lochhead's work is usually open to becoming fluid'.[71] S. J. Boyd quotes an interview with Lochhead where the playwright mentions *Jekyll and Hyde* and the Scottish sense of being split, with the different halves communicating with each other (Scottish and English, masculine and feminine).[72]

Indeed, Lochhead can seen as a precursor of those modern Scottish writers who have re-energised the fictional exploration of the double, from the Stevenson and Hogg-influenced *A Method Actor's Guide to Jekyll and Hyde* by Kevin MacNeil (2010) to James Robertson's *The Testament of Gideon Mack* (2007), a response to *Justified Sinner*. As an indication of the story's continuing pertinence to Scottish identity, and its theatrical potential, Hogg's novel was adapted and directed by Mark Thomson for the Edinburgh Lyceum in 2009.

Yet Lochhead belongs to a more distinct strand of this history, too, that of Scottish women writers, who experience what Monica Germanà refers to as the 'double marginalisation' of being a Scot within the UK, and a woman within a patriarchal culture.[73] Germanà's study of the double in modern Scottish literature draws on Alison Fell's *The Bad Box* (1987) and Emma Tennant's *The Bad Sister* (1978) and *Two Women of London: The Strange Case of Ms Jekyll and Mrs Hyde* (1989), all of which draw powerfully on the Hogg and Stevenson tradition. Both Germanà and Ian Rankin also point to Muriel Spark's influence as a Scots novelist preoccupied with doubles and split selves, in such works as *The Ballad of Peckham Rye*, *The Driver's Seat* and *The Prime of Miss Jean Brodie*.[74] As Germanà suggests, the Gothic 'presents characteristics which make it akin to postmodernism' in its restless reinterpretation of history, and of its own traditions and motifs.[75] Lochhead is the prime theatrical example of this: her plays up to and including *Dracula* reimagine either Scottish history or the history of the Gothic.

Hence, looking back at early dramatic works like *Blood and Ice* (1982) and *Mary Queen of Scots Got Her Head Chopped Off* (1987), this motif of duality is strongly evident. *Blood and Ice* features a series of shifting and merging dualities, from Byron as Polidori's 'vampyre' to Mary Shelley as Dr Frankenstein. Frankenstein himself laments his monstrous creation as 'My own vampire, my ugly one, my own spirit let loose from the grave to destroy all that is dear to me', while Byron refigures both himself and Mary as Frankenstein's monster when he says to her, 'there is something in us which is very ugly. Do you not think we are somewhat alike? We are put together all wrong'.[76] In *Mary Queen of Scots*, La Corbie makes the doubling conceit of the play plain at the outset: 'Once upon a time there were twa queens on the wan green island, and the wan green island was split inty twa kingdoms.'[77] It is clear that this island is not big enough for both of them, and one must die. There are echoes of *Dracula*'s link with Mina when Bothwell kisses Bessie's neck, which sends a shiver through Mary ('*Sexual current as electric shock*', as the stage directions say), and when Mary and Bothwell make love on the floor during an explosion, with rose petals strewn on that floor.[78] At the end, there is a repetition of *Dracula*'s uncanny doubling of the cast as they become twentieth-century Scottish children, bullying Mary for being a Catholic girl and poking fun at 'Wee Knoxxy'.[79]

The 'Modern Gothic' Double in Lochhead's Later Drama

However, it is not until Lochhead takes on more contemporary settings and comedic situations in her original drama that a further, more surprising sense of the uncanny double begins to emerge. Just as works of the 'Victorian Gothic' (or 'modern Gothic' as it was termed at the time), such as *Dracula*, moved their stories from the 'exotic and historical settings' of eighteenth-century Gothic to the more disturbingly familiar world of 'bourgeois domesticity' or 'the new urban landscape',[80] so Lochhead's plays take on an extra, disturbing edge when they are set in contemporary Scotland, and when they appear superficially as comedies. To take *Quelques Fleurs* (1991) as a first example of this, the piece bears a superficial resemblance to other types of class-conscious comedy popular at the time, from the observational sketches of Victoria Wood, to the BBC television situation comedy *Keeping Up Appearances* and Alan Bennett's *Talking Heads* series. However, it draws on several of Lochhead's recurring contrastive pairs in its story of sibling rivalry between Verena and Joy (which is also a working-class/middle-class comparison), delivered to the audience in a male/female pair of contrasting monologues. Verena, whose husband Derek works on the oil rigs, tells us of the surrogate child that her highly-fertile sister was supposed to have for them, yet we are invited to conclude that Derek may have drunkenly slept with Joy. Derek's monologues to the audience work backwards, so that he becomes progressively more sober and lucid, an uncanny effect that could be said to echo the narrative experimentation of *Jekyll and Hyde* as much as theatrical antecedents like Harold Pinter's *Betrayal* (1978), the story of an affair told from the end and working backwards. In *Quelques Fleurs*, the social 'winner', Verena, becomes the loser and the 'loser', Joy, if not a winner then the person who holds onto herself and her position; the superior, sniping, house-proud Verena loses her composure, whilst the slobbering drunk regains his.

What is more, the account of Verena's attempt to adopt Joy's seventh child is shot through with dark circumstance and gallows humour, from Derek's 'Gothic-horror' approach to describing his job as a diver on an oil rig to his exasperation at his colleague's anecdote about the Yorkshire Ripper, a monster made domestic and familiar in the retelling. As with much of Lochhead's drama, questions of coincidence or predestination recur with Verena's accurate reading from the fortune-teller. Perhaps most characteristically for Lochhead, the play's dénouement reveals, from Verena's point of view at least, the monstrousness of wished-for things: the Frankenstein image once more. The title of the play is itself a metaphor for the ersatz renamed as the bewilderingly alive. 'Quelques Fleurs' is the name of a jumbo gift basket of toiletries that Verena had bought for her much poorer sister, and can be linked with the 'bloom' of pregnancy, as well as a washing one's hands of someone, which is what Verena does to Joy.

Lochhead's contribution to the London-based Royal National Theatre's New Connections series of plays for young people, *Cuba* (1997), has several points of overlap with these themes. The two 1960s schoolgirls, Barbara and Bernadette, are close friends but become 'blood sisters' in the course of the play, following in the footsteps of Lochhead's Lucy and Mina, of Tennant's *The Bad Sister*, of – in the male version – Stevenson's *Master of Ballantrae*, and before that Hogg's George Colwan, innocent half-brother to Robert Wringhim. The older woman at the start of *Cuba*, looking through the souvenirs of her school days, is named as 'B', and so initially could be either of the two. Certainly, there are the familiar contrasts from *Quelques Fleurs* between a working-class and a middle-class background, and the enormous difference that opens up between how the two girls are treated when they get into trouble for spray-painting graffiti on their school as a political protest. Equally, there is the familiar contrasting between male and female in the figures of the two teachers; the bluff Mr Shaw's complacent conservatism contrasted with the impassioned radicalism of Miss Arthur. However, what lingers about the play is the supernatural imagery with which Bernadette's ejection from the selective high school is achieved. Keats's 'La Belle Dame sans Merci' becomes a metaphor, not only for the nuclear apocalypse threatened by the Cuban missile crisis, but for Barbara's casting-out of her blood-sister into the underworld. She sees Bernadette, walking with her friends from the 'rough' school, her gaze passing straight through her. B's last words on her friend are the lines of the poem, 'Her hair was long, her foot was light / And her eyes were wild';[81] the flip-side of this seems to be that her eyes are no longer wild, her foot no longer light, having been denied the chance of social mobility at a selective school, which her talent had earned her. Instead, vampire-like, her middle-class blood-sister has fed on Bernadette, and turned her into a 'pale warrior'.

The highly popular *Perfect Days* (1998), a topical, touching comedy about a TV makeover artist and celebrity hairdresser, again might appear to be far removed from the world of the Gothic. Indeed, Lochhead writes that she set out to create a play, at last, with a happy ending, a stage version of the rom-com genre that held out new hope for the British film industry in the 1990s.[82] However, it is a happy ending achieved only through the betrayal of a sister-figure (Barbs's ex-sister-in-law Alice), and the destruction wrought in this relationship, as in *Quelques Fleurs*, by a child, the now grown-up Grant. For him the women have different uses: Alice wants to establish a relationship with her son, while Barbs takes him as a lover. There is also the rather bleak suggestion that Barbs is still in some way bound to her mother Sadie, who appears as a ghost at a late stage in the play, and that she only becomes free to make her own choices – is only free to be a mother – once her own mother is dead. While Lochhead specifies in the script that the version of the song 'Perfect Day' be 'the current multi-voiced and soaring BBC version' (the BBC's Children in Need charity had released the song the previous year),[83] many audience members at the play's Edinburgh première will have been aware of the song's original recording by Lou Reed. This is often interpreted as a paean to heroin addiction, and is certainly used ironically as such in the 'cold turkey' sequence of the Danny Boyle film *Trainspotting*, released two years earlier and set in 1980s Edinburgh. Even while the play attempts a rom-com-style happy ending, then, the tools it uses remain double-edged.

The published script of *Good Things* (2004), which premièred at the Tron Theatre, Glasgow, describes it as a 'sister-play' to *Perfect Days*,[84] and this is true in the sense that it explores the dilemmas faced by a woman approaching fifty rather than Barbs's forty; a woman, Susan, who has not delayed having a child, but who is dealing with the fallout of a more recent divorce. She has an offstage, fifteen-year-old daughter called Stephi, and has lost her home as a result of the divorce. Susan is now unemployed and working as a volunteer in a charity shop. She meets David, a man of about her age, recently widowed, who brings his late wife's clothes into the shop, including a fabulous pair of unworn shoes that fit Susan perfectly. The imagery of stepping into someone's shoes, of becoming David's new partner, is clear, but of course there must be obstacles – objects and people – placed in the way of this happy ending. There is an insistence in the play upon patterns of loss and retrieval (silk ties, shoes and a copy of *Doctor Zhivago* are all thought lost and then found again). Indeed, David himself is redeemed in Susan's eyes when it is revealed that he does not have a twenty-something girlfriend, but a daughter-in-law instead.

What gives the play a melancholy undertow is the pervading sense of loneliness, separation and mourning. There is a distinction made between proximity and closeness. Susan has moved in with her father, who is in his eighties and suffering from dementia, physically close but mentally hard to reach. The uncanny element in the play is the shadowy offstage figure of Robert Gilmartin, talked about but never seen, Susan's stalker who is killed by a bus. He can be taken as both a parallel figure for David, or for Susan: a bad, deranged kind of loneliness, which mistakes proximity for closeness. The name 'Robert Gilmartin', of course, welds together the names of the split personalities in James Hogg's *Confessions of a Justified Sinner*, Gil-Martin and Robert Wringhim. One reading of the play's title is as a truncation of the expression 'good things come to those who wait'; this is an adage that can be applied positively – to Susan's eventual happiness and hopefulness – or negatively, to the unseen Gilmartin. For a stalker, waiting becomes an obsession and a proof of devotion; like Hogg's Gil-Martin, he is Susan's 'persecutor and defender',[85] and in the play as in the novel, good things do not come to him. So Lochhead's Gilmartin the stalker works as a modern Gothic interpretation of Hogg's Gil-Martin; in place of the loneliness of being one of the Elect, as Wringhim believes himself to be, there is the loneliness of the modern city. Instead of the tortured relationship between Wringhim and his supernatural pursuer, there is the stalker's imagined relationship with Susan, and the sense of grievance that is fostered by being ignored: as Gil-Martin tells Wringhim: 'turn your eyes on me, and behold to what I am reduced'.[86] Yet Susan's Gilmartin does not pursue her until death, but is killed himself. This is either, according to interpretation, a reflection on the randomness of city life (and therefore a rebuttal of Wringhim's Gil-Martin and Gilmartin's belief in predestination), or an accident that Lochhead found structurally necessary for Susan to throw off her unhappiness without making her into a more aggressive character.

So we have seen how in Lochhead's drama doubling occurs within individual characters' psyches, between characters, between the adaptation and the source text(s), and between plays within the Lochhead canon. Finally, then, in the spirit of sibling rivalry, I propose a different (bad?) 'sister-play' for *Good Things*, and that is Lochhead's version of Euripides's *Medea*, on which she was working, for a period, at the same time. Medea expresses the fury with a feckless husband that Susan in *Good Things* must keep under control for the sake of her relationship with her daughter Stephi. Lochhead actually adds an encounter in the play between Medea and Jason's new bride, Glauke, who, like Stephi's new stepmother Natalie in *Good Things*, is '*a very pretty, very young girl*'.[87] Medea confirms men's worst fears about a scorned woman: she responds to Jason's name calling (tigress, fury, harpy, witch, she wolf, monster) with 'yes I am!'.[88] She is a creature of nightmare made real, her fury a contagion that literally drags Kreon down with his doomed daughter when he reaches out to hold her and the melted corpse – with its poisonous crown and gown, Medea's deadly gifts – sticks to him:

> a dance macabre well enough
> as the auld fellow tried to struggle free
> and the deid weight of the deid daughter
> pu'ed him to his knees again . . . corpse on corpse
> in a horrid parody of an unnatural embrace.[89]

Lochhead insists that her Medea is 'not supernatural', but 'all too human'.[90] Yet Medea certainly has the supernatural at her disposal; she calls herself the queen of 'pretty poison', refers to 'my certain expertise' and calls on Hecate to help her cook up a 'black black wedding breakfast'.[91] So the witch is in us, as, by another analysis, Hyde, Gil-Martin and the vampire are in us. They are part of what we are, horrid versions, but still us nonetheless. *Medea* performs the triumph of revenge and the death of redemption, just as *Good Things* performs the opposite. And, just as playing Medea is part of the everyday experience of women – as the representative chorus of '*women of all times, all ages, classes and professions*' suggests[92] – so the uncanny is to be found in the loft apartment, outside the charity shop and in the school yard, as much as in Castle Dracula.

'Invite him in': The Popularity of Lochhead's *Dracula*

This chapter will end with some reflections on the longevity of Lochhead's *Dracula* as an adaptation. David Glover notes of Stoker's Dracula, that, although his 'likeness cannot be captured either by painting or photography, the vampire continues to reproduce itself in a seemingly endless series of copies, always resourcefully different from previous incarnations'.[93] Hence, the vampire is always somehow absent, deferred, lost. Yet, from the vantage point of the early years of the twenty-first century, it is hard to remember a time when vampires were unfashionable, or a niche enthusiasm. Stoker's *Dracula* is a staple of school and university reading lists, available in a range of annotated and critical editions, and since 1999 there has been a scholarly journal solely concerned with *Dracula* studies.[94] The phenomenally successful Twilight series of books and films by Stephenie Meyer have made the vampire love story almost taken for granted as a popular culture staple, and have been followed onto screens by vampire–human romances in *The Vampire Diaries* (2009–), *True Blood* (2008–) and, originally for British television, *Being Human* (2008–), while the television series *Buffy the Vampire Slayer* (1997–2003) enjoyed phenomenal success. Far from being threatened by parody, there is almost a danger that our culture is taking these vampires as seriously as they take themselves.

What these films and series demonstrate is the transformation that Dracula has made over the last century, from monster, to villain, to alienated anti-hero, to hero. The focus has shifted from a heuristic process directed at the vampire ('What is this thing we are dealing with?') to a hermeneutic one directed by the vampire ('What am I doing here? What is my purpose?'). The ambiguity in Lochhead's version, between a vampire that is out there and a vampire that is in here, has been abandoned for a model of the vampire as more sensitive, and human, than us, because of his superior suffering and greater worldly experience. A landmark in this developing trend came with the release of Francis Ford Coppola's *Bram Stoker's Dracula* (1992). Gary Oldman played the title character as the archetypal loner, the dandyish outsider, the victim of tragic fate: centuries ago, as Prince Vlad, he had lost his wife in a *Romeo and Juliet*-style misunderstanding, and is in Victorian London seeking out her reincarnation, Mina.[95] As Glover comments,

> in Stoker's work the vampire is essentially mysterious and much of the novel's psychological interest stems from the struggle within the victims between their good and demonic selves. Here, however, it is the vampire himself who is torn between conflicting forces, who is looking for a way out. And clinically this turns him into something of a borderline case.[96]

The film is as much an elegiac tribute to twentieth-century screen Draculas as an adaptation of the novel, using studio sets, tricks of perspective and double exposure photography, just at the historical point when the cinematic photography (that late-Victorian new technology, along with the typewriter and the phonograph in Stoker's novel), was being superseded by computer-generated imaging.[97] Yet despite its visual complexities and ambiguities, the film's explanatory conceit of reincarnation destroys all notions of a double self, since the borders that separate life and death, self and other, are made porous. As Glover notes, Coppola in this film not only romanticised the vampire but sentimentalised him; as a result his desires are normalised and 'stabilized into a firmly heterosexual frame'.[98]

While readings of the vampire have become in some ways more sentimental, the treatment of Mina has become progressively more radical. Mina Harker in Coppola's film is a long way from the none-too-intelligent and rather passive Dianas, Marias and Alices, who play the Mina roles in the successive Hammer movies.[99] This Mina (Winona Ryder) is lively, assertive and intelligent, corresponding to recent assessments of her role in Stoker's novel.[100] It is only the reincarnated love story of the Coppola film that makes her role necessarily passive. Lochhead's adaptation was one of the first to read

Mina as neither victim nor whore, and has paved the way for further fiction featuring an 'empowered' Mina, such as Alan Moore's *League of Extraordinary Gentlemen* graphic novel series (adapted into a film in 2003). Most tellingly, when Bram's descendant Dacre Stoker co-wrote *Dracula the Un-Dead*, the 'official sequel' to *Dracula*, the version of the narrative chosen had more in common with Oldman and Ryder (or indeed, Edward and Bella from *Twilight*) than with Stoker's original: reincarnation, lost loves and Mina as an experienced, sexual and resourceful woman. Both the Stoker sequel and the Moore series, moreover, develop the idea, suggested by Lochhead's, and later Godber and Thornton's versions, that Mina remains part-vampirised by her encounter with Dracula.[101]

Lochhead's contribution to a modern Gothic sensibility, then, appropriately enough, has been double. Firstly, her adaptation of *Dracula* incorporated both popular knowledge of Dracula and more recent academic interpretations, creating a version that deconstructs itself in the production of its own narrative. In doing so, she provided an early stage model of the new vampires that were to dominate adaptations in other media from the 1990s on. But secondly, the suggestion, in Lochhead's *Dracula*, that we all carry our doubles within us as well as drawing them to us from outside, has been built, in the later plays, into a series of Gothic ruptures in the fabric of modern-day Scotland. And through these ruptures, a vengeful (usually female) double of Hogg's Robert Wringhim, the rejected sibling and unacknowledged child, can be seen peeping through.

CHAPTER EIGHT

Liz Lochhead's Theatre for Children and Young People

Anne Varty

I have never thought of children's theatre as anything separate. It's the same as theatre for everyone else – granted that you have to make everything very clear.[1]

Liz Lochhead's experience of her childhood lies at the heart of her work and she openly acknowledges its shaping influence. The memory poems in section II of *The Colour of Black and White*, 'Kidspoem/Bairnsang', 'Little Women', 'The Metal Raw', 'Lanarkshire Girls', 'Your Aunties', 'Clothes', '1953',[2] show how closely she holds to the pleasures, pains and retrospectively understood politics of her youth. Her experience of school surfaces much earlier, in, for example, the Gothic nightmare of 'In the Dreamschool',[3] reversed in her cabaret monologue 'Mrs Rintoul: Standard English'[4] to draw out the teacher's perspective. Lochhead's ability to filter the sensibility of the child through the lens of the adult is also a compelling strand of her work; she conveys an acute sense of the dynamic between the self as adult and child, captured by the dark refrain 'And there's grown-up mothers / Who are still little children / In the darkness of their heads' in the cabaret song 'The Sins of the Fathers'.[5] Oppression, whether social or sexual, can align children with women, and in some contexts, as she demonstrates in the final stanza of 'Kidspoem/ Bairnsang', also with Scotland. Yet even in naming 'the way it had to be said' Lochhead liberates the imagination.

The challenge to adult authority, the charting of the successes and failures of the younger generation's quest for freedom and identity, run as power-ful strands throughout Lochhead's theatre for children and young people. This chapter focuses on *Shanghaied* (Borderline, 1982), *The Magic Island* (Unicorn, 1993), *Cuba* (RNT Connections, 1997) and *Elizabeth* (Royal Lyceum Theatre, 1998).[6] The first and last of these, published as the double bill *Britannia Rules* and *Cuba*, are frequently performed and are embedded in contemporary Scottish culture through the school curriculum. Yet only the unpublished *Magic Island* is a conventional script for the entertainment of young people; *Shanghaied*, set in 1939, is a play 'about children' rather than 'a play for children' in which adults play children on an outsized set;[7] *Elizabeth* is 'about what happened to the same four characters as grown-ups on Coronation Day';[8] *Cuba*, and the early work for Scottish Youth Theatre, are written for young people to perform rather than to watch. The extraordinary success of these plays for young performers and audiences derives from their emphasis on theatre as process rather than product, levelling difference between performer and audience by requiring active collusion from the audience in the theatre making. The uninhibited imagination of the young is matched by Lochhead's zest for experiment; she asserts of *Shanghaied*, '[i]n the theatre you can do anything as long as you do it with truth and conviction'.[9] Invisible dog and budgie, movement between time zones and levels of stage 'reality', stage magic to make characters visibly invisible are some aspects of how Lochhead suspends the disbelief of her young audiences and requires them to join in. These plays also address adult audiences by using memory, whether biographical or cultural, as a theatrical device. Period settings, or the retrospect of adult characters, enlarge the apparently trivial encounters of youth with a sense of place in history, embedding individual development within political process, and affirming the value of the demotic and the local within a larger vision of global time and place. The oversized 'pine-apple' in the first scene of *Shanghaied*, for example, is brought to life from 'wir Empire reading book' and contrasts with the tinned chunks in Clydebank.[10] Lochhead notes how mixed audiences responded to that play, 'there'd be adults in fits of laughter at Billy and Morag concluding Emily was a spy and little kids wondering why – they were with Billy and Morag and this was *serious*'.[11] These plays create and engage communities by validating their sense of place and significance in history.

Lochhead states that the title *Shanghaied* came from the Glasgow East End Writers' Workshop where one member looked back at his evacuation as 'Shanghaied to Castle Douglas among all the coos and how he didnae like it. At all'.[12] Local and global come together in the title itself and provide the layered stage on which the play is set. Written after a week of workshops with Borderline Theatre Company, Lochhead states that the plot was of secondary interest: 'Thanks to working with those actors the play was all about relationships: the moment to moment dance of shifting alliances as they bonded together or re-aligned themselves under new pressures.'[13] The charm and energy of the piece are indeed in the kaleidoscopic rearrangements of loyalties, and the micro-dramas that play out against the sombre backdrop of wartime evacuation. The collision of values between rich and poor, town and country, girls and boys, older and younger, Catholic and Protestant, ensures that the tone is buoyantly comic. Yet the source of this fast-paced comedy is the fundamental instability of the group of children. The fault lines of their shifting alliances mirror those that divide contemporary Scotland. Each child has the potential to become 'other', alien, challenged or rejected by a larger or more powerful grouping; allegiances of the audience are given nowhere to settle except with the community of children, microcosm of Scotland, as a whole. The wartime certainties of ally and enemy are called into question through the experience of the drama itself, just as the divisions of an 'adult' Scotland, revisited in *Mary Queen of Scots Got Her Head Chopped Off*, are foreshadowed.

Shanghaied ends on a celebratory fusion of language and friendship in which posh Emily can say authentically 'Nae kiddin' and poor Morag can assert 'Share everything, actually.'[14] However, *Elizabeth* draws out the latent dramatic irony of this embodied optimism. Just as young Billy's 'I . . . hope they willny bomb Clydebank either. My Uncle Jackie thinks the Clyde's too far fur them tae fly',[15] with its nod to Stewart Conn's *I Didn't Always Live Here* (1967), is known by the adults watching to be in vain, so too is the assertion of unity. While in Janetta Street, Clydebank in 1953 'sharing' is a way of life conditioned by austerity, the notion that society can thrive by the levelling of difference has become party political and is paradoxically an instrument of division. It is represented by Billy's comic republican attitude to the Coronation; during his wallpapering routine he explains his Communist Party creed and tells Emily, 'the whole world over people are exactly the same'.[16] Written sixteen years after *Shanghaied*, and aging the characters by fourteen years (a trope shared with Caryl Churchill's *Cloud Nine*, 1979), *Elizabeth* shows how trivial differences in childhood become culturally entrenched. There is the same enlargement of the local by the global, with Morag's dreams of emigration to America and the context of the Coronation, but the drag of the past is too powerful to overcome. Billy is forced by Aunty Betty, and the values she represents, to marry his pregnant ex-girlfriend, and the play ends with both Billy and Hughie following Auntie Betty off stage '*slowly as a procession down a catwalk*' to the sound of the national anthem.[17] Only Hughie, whose parade costume as Britannia gives the title to the double bill, suggests hope for future change and liberation. Hughie, cross-dressed, androgynous, gay, with his anarchic good humour, warm pragmatism, his rejection of his father's hostile Catholicism, resists conformity where Billy and the rest capitulate. Reviewing the première of the double bill at the Royal Lyceum Theatre, Edinburgh, Mark Fisher noted, '[t]he first half of Tony Cownie's delightful production anticipates the post-war challenge to the class system, the second isolates the moment of uncertainty between the reliable austerity of the old era, and the unpredictable expansionism of the new'.[18] The double bill reflects a nation's coming of age.

The Magic Island, commissioned by the Unicorn Children's Theatre as an adaptation of *The Tempest* for seven- to eleven-year-olds, premièred in London in February 1993, directed by Richard Williams. Its Scottish première was directed by Leslie Finlay for TAG (Theatre About Glasgow) which was at the time the only company in Scotland devoted exclusively to theatre for young people. It opened at the Glasgow Mitchell Theatre as part of the Mayfest in May 1995, before embarking on an extensive Post Office-sponsored tour of Scotland, travelling as far north as Orkney and as far west as its final destination, Islay, where it closed in July 1995.

Lochhead reframes the story as Miranda's reminiscence, anchoring the allegiances of the young target audience. She reconfigures the Renaissance politics as a feud within an Edwardian theatre family, building astutely on the theatrical conceit of Prospero's 'we are such stuff as dreams are made on', and her script allows liberal space for stage business, closing, for example, with the direction *'finale of entire company doing tricks'*.[19] Most importantly, the primary relationship of Miranda's journey into adolescence is friendship with her cousin Fernandelle, rather than love with Ferdinand. The partnership that emerges is one of shared theatrical enterprise, 'play' both personal and professional, opening futures, not foreclosing them with the narrative device of marriage. Reviewing the first production, Sarah Hemming identified the focus on girls' friendship as 'a resounding success', asserting that it enabled 'some of the central ideas of betrayal and allegiances' to be tackled for a young audience.[20] The focus on friendship sounds Lochhead's most dominant note throughout her theatre for young people. It respects the perspective and needs of her audience, and fashions a crucial platform from which the values of the parental generation, their authority and traditions, can be safely questioned, assimilated, defied or rejected as the microcosmic society achieves maturity and independence. In interview with Marianne Brace for the *Independent* at the time of the London première, Lochhead identified freedom and responsibility as her themes and asserted that 'writing for kids, you're able to deal with these very large concepts'.[21]

Miranda opens the play, in an outer frame of action, addressing the audience. She is performing her backstage chores at the Empire Theatre where she works in a double-act with her cousin Fernandelle. Setting aside Lochhead's playful acknowledgement of postcolonial interpretation of *The Tempest*, attention is immediately focused on surprising transformation:

> I was [. . .] just running up a ladder – no, not 'running up a ladder' don't be daft – I mean running up a ladder in my new flesh tights, I mean 'invisible mending' – doesn't that sound magic? [. . .] I was delving in the hamper where we keep the cossys [. . .] two or three of these greeny-silver sequins stuck to my hand and they reminded me of fish scales and that reminded me of the island . . .[22]

Overlaying the verbal and the visual, demonstrating a punning metamorphosis and duplicity of language, Miranda tunes her audience's attention to the business of theatre. The rabbit she is holding is no longer just a fluffy pet, it is the rabbit that will be conjured out of the hat in her father Prospero's act as stage magician. Her words foreshadow Prospero's description, in the inner frame of the action, of the transformations he performed as star magician at the Empire, some twelve years earlier, before he was ousted by his avaricious brother Antonio, theatre manager, who invested their business fortunes in the new 'movies'.

The play itself is about invisible mending, healing the family fractures of the past which saw Prospero board the *Titanic* as ship's entertainer with his two-year-old daughter, to find himself washed up on the Magic Island and acquiring the real magic of Caliban's mother, witch Cora. It is theatre, the enacting of spectacular transformations, which achieves the healing change Prospero seeks, and which makes the meta-theatricality of the piece not simply an arch means of re-visioning Shakespeare, but a complete integration of form with content. At the heart of this mending is Prospero's wish to reveal the past, and the understanding of identity it holds, to his daughter. Aged fourteen, it is time for her to become integrated in a society larger than the microcosm Prospero has created around her on the Magic Island. As he tells the story of her origin, he performs, at the same time as he describes it, the old-fashioned stage magic on which his career was based: 'Rose to dove, dove to fan and / Fan to big fat ticking watch again / And all before the second hand described / One full circle'.[23]

Lochhead here deploys the symbolism of history, time and patriarchy with a deft lightness of touch. Miranda must now take her place in this cycle of metamorphosis, negotiating her own position in relation to her father, and begin to assume an adult identity which means stepping away from the past and the rules of her father. Prospero hypnotises Miranda with his stage magician's watch, a performance which neatly captures the commanding power of time, while it also embeds the urgency of Shakespeare's Prospero in stage action by at once recalling and submerging his lines to Miranda: 'The hour's now come; The very minute bids thee ope thine ear.'[24] The hypnotising of Miranda brings about a fusion of the drama's outer frame with its inner action as she is made to occupy a liminal space to prepare for her journey into adulthood.

Lochhead's Prospero summons Ariel to give an account of the storm:

Not a hair is harmed.
Their garments are dry, unmarked
And fresher than before.
As you commanded, I've split them up
In odds and sods and scattered them about the isle.
The brother's brat I landed all alone

And left it sighing up a storm,
Weeping torrents, in an odd angle of the isle.[25]

The speech typifies Lochhead's blending of Shakespeare's verse with her own
at key points throughout *The Magic Island*, recalling Ariel's words:

Not a hair perish'd;
On their sustaining garments not a blemish,
But fresher than before: and, as thou badest me,
In troops I have dispersed them 'bout the isle.
The king's son have I landed by himself;
Whom I left cooling of the air with sighs
In an odd angle of the isle and sitting,
His arms in this sad knot.[26]

Lochhead seizes her opportunity to veil the gender of 'the king's son' with 'the
brother's brat', just as she negotiates her own position as poet and playwright
in relation to the patriarchal authority of this text and its history. Caliban,
too, is drawn into this negotiation as his first long speech opens with a line
in idiomatic Scots, 'Ach, I'm away to eat my dinner!',[27] lending the nuance
of British politics to Lochhead's critique of Prospero's imperial designs and
Caliban's diatribe about the benefits of learning language.

The arrival of Fernandelle is heralded by a direct address to the audience
by Miranda, breaking the inner frame of action. Her speech links her own
growing-up with political difference between generations. She speaks with
the authority of generational difference and the acquired cultural maturity of
postcolonial values:

Maybe you think what Prospero did to Cora's son Caliban was no better than
what Prospero's wicked brother did to him? [. . .] maybe nowadays I'd agree with
you, but see, at that time my dad, he couldn't do no wrong, not in my eyes [. . .]
I still love him, but, see nowadays I don't seem to need to think he's perfect [. . .]
I was only fourteen and to be fair to my dad, he honestly didn't think there was
anything wrong with trying to civilise old Caliban. Ask your Mums and Dads,
wasn't there a time when you went to the cinema, and the Indians were the
baddies and the cowboys were the goodies, no question. Also – I've got to tell
you the truth – I was afraid of Caliban [. . .][28]

To show the crucial process by which Miranda acquired the perspective she
demonstrates here, the inner frame turns to the entrance of Fernandelle.
Prospero '*as if on stage in a theatre, binds Miranda's eyes, and puts them both
somewhat out of Fernandelle's sight while he watches*', to reinforce the contrived
theatricality of the revelation. Fernandelle is '*a girl as almost identical as pos-*

sible to Miranda in appearance'. As she grieves for her supposedly drowned father, Prospero removes Miranda's eye mask and asks her what she sees. Only on second bidding does she reply, 'A friend.'[29]

The action slows down for this resonant scene as both girls, *'astonished, stare at each other and slowly circle, staring into the mirror of each other. A magical, silent moment'*.[30] The technique of doubling, a Gothic trope which Lochhead always uses expertly, including in *Cuba*, suggests how the self must recognise itself as both unique and other to take an adult role. Miranda, and indeed Fernandelle, must learn to recognise themselves from the outside as well as from within. At the same time, each girl is introduced to a community of sameness, so that the experience of the uncanny is matched by the comfort of recognition, and resonates with every child's wish to be the same as their friends.

Fernandelle tells Miranda how she used to perform a double-act in the theatre with her sister Claribel. Miranda, confessing that everything she has practised with her father has been 'solo', does not understand this concept. Fernandelle explains by distinguishing between singing melody and harmony, a metaphor to indicate that friendship works by enabling partners to contribute differently to a shared activity, each enhancing the performance of the other. This is theatrically embodied when they begin a duet: 'Come to this yellow sand, / and find your friend. / When you will forgive, make peace / All storms will cease.'[31] Prospero tests Fernandelle's integrity, forcing her obedience with magic, but her faith in her new friendship wins through, 'I am as weak as a kitten [. . .] I'm sure that somehow everything will be well, because I have this friend, Miranda.'[32] Miranda, for the first time, finds herself at odds with her father, protesting at his apparent persecution of Fernandelle.

Act II opens on Fernandelle alone outside Prospero's cell balling and darning a mountain of socks. Prospero, unseen, watches as Miranda approaches Fernandelle and offers to help in an act of primal disobedience.

FERNANDELLE I'm supposed to darn every last pair [. . .] before I'm allowed to see you again. What are you doing here, Miranda, if your dad comes [. . .]
MIRANDA I'll help you.
FERNANDELLE That's disobedience. Did you ever disobey your Dad before?[33]

Prospero watches with satisfaction, 'Look at them! Two heads bent together over the same task. I never thought I should rejoice to see my own Miranda disobeying me!'[34] The test is for Miranda too, as her father gauges her independence of mind, her necessary fall, as she approaches integration into larger society.

The girls' togetherness gives them authority, which contrasts with the comically chaotic disputes amongst the triumvirate of fools, Caliban, Drinculo and Antonio, who attempt their own form of disobedience against Prospero. Eventually Antonio is humbled, and rewarded by reunion with his daughter. He first sees her acting out her integration in a new society through a skipping game with her cousin. Reunion complete, local island politics resolved, the restored family sets sail to buy back the Empire Theatre and relaunch their business.

Reviews judged *The Magic Island* on its fidelity to *The Tempest*. 'This is naturally not a production that attempts to get to grips with the profundity of this great play. But it does keep faith with many of its themes and its mysteriousness, celebrates the writing, and is performed with pace and humour,' Sarah Hemming asserted.[35] The Scottish revival met with a mixed reception, typified by *Scotland on Sunday*, which found 'the device of turning Prospero into a persecuted stage magician rather than a deposed king [. . .] confusing and [. . .] diminishing'.[36] Yet these responses overlook Lochhead's enterprise in this play, to speak directly and unpatronisingly to a young audience, without compromising her own voice.

In 1997 Lochhead returned to the theme of friendship with *Cuba*, a commission by the Royal National Theatre for its Connections series of scripts designed for performance by eleven- to nineteen-year-olds. The play was entered in the national competition by the Cumbernauld Junior Youth Theatre in March 1997 and has since been frequently performed by youth theatre groups across the world. Set against the Cuban missile crisis of October 1962, two fourteen-year-old grammar school girls, Barbara and Bernadette, find their friendship tested and discover how class differences as well as personal integrity shape relationships and life chances.

Lochhead has written about her own intense feelings during that historic period:

> The first time I fell in love with poetry – Mr Valentine was reading Keats 'La Belle Dame Sans Merci' out loud to us. We were in our third year, none of us 15 yet, and we were 'walking in the valley of the shadow of death'; I remember thinking just that, in just those words out of the psalm on the way to the school that morning. It was the time of the Cuba crisis and everybody was scared, even the grown-ups [. . .] As Mr Valentine read to us about [. . .] the lake where no birds sang – out of the flat normal November sky behind his head we really expected that death. And the bombs might come falling. The poem hurt us. Everyone in the class felt it, even the science boys and the maths geniuses who hated English, and the sporty class captain and Mr Valentine himself. You could feel it in the silence and the shared held breath when the voice stopped.[37]

This experience surfaces again in her short story 'La Belle Dame Sans Thingwy' broadcast on BBC Radio 4 on 24 September 1991.[38] The unnamed narrator recalls 'The Day' of revelation on which she fell in love with poetry as her beloved English teacher Mr Luff read out Keats's poem to the unwilling class of 3A:

> There would be just one gigantic groan, telling you mines would definitely be the loudest. Aw naw, an ode or something. The usual. To a skylark [. . .] or a Greek vase or something. A vase! Please [. . .] What were these guys on?[39]

The speaker remembers her fear of imminent death in the light of the Cuban crisis then unfolding in their midst, which fuses with her intense jealousy of her classmate Aileen Walkenshaw who left school at Christmas in order to marry Mr Luff. Keats's poem of enchantment and betrayal reflects her complex feelings in relation to Aileen, Mr Luff and Cuba: 'And this was the Day of the Poem. See it all connects up.'[40]

These motifs recur in *Cuba*, which, like *The Magic Island*, is told as a memory play, triggered by Barbara's 'sorting through' boxes in her dead mother's house.[41] Finding a class photograph of herself, and her best friend Bernadette, she is transported to the crisis of 1962. Just as the British foreign secretary announced on 23 October 1962, 'Man is now at the point of choice [. . .] whether we blow ourselves to bits or whether we [. . .] negotiate,' so the play culminates at a point of choice for the two girls, whether to destroy their friendship or to honour their secret pact as blood-sisters. At the start of the play Barbara and Bernadette are indistinguishable and inseparable; it is not initially clear to the spectator which one of them is reminiscing. However, class differences quickly become apparent: Barbara's father, Dr Proctor, fills out the crossword while Bernadette's father, Mr Griggs, completes his football coupon.[42] The socially constructed aspect of these differences is inscribed in the script; they can be enhanced in performance, as was done, for example, in a Brechtian production by the 16/22 Company at the Oxford Playhouse in 2009 in which the girls' parents were cross-dressed. The mothers were played by young men wearing white aprons, quickly set aside for the same actors to play school boys; the fathers were played by young women who adopted masculine poses. This comic technique underlined stereotypes and exposed the differences between class, gender and nation as ideological rather than inevitable and natural.

Political tension and uncertainty dominate life at home and at school; the girls, on Bernadette's prompting, decide to support Cuba, 'the prawn' in 'Krushchev's game'.[43] The movement of scenes and dialogue is swift and witty up to the point at which anxiety overwhelms the English lesson at school when 'La Belle Dame Sans Merci' is recited stanza by stanza round the class. Dialogue is suspended as the poem unfolds. Barbara breaks down as she recites:

I saw their . . . starved lips in the gloam,
With . . . with horrid warning gaped wide,
And I a- And I awoke . . .[44]

The scene embodies the way inscrutable forces lead the heroic to perdition, and mirrors the mesmerising power of the Cold War over global politics and its threat to individuals. It is a daring episode in the drama, a yielding to poetry that flips the everyday experience of the play inside out. Up to this point in the play teenage experience had been focused by chat of magazines and clothes, make-up and men, comically tinted with the surreality of imminent death. During the reciting of the poem the uncanny is unleashed to dominate the stage, and teenage experience can be traced only in reluctant giggles or hesitant delivery. The recitation sits at seeming odds with the surrounding drama, yet it is the poetic climax of the play, drawing its complex themes together. The tone of the drama that follows is unrelentingly dark as the girls are captured by the desolation of the zeitgeist.

Hiding in the toilets of what they believe to be their deserted school, they enact a ritual of blood-sisterhood, stepping firmly into a world of their own making. Then they spray 'Cuba Libre', one word each, in stolen red paint across the headmaster's door. The colour of the paint and the colour of the blood they have just exchanged unite their solidarity with rebellion and anticipate larger bloodshed. Caught and called to account, they are discussed by the headmaster before the interview. He recalls his circulation in the same society as the parents of 'the doctor's daughter', ending 'Who's the other girl?'[45] Bernadette's fate is sealed. Other, alien, foreign, not one of us, the battle lines of Kennedy and Krushchev are clear; the Cuban crisis simply magnifies mutual suspicions within civil society, serving a function akin to that of war and coronation in *Britannia Rules*. This is the moment of choice, the dramatic climax of the play that speaks to generations of young people. Will they have the courage to stand up to authority, to honour friendship, sisterhood and dissent, or not? Bernadette confesses, expecting Barbara to follow, but Barbara remains silent. Bernadette is expelled and has to attend the 'rough school';[46] Barbara is scolded for allowing herself to be led astray by her disreputable working-class friend. The middle class maintains its power. Their ritual was instantly betrayed, and both girls become ghosts, carried into the 'gloam' of Keats's poem. B tells us that if they met on the street Bernadette 'would look straight through me and I would just look away'.[47] And B, the adult Barbara, is consumed by her reminiscence into being the unseen observer of the entire drama.

Lochhead has written vividly about her own schooldays at Dalziel High in Motherwell, not only in her poetry but also in a short autobiographical memoir, 'A Protestant Girlhood'. Here she describes how she felt alienated from her own education:

> Nothing in my Education had ever led me to believe that anything among my own real ordinary things had the right to be written down. What you wrote could not be the truth. It did not have the authority of English things, the things in books. Muffins and jam. I knew what they wanted you to write. My grown-up writer's fear is that this might still be so.[48]

Her strength as a writer for young people comes precisely from this determination to write 'the truth', drawing on experiences so keenly felt and remembered even as they were subverted by a phantom authority that simultaneously possessed and estranged her. The authenticity of her plays for young people derives from her uninhibited scrutiny of youthful experience, in particular the vicissitudes of friendship located within a particular time and place. Even the archetypal, mythical friendship depicted in *The Magic Island* affirms the conditioning role of social and historical specificity. *Shanghaied* presents friendship as unexpected yet mutually nurturing; it salutes the binding quality of shared language which is often literally denoted by an exchange of food and words as, for example, Emily discovers what 'sair haun' means and Hughie learns how to eat boiled eggs for breakfast. *Elizabeth* shows these relationships buckling under overwhelming pressures. *The Magic Island* brings cousins together to learn independence from their parents' generation. *Cuba*, like *Elizabeth*, examines friendship destroyed by the interference of cultural and social norms:

> Sometimes I think the whole different backgrounds thing was grossly exaggerated, although much was made of it at the time . . . Different sides of the track maybe, but I'd say they were far more alike than – well, certainly *much* more alike than they thought they were.[49]

In every case, the bonds of youthful friendship, made or broken, are seen as integral in the shaping of both the individual and the society in which they become adults. Lochhead moves effortlessly from the specifics and idiosyncrasies of the individual to the larger picture of communities, cultures and political futures.

CHAPTER NINE

A Woman's Voice

Adrienne Scullion

She will bring enthusiasm, the ability to communicate with youngsters in particular, to represent Scotland [. . .] particularly with an accent on the role of women in Scottish society.

(First Minister Alex Salmond announcing appointment of Liz Lochhead
as the Scots Makar, 19 January 2011)[1]

Commenting in 2011, First Minister Alex Salmond proposed that, '[i]n creating the post of national poet, the communities of Scotland demonstrated the importance it [*sic*] places on the many aspects of culture which lie at the heart of our identity'.[2] In many ways this is an attitude that places the arts and artists at the heart of the national conversation, and certainly the nomination of Lochhead to the role underlined her public profile within Scotland and signalled the reach of her work in the context of Scottish education and in a wider popular consciousness. But, while her confirmation as Makar was flagged as being 'a non-political appointment',[3] it was clear that both political and cultural institutions anticipated her potential to make an impact within and without the nation:

> With a natural ability to reach all ages and touch both sexes through her writing, Ms Lochhead has also been immensely successful at championing the Scots language. She continues to reach out to school pupils through her work which is widely read in Scotland's schools and she is also a much valued role model, advocate and inspiration for women who are given a strong voice in her writing.[4]

Such sentiments reflect Lochhead's position as a performer, communicator and educator with an acknowledged high-profile presence at the heart of civic Scotland; but as her public profile and civic role have grown over the years, these same reflections might also prompt a review of the cultural role of her plays and, by extension, a reassessment of the changing voices of the women that populate her dramas from *Blood and Ice* (1982) and *Mary Queen of Scots Got Her Head Chopped Off* (1987) through to *Perfect Days* (1998) and *Good Things* (2004).

Lochhead's is certainly a repertoire that places a woman or women at the centre of the drama and at the heart of the narrative: Elise, Mary Shelley, Mina Westerman, Mary Stuart, Elizabeth I, Barbs Marshall, Susan Love, even Medea and Agnes in her translations, are characters that drive the narrative forward. So doing, they give voice to the social and domestic, sexual and creative roles of women within societies that politically and culturally marginalise and devalue their work and their lives. Lochhead takes the common view of these women – Mary Stuart as *femme fatale* and Elizabeth I as scheming politician in *Mary Queen of Scots Got Her Head Chopped Off*, Mary Shelley merely as daughter of Mary Wollstonecraft and William Godwin or lover and wife of Percy Bysshe Shelley, Elsie as downtrodden maid in *Blood and Ice* – and peels back the mythology, drawing out the person's essential humanity. Lochhead's feminism strives to find in each of her creations a more empowering identity than has traditionally been projected.

Reviewing the repertoire overall, however, Lochhead's trajectory is also one where both plays and dramaturgy move from the epic, historical and allegorical to the sentimental and domestic. This may indicate a parallel journey from a voice and role at the heart of national and international feminist practice and scholarship to a different role and voice – arguably a more consensual position – within and for post-devolution Scotland. Certainly, in the thirty years since *Blood and Ice* Lochhead has moved into higher-profile public roles within Scottish civil society, not only as Makar, but in advisory and advocacy positions regarding Scottish primary and secondary education – with a particular commitment to championing the study of Scotland's cultures and languages in Scottish schools – and making public her personal support of Scottish independence. In parallel with this growing post-devolution role, the focus and potential of her theatre work, and the critical literature around it, have changed hugely. Indeed, my proposition is that, as Lochhead has developed a voice and influence within aspects of the post-devolution national conversation – specifically concerning poetry, education and language – she has turned from drama as mode of investigation or communication. Arguably, her political engagement is now firmly made in her own voice – unmediated via stage representations or other performance metaphors. Reflection on her position in Scottish culture over some thirty years raises a set complementary questions: has Lochhead's dramaturgy moved from the cultural or political cutting-edge; has theatre itself become less productive for her as a site of social engagement; has the critical literature around Lochhead faltered and, consequently, overlooked more recent works that do retain critical and political potential; does the perceived changing nature and status of Lochhead as a leading voice in Scottish culture and cultural studies raise more general issues about the post-devolution national conversation, about negotiation of institutional engagements, relationships and questions?

Earlier critical discussion pushed towards a reframing of the historical 'absence' of a Scottish dramatic literature by focusing on the representation of the working class and on a particular performance tradition, specifically the popular tradition in Scottish theatre and its roots in and connection to popular stages of all kinds, not least music hall and variety theatre. This reinforced a mythos of Scottish theatre as popular and political, rather than literary or play-based, and proposed a distinctive and exciting combination of tropes for Scottish theatre that were very different from the modes and traditions of English or Irish theatre. But it still excluded the voice and representation of women as a radical – or even visible – force in what, like so much of wider Scottish culture, remained dominated by patriarchal and phallocentric discourses. It was about recovering a marginalised and neglected tradition of Scottish working-class theatre making and writing.

Marked by essays by John Hill and Douglas Allen in the late 1970s, it had its most visible apotheosis in 7:84 (Scotland)'s 'Clydebuilt' season in 1982.[5] A particular feature of this was the combination of contemporary theatre practice and historical inquiry, which has proved a model of subsequent theatre scholarship within Scotland. So, in addition to revivals of George Munro's *Gold in his Boots* (1947), Joe Corrie's *In Time o' Strife* (1927), Ewan MacColl's *Johnny Noble* (1946) and, most influentially, Giles Havergal's production of a revised version of Ena Lamont Stewart's *Men Should Weep* (1947), the 'Clydebuilt' season saw parallel publication of a number of core plays, in volumes including other primary sources like contemporary reviews, interviews and photographs. *Men Should Weep* apart, however, the recovered plays of the 'Clydebuilt' season and a high-profile subset of 1970s plays – Bryden's *Willie Rough* (1972), Roddy McMillan's *The Bevellers* (1973), Tom McGrath's *The Hardman* (1977) – attended to narratives of the nobility of male labour, wounded masculinities and beleaguered communities of urban men. This focus – according to Lochhead this 'macho flowering'[6] – was challenged by a second phase of scholarship around Scottish theatre specifically marked by commitment to feminist theatre practice, critical practice and historiography – and, while this work did address other contemporary women writers, like Sue Glover and Rona Munro, it was Lochhead's plays that served as a shared point of reference for scholars publishing internationally.[7]

The pillars of Lochhead's early reputation – key foundations of her critical canonisation in this phase of Scottish theatre scholarship – were *Blood and Ice* (1982) and *Mary Queen of Scots Got Her Head Chopped Off* (1987), plays about literature, history and politics, about myths and metatextuality, about women and about representation. The context of their reception was sustained public debate about political nationalism that impinged strongly on the critical and scholarly agenda of Scotland. The roots of this nationalism – and indeed the roots of the first phase of Scottish theatre studies – lay in the 1960s and a generation of Scottish historians taking seriously the past of Scotland, and the academic and popular recovery of Scottish folk traditions. Such nationalism took on a new urgency in the 1970s with North Sea Oil's discovery and economic exploitation. Taking popular and cultural as well as political forms, this led to the 1979 devolution referendum. Controversially, that required the support of 40 per cent of the electorate and, while a majority voted in favour of devolution, that tariff was not met. The Scottish Nationalists joined the Conservatives and Liberals in passing a vote of no confidence in the Labour government, which lost control of the House of Commons. This was a prelude to the 1979 election of a Conservative government under Margaret Thatcher's divisive leadership.

After the failure of the 1970s devolution movement and election of the Conservative government, the culture of Scotland seemed most confident when oppositional. Frustrated and alienated by London's political, cultural, social and financial ideologies, Scottish culture worked in two contrasting, but complementary, ways. On the one hand, new work for and in Scotland looked afresh to the past, creating texts of linguistic and visual specificity, reassessing the cultural influences that make Scotland: Lochhead's *Mary Queen of Scots Got Her Head Chopped Off*, John Byrne's *The Slab Boys* (1978) and Tony Roper's *The Steamie* (1987) can be seen as texts working in this way. On the other, there was increased internationalism of outlook in terms of influence, process and market in the careers of new artists, most famously the 'New Glasgow Boys' – Stephen Campbell, Ken Currie, Steven Conroy and Peter Howson – but also in critical questions that tested Scotland's cultural and political nationalisms and representations against national movements in a range of postcolonial environments – Quebec, Catalonia, the emerging Baltic states. The former was marked by use of feminism and the representations of women as a new lens with which to integrate established and canonical representations; the latter drove Scotland's feminisms – and Scotland's critical feminists – into a range of international contexts and conversations, including the body of secondary literature inspired by Lochhead's plays.

In this period and context, bold reframing of the historical and literary past typified Lochhead's work; the critical work engaging with it was similarly political, finding critical cohesion in aligning feminist praxis with nationalist theory. Recovering women's stories, reframing women's histories, restaging the history play, reinterpreting folk tales by prioritising the view of women underpin feminist culture in the 1970s, 1980s and beyond. This imperative is central to Lochhead's early work. But what made her work particularly appealing within emergent critical discourses both without and within Scotland was her explicit engagement with and paralleling of gender and national identities and, specifically, her exploration of links between representing women and representing Scotland. In this phase of her playwriting – and the dramatic monologues and poetry she was writing at the same time – Lochhead adopts a classic feminist strategy of retelling history from women's viewpoints and uses a feminist dramaturgy to reimagine both history and the history play. With Lochhead and *Mary Queen of Scots Got Her Head Chpped Off* at the centre of a nexus of plays and critical responses, Scottish theatre-making and theatre criticism undertook intersecting exploration of history and historiography, national identity and nationalism, gender identity and feminism. In this body of critical literature, *Mary Queen of Scots Got Her Head Chpped Off* is valued as typical of Lochhead's feminist dramaturgy, re-presenting the hegemonic myths of Scottish national identity, deconstructing both legitimate history and popular culture, and activating metaphors of playing, acting, story-telling, performing: 'Once upon a time', La Corbie, the play's fantastically grotesque narrator, female chorus and sometime-conscience, begins, 'there were *twa queens* on the wan green island.' The play boldly re-enacts their stories and lives, lies and legends. Just as received images of Mary Shelley are dissected in *Blood and Ice* so, in *Mary Queen of Scots Got Her Head Chppoed Off*, Lochhead deconstructs the mythology associated with Catholic Mary and Protestant Elizabeth and, again, finds disturbing parallels between the demands made of women in the play and in the past, and the prejudices that still limit their expectations and ambitions.

Lochhead's re-examination of the history, mythology, legends and even iconography of Scotland's past attracted contemporary feminist critics who read and reread her iconoclastic version of one of the 'privileged moments' of Scotland's political past. Engaging with Lochhead's version of history, the critics' readings influenced wider debates about Scottish literature within and without Scottish studies. This influence can be identified in an early (1992) essay on Lochhead in an anthology using the postcolonial to critique British literary canons. Here, Marilyn Reizbaum interrogates the '"double exclusion" suffered by women writers in marginalized cultures [. . .] where the struggle to assert a nationalist identity obscures or doubly marginalizes the assertion of gender (the woman's voice)'.[8] Reizbaum explores this proposition via case studies of modern Ireland and Scotland: her particular concern is the canonical trends complicit in colonial or other dominant ideologies of place and gender. She proposes that, within the marginal and/or the postcolonial place – within Scotland in fact – two canons exist: 'one that is for the most part contained by geographical and cultural boundaries; and one that is presented as universal, is "universally" responsible by omission from the creation of the "inside" canon'.[9] For her the marginalised culture, its cultural apparatus and infrastructure, have been fatally compromised by servicing and supporting an externally approved (denationalised) canon and colluding in devaluing the circulation and reception of the 'inside' canon within the culture. In many ways, it is a classic reading of the dichotomous position of Scotland within the Union, played out by some as 'cultural sub-nationalism' or 'the Scottish "heart" split from the British "head"' or the 'Caledonian antisyzygy'.[10] However, for Reizbaum, a feminist praxis combined with a nationalist imperative has the unique potential to expose and change the 'double exclusion' of place and gender. Her explication is a reading of *Mary Queen of Scots Got Her Head Chopped Off*:

> Mary and Elizabeth are presented as personally and historically trapped: the former is remembered for her sexual exploits and her infamous death [. . .] the latter as a powerful ruler, albeit a sexual curiosity. What is new here is Lochhead's dramatic proposition that these figures are united, not by political defeat and conquest and not by gender alone, but by a re-vision of the interplay among their roles as women, heads of state, and defenders of the faith. Lochhead involved the historical linkage of cultural marginalization, gender, and religion, but she disrupts the essentialist fiction by suggesting it is a loss of autonomy that joins them.[11]

Or, as Lochhead summarises, 'when's a queen a queen / And when's a queen juist a wummin?'[12]

Lochhead's work and the critical canon around it were part of an interaction that changed the nature of Scottish theatre and Scottish theatre scholarship. The work made important and necessary contributions to both Scottish studies and theatre studies: while women artists had been frequently overlooked in the former and Scotland was often just a footnote or token add-on in the latter, the international reach of Lochhead's plays – and the critical agenda that drove, extended and reinforced this – achieved an deep, unexpected and sustained influence within and without Scotland. The plays and their interrogation affirmed the popular theatre tropes of Scottish theatre-making – identifying in Lochhead's work a distinctively national use of cabaret-style, mix of genres, heightened language and direct address that was celebrated as counter-cultural, radical and feminist. A growing secondary literature – almost all (self-) identified as feminist – circulated to an international readership as flag-bearers of a new set of images, questions and discourses about Scottish theatre. Work by and around Lochhead pushed (the study of) Scottish theatre out from the footnotes of studies of English (language) dramaturgy and into international feminist debate.

For all its combined local and international influence, however, the critical work that might be connected to Lochhead is also an interrupted or stalled literature: stalled by shifts in Lochhead's own playwriting – leaving aside her important series of translations discussed by John Corbett – towards the contemporary comedies of *Perfect Days* and *Good Things*, and interrupted by the relative infrequency of revivals of her work. And part of the reason for

this navigates back to Lochhead's career. At the same time as a critical ortho-
doxy was growing Lochhead found her original playwriting all but frozen out
of actual theatre-making. Despite the intellectual excitement that so many
scholars found in her work, the same did not seem to hold true for theatre-
makers; revivals were few and far between and, until recently, were certainly
not undertaken by Scotland's major companies.[13] When Lochhead did come
back to original playwriting it was with an unexpected sequence of plays –
Perfect Days and *Good Things* – that did not really fit into the canonised – or
even mythologised – critical paradigm that had coalesced around her work.

In *Perfect Days* successful Glaswegian businesswoman Barbs Marshall is
presented as having all the trappings of a trendy urban lifestyle – stylishly
appointed loft apartment, wardrobe of designer clothes, bantering gay
(male) best friend, quirky assortment of bickering-cum-supportive childhood
friends. But with her fortieth birthday fast approaching, and without any
reliable sexual partner on the horizon, Barbs is increasingly desperate to have
a baby. Her story, the play's narrative, is about her finding an appropriate
sperm donor and, by extension, negotiating and reimagining her networks of
friends and business acquaintances into a new kind of family for a new urban
economy. So far, so conventional. As in Lochhead's earlier plays, there is a
paralleling of the woman and the place – here Barbs and Glasgow – but the
reach of that metaphor is arguably more limited than in previous iterations.
Randall Stevenson was all but alone in his critical engagement with *Perfect
Days*, making a committed effort to link it to Lochhead's earlier plays and, in
particular, to *Mary Queen of Scots Got Her Head Chopped Off*. He argued that
the earlier play

> interrogate[d] national behaviour and identity in terms of historical origins or
> analogues. In *Perfect Days*, by contrast, national life and outlook are much less
> pressing issues in themselves and form instead part of a more familiar, estab-
> lished background against which still wider questions may be highlighted.[14]

This is a bold claim, given the alignment of political and cultural nationalism,
feminism and socialism that many critics identified and championed in the
earlier play – and that, in my reading, drove both the play and the connected
scholarship into a genuinely international space of critical engagement.
Stevenson's premise is that a play that begins 'Country: Scotland. Whit like
is it?', and then attempts to answer that, is introspective and narrow. He
continues by arguing that, in comparison, *Perfect Days*:

> [p]erfectly exemplifies the change of idiom the actor and director Sandy
> Neilson anticipated when he remarked that:
> > In any form of development in drama, you're going to go through the classic
> > syndromes of [. . .] playwrights writing about, first of all, their own identity

[. . . a] fairly introspective sort of drama – who are we?, who are the Scots?, how do we actually relate, culturally speaking, to all those other people around us? Surely we have an identity and a voice of our own. Then, eventually, that gets written out and [. . .] we can then go on and expand the subjects to become truly international, yet with a distinctive Scottish voice.[15]

Stevenson's argument is, then, that *Mary Queen of Scots Got Her Head Chopped Off* is introspectively and narrowly about Scotland, while *Perfect Days* demonstrates Lochhead widening the locus of the Scottish playwright, expanding her subject, as he puts it, to become internationally relevant. Even to attempt this reading, Stevenson has to put aside any interrogation of Lochhead's work from a feminist perspective and focus on its metonymic engagement with nation. For me, this is a retrograde step, reading against both the allegorical potential of Lochhead's earlier plays and their feminist imperative, critical purchase and surrounding scholarship.

Perfect Days is certainly about the changing nature of (representations of) Glasgow. This is explicit in the paralleled cultural values and social competencies of the play's principal mothers – Barbs and her mother Sadie – and its contrasting masculinities in Hannegan (an off-stage presence of a long-dead archetypal hard man) and the heightened stage camp of Barbs's gay assistant Brendan. Much of the humour depends on the audience recognising and balancing these two identities and what lies behind them, the old-fashioned respectable working class of fixed and predictable gender roles and a new or aspiring middle-class identity and metrosexuality. Lochhead finds much visual and verbal humour in contrasting the two 'worlds' of a working-class past and a middle-class present – Barbs's 'brand new . . . La Perla flimsies' are contrasted with the 'vintage whateveryonewants [. . .] hot pink acrylic garment with appliquéd pearls' that her mother buys for her birthday. Stevenson develops a compelling analysis of the play in respect of class and place, key values of Scottish theatre studies, but he also excuses some remarkably broad representations and convoluted plotting as witty reworkings of film rom-com.

While the characters, the language, the stories of *Perfect Days* and *Good Things* may have resonated within Scottish popular culture – the distinctive localism of the cultural references that site the plays in contemporary Glasgow and reward audiences for an insider knowledge of this – the generic reference points for each were, indeed, film rom-com and television sit-com, not musical hall, variety theatre or cabaret, useful points of reference in framing and exploring Lochhead's previous works. The representations of desperate single women and camp gay men jarred with many feminists and the rom-com/sit-com frames suggested formal and generic conservatism where previously there had been complex, if playful, referencing of forms of popular theatre. Nevertheless, both *Perfect Days* and *Good Things* maintained Lochhead's commitment to plays with women at the centre of their narratives and importantly, even provocatively, these women were of a 'certain age' – Barbs in *Perfect Days* is turning forty and Susan in *Good Things* is almost fifty – negotiating relationships and identities in the harsh contexts of biological clocks and of a contemporary youth-fixated society. These plays provoked raucous laughter and loud gasps of recognition from audiences in Scotland, in London and on tour elsewhere in the UK. They also reconnected Lochhead's theatre writing with the imagined and the linguistic worlds of her poetry and her dramatic monologues – very specifically they shared a space, language and set of representations and life stories with Verena and Derek in *Quelques Fleurs* (1991).

Blood and Ice, *Mary Queen of Scots Got Her Head Chopped Off* and *Dracula* had been something of an inspiration to a cohort of scholars – and, in this reading, to feminist scholars in particular. They represented a coherent body of work that facilitated participation in a timely and important feminist debate about national identity, cultural values, the state of the nation and theatre. *Perfect Days* and *Good Things* – separately and together – appeared to offer none of the same critical opportunities nor did they engender in critics new questions, approaches or conversations. Immediate critical reaction was that, at best, there was nothing new or challenging in the plays or productions and, at worst, that these were unrecoverable in any kind of radical or political or feminist discourse. *Pace* Stevenson, these were plays that were determinedly – even embarrassedly – ignored by cultural critics, theatre critics and above all by feminist critics.

Even the earlier plays and, more particularly, the earlier scholarship, for all its positives, were, however, not without their limitations and challenges. The critical focus on Lochhead's core repertoire of *Blood and Ice*, *Mary Queen of Scots Got Her Head Chopped Off* and *Dracula*, and even on her translation of *Tartuffe* (1986), certainly pulled Scottish theatre scholarship to the international and the comparative, but it also narrowed the focus on a small segment of the culture and the industry, and probably festishised the work of one writer over a rounded analysis of the industry and its range of representations and voices. This may be a sign of an immature, or emerging, scholarly culture, or the inevitable consequence of a limited number of voices in sustained play. In reflecting on the contemporary orthodoxies of Scottish theatre studies – and from the perspective of writing within it – it is judicious to recognise that it remains an emergent subject with a comparatively limited number of commentators maintaining an active contribution. All but uniquely, Lochhead provides a sustained object of study across some three decades of that scholarship. Nevertheless, and referencing again what I see as the key tropes, trends continue to emerge. It is observable that recent

Scottish theatre scholarship has been much less concerned with the play text and its representations and much more focused on policy, politics and institutions. If socialism underpinned a first phase in the study of modern Scottish theatre and feminism a second, then it is nationalism and its cultural politics that underpin a third phase, manifest in scholarship with a focus on the politics and institutions of Scottish theatre, specifically on the policies of devolution and post-devolution Scotland and, in particular, the establishment of the National Theatre of Scotland.[16]

Lochhead remains one of the best known of modern Scottish playwrights, but that identity and role have been superseded by a different presence and purpose in contemporary debates about cultural, educational and social institutions and infrastructures in post-devolution Scotland. Lochhead has, perhaps, moved from a role and identity as playwright – from entering the national conversation through the medium of plays – and into more direct interventions and advocacy roles about, for example, the agency of language.[17] In recent years, what Lochhead has not done is engage in these conversations as a playwright, but instead, and perhaps reflecting our new focus on debates about cultural policies and national politics, she has chosen roles that facilitate her speaking in her own unmediated voice rather than via characters on stage or even through the interpretative lens of other critics. As public funding is squeezed and as it becomes more difficult than ever for new plays to find their way to production, Lochhead's speaking as and for herself may be a pragmatic as much as it is a political choice. Nonetheless, in the context of post-devolution Scotland and with culture as clear and privileged driver of the values of the nation, her responsibilities in the national conversation are as important as ever.

Endnotes

Introduction – Varty

1. Robert Crawford and Anne Varty (eds), *Liz Lochhead's Voices* (Edinburgh: Edinburgh University Press, 1993).
2 Liz Lochhead's inaugural poem, 'Poets Need Not', http://www.scottish poetrylibrary.org.uk/poetry/our-national-poet/inaugural-poem
3. See for example, 'Liz Lochhead – The SRB Interview', *The Scottish Review of Books*, 7.4, 12 Nov. (2011); interview with Kate Shannon, *Holyrood*, 5 Jul. 2012.
4. 'Liz Lochhead – The SRB Interview'.
5. David Barnett, 'My belated thank you to Liz Lochhead', *The Guardian Books Blog*, 17 Aug. 2012; http://www.mediamatters.co.uk/LizLochhead Collection/
6. Interview, *Holyrood*.
7. *The Guardian*, 19 Jan. 2011.
8. Quoted in Ian Brown, 'Cultural Centrality and Dominance: The Creative Writer's View – Conversations with Scottish Poet/Playwrights', *Interface*, 3 (Summer 1984), pp. 18–19, reprinted in *International Journal of Scottish Theatre and Screen*, 4.1 (http://journals.qmu.ac.uk/index.php/IJOSTS/article/view/118/pdf), p. 2.
9. 'Re-enter Houghmagandie: Language as Performance in Liz Lochhead's *Tartuffe*', in Robert Crawford and Anne Varty (eds), *Liz Lochhead's Voices* (Edinburgh: Edinburgh University Press, 1993), pp. 116–17.
10. Ibid., p. 117.
11. Liz Lochhead, *Perfect Days* (London: Nick Hern Books, 1999), p. 22.
12. Ibid., p. 41.
13. Ibid., p. 49.
14. Ibid., p. 78.
15. I am indebted in this and the previous paragraph to Ian Brown for his helpful thoughts on Liz Lochhead, Glasgowness and dramatic language.
16. *The Scotsman*, 20 Jan. 2011.
17. *The Guardian Book Blog*, 19 Jan. 2011.

18. *Scotland on Sunday*, 3 Aug. 2003.

19. http://scotlandonscreen.org.uk/database/record.php?usi=007-000-004-209-C

Chapter 1 – Practitioners

1. http://www.royal.gov.uk/TheRoyalHousehold/OfficialRoyalposts/PoetLaureate.aspx

2. Ibid.

3. 'For the opening of the Scottish Parliament', *A Book of Lives* (Manchester: Carcanet, 2007), pp. 9–10.

4. Personal communication. Liz Lochhead has been an honorary president of the Scottish Poetry Library since 2004.

5. http://www.scotland.gov.uk/News/Releases/2011/01/19141814

6. James McGonigal, *Beyond the Last Dragon – A Life of Edwin Morgan* (Dingwall: Sandstone Press, 2010), p. 410.

7. 'There's lots to enjoy in this revival of Liz Lochhead's translation of Moliere's *L'ecole des femmes*, but perhaps the greatest pleasure comes from the wit and dynamism offered by the text itself. A palpable sense of anticipation grips the audience as we await the culmination of another couplet to see what irreverent rhyme the new Makar has found to make the great French comedy sing in the Scots vernacular.' Allan Radcliffe, *The List*, 28 April 2011.

8. 'It's not a neat piece of theatre, and not everything about it works perfectly; but its warmth, its complex texture, and its dynamic, questioning quality express truths about Morgan that a tidier drama could not begin to contain.' Joyce McMillan, *The Scotsman*, 4 November 2011.

9. http://www.scottish.parliament.uk/newsandmediacentre/31671.aspx

10. http://www.scottishpoetrylibrary.org.uk/connect/blog/connecting-cultures

11. http://www.scottishpoetrylibrary.org.uk/connect/blog/trouble-not-my-middle-name-new-poem-liz-lochhead

12. http://www.scottishbooktrust.com/myfavouriteplace/celebrities/liz-lochhead

13. Liz Lochhead, *Memo for Spring*, in *Dreaming Frankenstein and Collected Poems* (Edinburgh: Polygon, 1984), pp. 138–9; printed here with the author's permission.

Chapter 2 – McMillan

1. Liz Lochhead, *A Choosing: Selected Poems* (Edinburgh: Polygon, 2011).

2. Liz Lochhead, *Memo for Spring* (Edinburgh: Reprographia, 1972).

3. The collection was reviewed by Stewart Conn, *Glasgow Herald*, 19 August 1972; Robert Garioch, *Scottish International*, 5.6, Aug. (1972), p. 35; Philip Hobsbaum, *Lines Review*, 42/43 (1972), pp. 148–9; Alexander Scott, *Studies in Scottish Literature* XI, 1 and 2, (1972), p. 20.

4. Alison Smith, 'Liz Lochhead: Speaking in Her Own Voice', in Robert Crawford and Anne Varty (eds), *Liz Lochhead's Voices* (Edinburgh: Edinburgh University Press, 1993), p. 7.

5. Carol Ann Duffy, 'Foreword', *A Choosing*, p. ix.

6. Michael Schmidt, Stanza Lecture, Stanza Festival of Poetry, St Andrews, 2006. http://www.stanzapoetry.org/stanza06_archive/lecture06.htmhttp://www.stanzapoetry.org/stanza06_archive/lecture06.htm

7. *A Choosing*, p. xi.

8. 'Revelation', *Memo for Spring*, in *Dreaming Frankenstein*, p. 124. In all quotations from poems originally published in the collections *Memo for Spring*, *Islands* and *The Grimm Sisters*, I give first the title of the original collection followed by the page reference in *Dreaming Frankenstein & Collected Poems* (Edinburgh: Polygon Books, 1984).

9. 'Some damage was done to English verse by too close an imitation in the 1930s of the American idiom as evidenced in such poets as Eliot and Pound', Philip Hobsbaum, *Tradition and Experiment in English Poetry* (London: Macmillan, 1979), p. xii.

10. 1992 radio programme, later published lightly edited Crawford et al., in *PN Review*, 89, Jan.–Feb. (1993): http://www.pnreview.co.uk/cgi-bin/scribe?item_id=3588

11. *Bagpipe Muzak* (Harmondsworth: Penguin, 1991), pp. 79–81.

12. *The Colour of Black and White* (Edinburgh: Polygon, 2003), p. 107.

13. Ibid., p. 97.

14. *Memo for Spring; Dreaming Frankenstein*, p. 158.

15. http://www.picador.com/poetry/prize/anthologise

16. http://scottishpoetrylibrary.wordpress.com/2011/09/07/anthologise/

17. Geoffrey Summerfield (ed.), *Voices, the First Book; Voices, the Third Book* (Harmondsworth: Penguin Education, 1968).

18. *Grimm Sisters; Dreaming Frankenstein*, p. 131.

19. *Dreaming Frankenstein*, pp. 8–9.

20. Dorothy McMillan, 'Liz Lochhead and the Ungentle Art of Clyping', in Robert Crawford and Anne Varty (eds), *Liz Lochhead's Voices* (Edinburgh: Edinburgh University Press, 1993), pp. 17–37.

21. Kathleen Jamie, 'Author Statement', British Council Writers at http://literature.britishcouncil.org/kathleen-jamie

22. Directed Tony Cownie, Royal Lyceum Theatre, Edinburgh, 16 Sept.–15 Oct. 2011.

23. *Grimm Sisters; Dreaming Frankenstein*, p. 72.

24. *Colour of Black and White*, p. 126.

25. *Memo for Spring; Dreaming Frankenstein*, p. 126.

26. 'Bagpipe Muzak, Glasgow 1990', *Bagpipe Muzak*, p. 24.

27. http://www.scottish.parliament.uk/newsandmediacentre/31671.aspx

28. *Memo for Spring; Dreaming Frankenstein*, p. 142.

29. Christopher Whyte, *Modern Scottish Poetry* (Edinburgh: Edinburgh University Press, 2004), p. 189.

30. *Islands*; *Dreaming Frankenstein*, p. 115.

31. Roald Dahl, *Revolting Rhymes* (London: Cape, 1982); Carol Ann Duffy, *The World's Wife* (London: Picador, 1999); *The Grimm Sisters* (London: Next Editions, 1981).

32. H. D. (Hilda Doolittle), *Helen in Egypt* (New York: Grove, 1961); Angela Carter, *The Bloody Chamber, and Other Stories* (London: Gollancz, 1979).

33. Anne Sexton, *Transformations* (London: Oxford University Press, 1972). The fairy tales retold in the collection include *Snow White*, *Rumpelstiltskin*, *Rapunzel*, *The Twelve Dancing Princesses*, *The Frog Prince* and *Red Riding Hood*.

34. *Blood and Ice* was performed at the Traverse Theatre, Edinburgh, in 1982. It has been much revised. The quotation in the text is from the 2009 revision (London: Nick Hern Books, 2009), p. 62, but the suspicion of the sentiment was in the earliest version.

35. *Grimm Sisters*; *Dreaming Frankenstein*, p. 70.

36. Ibid., p. 72.

37. Ibid., p. 77.

38. Ibid., p. 74.

39. Ibid., p. 76.

40. Ibid., p. 93.

41. Ibid., p. 86.

42. Ibid., p. 87.

43. Ibid., p. 78.

44. Ibid., p. 89.

45. *Dreaming Frankenstein*, p. 9.

46. Ibid., p. 11.

47. Ibid., p. 61.

48. Ibid., p. 67.

49. *Bagpipe Muzak*, p. 71.

50. Ibid., p. 77.

51. 'Clothes', *Colour of Black and White*, p. 32.

52. Colin Nicholson, 'Towards a Scottish Theatrocracy', in Berthold Schoene (ed.), *The Edinburgh Companion to Contemporary Scottish Literature* (Edinburgh: Edinburgh University Press, 2007), p. 166.

53. *Colour of Black and White*, pp. 3, 4.

54. Ibid., p. 19.

55. I quote from a review by Charlie Louth, 'Death the Teacher', *TLS*, 7 Oct. 2011, p. 8. Louth is translating a marginal note by Célan on one of Éluard's poems: *Qui ne donne pas au poème la force de résistance de l'incommunicable, n'a pas écrit de poème.*

56. 'The Bee Meeting', 'The Arrival of the Bee Box', 'Stings', in *Ariel* (London: Faber, 1965), pp. 60–7.
57. Carol Ann Duffy, *The Bees* (London: Picador, 2011).
58. 'Persimmons', *A Choosing*, pp. 4–5.

Chapter 3 – Severin

1. Liz Lochhead, 'Inner', *Dreaming Frankenstein and Collected Poems* (Edinburgh: Polygon, 1984), p. 113.
2. Cairns Craig, *Out of History: Narrative Paradigms in Scottish and English Culture* (Edinburgh: Polygon, 1996), p. 12.
3. Carla Rodriguez Gonzalez, '"Scotland, Whit Like?": Coloured Voices in Historical Territories', in Merete Falck Borch, Eva Rask Knudsen, Martin Loer and Bruce Clunies Ross (eds), *Bodies and Voices: The Force-Field of Representation and Discourse in Colonial and Postcolonial Studies* (Amsterdam: Rodopi, 2008), pp. 372–3.
4. Ibid., p. 372.
5. Richard Price, 'Love, Language, and Loss: The Colourful Confessions of a National Treasure', *Scotland on Sunday*, 22 June 2003, p. 4.
6. Liz Lochhead, *The Colour of Black and White* (Edinburgh: Polygon, 2003), p. 7.
7. Joel Finler, *Hitchcock in Hollywood* (New York: Continuum, 1992), p. 59.
8. Ibid., p. 59.
9. *Colour of Black and White*, p. 7.
10. Ibid., p. 26.
11. Ibid., p. 19.
12. Ibid., p. 20.
13. Ibid., p. 37.
14. Ibid., p. 35.
15. 'The Metal Raw', ibid., p. 25.
16. 'After the War', *Colour of Black and White*, p. 38.
17. *Colour of Black and White*, p. 33.
18. Ibid., p. 39.
19. Antony Griffiths, *Prints and Printmaking: An Introduction to the History and Techniques* (Berkeley: University of California Press, 1996), p. 18.
20. *Colour of Black and White*, p. 14.
21. Ibid., p. 37.
22. Alan Guest, 'The Linocut', in *British Printmakers: 1855–1955* (Devizes: Garton and Co., 1992), p. 237.
23. *Colour of Black and White*, p. 75.
24. Ibid., p. 77.
25. Edwin Morgan, *Sonnets from Scotland* (Glasgow: Mariscat Press, 1984), p. 58.

26. *Colour of Black and White*, pp. 83–4.

27. Ibid., p. 76.

28. Robert Crawford, 'The Two-Faced Language of Lochhead's Poetry', in Robert Crawford and Anne Varty (eds), *Liz Lochhead's Voices* (Edinburgh: Edinburgh University Press, 1993), p. 72.

29. Amy Houston, 'New Lang Syne: *Sonnets from Scotland* and Restructured Time', *Scottish Literary Journal*, 22.1, May (1995), p. 66.

30. *Colour of Black and White*, p. 99.

31. Ibid.

32. Murdo Macdonald, *Scottish Art* (London: Thames and Hudson, 2000), pp. 159–65.

33. *Colour of Black and White*, pp. 104–5.

34. Ibid., p. 105.

35. Ibid., p. 103.

36. Ibid., p. 45.

37. *Dreaming Frankenstein*, p. 70.

38. *Colour of Black and White*, p. 45.

39. Ibid., p. 46.

40. Ibid.

41. Ibid., p. 53.

42. Crawford, pp. 59–60.

43. Laura Severin, 'Distant Resonances: Scottish Women Poets and African-American Music', *Mosaic: A Journal for the Interdisciplinary Study of Literature*, 39.1, March (2006), pp. 44–59.

44. *Colour of Black and White*, p. 128.

45. Ibid., p. 129.

46. Ibid.

47. Ibid., p. 68.

Chapter 4 – Gish

1. Liz Lochhead, interview by Emily Todd, *Verse*, 8. 3 and 9. 1 (Winter/Spring 1992), p. 95 (pp. 83–95).

2. 'Scots English' is 'part of a "linguistic continuum" from "Broad Scots" to "Scottish Standard English"'. See John Corbett, J. Derrick McClure and Jane Stuart-Smith, 'A Brief History of Scots', in John Corbett, J. Derrick McClure and Jane Stuart-Smith (eds), *The Edinburgh Companion to Scots* (Edinburgh: Edinburgh University Press, 2003), p. 2.

3. *Shakespeare and the Goddess of Complete Being* (London: Faber and Faber, 1992).

4. It means 'with face muffled', *Oxford English Dictionary*, s.v. 'mobled'.

5. Liz Lochhead, *Mary Queen of Scots Got Her Head Chopped Off*, rev. edn (London: Nick Hern Books, 2009), p. 27.

6. Liz Lochhead and Margery Palmer McCulloch, interview by Nancy K. Gish in this chapter. Unless otherwise noted, statements by Lochhead or McCulloch are from this interview.

7. Anne Varty, 'Scripts and Performances', in Robert Crawford and Anne Varty (eds), *Liz Lochhead's Voices* (Edinburgh: Edinburgh University Press, 1993), p. 163.

8. Ibid., p. 163.

9. *Mary Queen of Scots*, p. 6.

10. English, Scots and Gaelic.

11. See, for example, chapters in Crawford and Varty, *Liz Lochhead's Voices*; Margery Palmer McCulloch, *Liz Lochhead's Mary Queen of Scots Got Her Head Chopped Off*, Scotnotes 16 (Glasgow: ASLS, 2000); Lochhead, interview, *Verse*.

12. *The Guardian Books Blog*, 'Scotland Has the Makings of a Great Makar in Liz Lochhead', www.guardian.co.uk/books/booksblog/2011/jan/19/

13. Hugh MacDiarmid, 'A Theory of Scots Letters', in Hugh MacDiarmid (ed.), *The Scottish Chapbook*, 1. 3 (1922), p. 210.

14. The *Concise Scots Dictionary*, s.v. 'oxter'. Other glosses in this text also draw on *Chambers Scots Dictionary* and *Jamieson's Scottish Dictionary*.

15. Liz Lochhead, 'Introduction', *Tartuffe* (Edinburgh: Polygon, 1985).

16. Lochhead, interview, *Verse*, p. 95.

17. David Crystal, *The Stories of English* (New York: The Overlook Press, 2004), p. 311.

18. Richard Proudfoot, Ann Thompson and David Scott Kasten (eds), 'Introduction', in *The Arden Complete Works*, rev. edn (London: The Arden Shakespeare, 2001), p. 11.

19. Derrick McClure, 'The Language of Modern Scots Poetry', in *The Edinburgh Companion to Scots*, p. 211.

20. Ibid., p. 223.

21. For an overview of the language debate, see Margery Palmer McCulloch, *Modernism and Nationalism: Literature and Society in Scotland 1918–1939* (Glasgow: ASLS, 2004).

22. Lochhead, interview, *Verse*, p. 94.

23. David Crystal, *'Think on My Words'; Exploring Shakespeare's Language* (Cambridge: Cambridge University Press, 2008), p. 9.

24. *Guardian Books Blog*.

25. *Mary Queen of Scots*, p. 4.

26. Ibid., p. 23.

27. Maurice Lindsay and Lesley Duncan, 'Introduction', in *The Edinburgh Book of Twentieth-Century Scottish Poetry* (Edinburgh: Edinburgh University Press, 2005), p. xxxvi.

Chapter 5 – Hagemann

1. Research for this chapter was completed in September 2010. A full bibliography of translations will be published in *Scottish Literary Review* 5.1 (Spring/Summer 2013). Detailed references for all translations mentioned here can be found in the bibliography.

2. For instance, Hamish Whyte's 'Checklist' excludes translations without even mentioning the omission, and Alison Walker and Craig W. McLuckie's 'Annotated Bibliography' includes only the Italian version of *Blood and Ice* (listed under 'Poetry Collections'). See Hamish Whyte, 'Liz Lochhead: A Checklist', in Robert Crawford and Anne Varty (eds), *Liz Lochhead's Voices* (Edinburgh: Edinburgh University Press, 1993), pp. 170–91; and Alison Walker and Craig W. McLuckie, 'Liz Lochhead: An Annotated Bibliography' (Vernon, BC: Kalamalka Institute for Working Writers, Okanagan College, 2000). <http://www.kalwriters.com/archive/lochhead.html> (accessed 4 August 2010).

3. This inevitably means that there will also be gaps in the present chapter. Resources used in addition to BOSLIT include: the Scottish Poetry Library Catalogue, the *Index Translationum: World Bibliography of Translation*, Google searches and personal communications from translators, editors and agents. Lochhead herself does not keep track of translations (personal communication, 4 August 2011).

4. See, for example, the contributions to Tom Hubbard and R. D. S. Jack (eds), *Scotland in Europe*, Scottish Cultural Review of Language and Literature 7 (Amsterdam: Rodopi, 2006), and to the 2006 ASLS Annual Conference on 'Scotland and the World: Translating Literature into and out of the Languages of Scotland', <http://www.arts.gla.ac.uk/ScotLit/ASLS/AnnConf2006.html> (accessed 4 August 2010), as well as Paul Barnaby and Tom Hubbard's three surveys on 'The International Reception and Literary Impact of Scottish Literature', in Ian Brown et al. (eds), *The Edinburgh History of Scottish Literature* (Edinburgh: Edinburgh University Press, 2007): vol. 1, pp. 164–7 (for the period 1314–1707); vol. 2, pp. 33–44 (for the period 1707–1918); vol. 3, pp. 31–41 (for the period since 1918).

5. 'My Rival's House' is included in the *Intimate Expanses* anthology, which was translated as a whole into Finnish, German and Hungarian; in these three languages, the poem was therefore not individually selected for translation.

6. Adele D'Arcangelo and Margaret Rose (eds and trans.), *Poesie – Och!*, Intrecci 1 (Salerno: Oèdipus Edizioni, 2005), p. 175.

7. Personal communication from Iain Galbraith, 1 July 2010.

8. To give just a few examples, the former group includes, for Lochhead's poems, writers such as Jan Baeke from the Netherlands, Virna Teixeira from Brazil, Charles Dobzynski from France, Michael Donhauser from Austria,

Ina Grigorova from Bulgaria, Mónika Mesterházi from Hungary, or Göran Printz-Påhlson and Jan Östergren from Sweden; and for her plays, Ehud Manor from Israel or Klaudyna Rozhin from Poland. Among the latter group are, for the poems, academics such as Giorgia Sensi and Andrea Sirotti from Italy, or Dan H. Popescu from Romania; and for the plays, David Drozd from the Czech Republic or Ksenija Horvat from Croatia. Some translators straddle the two groups, being active as both literary authors and academics. Full-time translators are rarer; they include Dörte Eliass from Germany for the poems, and Reita Lounatvuori from Finland for the plays. In addition, there are one-off translators such as Carla Sassi from Italy.

9. Virna Teixeira, 'O cidadão desconhecido', in Virna Teixeira (ed. and trans.), *Ovelha negra: Uma antologia de poesia da Escócia do século XX* (São Paulo: Lumme Editor, 2007), pp. 86–7.

10. It may be mentioned in passing that notes can occasionally obfuscate rather than clarify meaning. For example, in the Bulgarian translation of 'The Redneck', an editorial note explains who George Buchanan was; but the Buchanan reference in Lochhead's poem is of course to the tartan rather than the scholar.

11. Personal communication from Iain Galbraith, 1 July 2010.

12. *Poesie – Och!*, pp. 177–81, 174–6.

13. Lance Hewson, 'The Bilingual Edition in Translation Studies', in *Visible Language* 27.1/2 (1993), pp. 155–6.

14. Ibid., pp. 150–1.

15. See *Poesie – Och!*, pp. 181–2 for D'Arcangelo's description of the two translations.

16. Ibid., pp. 120–7.

17. Donny Correia and Frederico Barbosa, 'Ao meu modo', *Zunái: Revista de poesia & debates* (c. 2005), ‹http://www.revistazunai.com/traducoes/liz_lochhead.htm› (accessed 23 March 2010).

18. *Poesie – Och!*, p. 179.

19. Paul Barnaby, 'Three into One: Twentieth-Century Scottish Verse in Translation Anthologies', in *Translation and Literature* 9.2 (2000), p. 191; also online: ‹http://www.nls.uk/catalogues/resources/boslit/3into1.html› (accessed 9 June 2010).

20. Michael Donhauser, 'Das Haus meiner Rivalin', in Iain Galbraith (ed.), *Intime Weiten: XXV schottische Gedichte*, intro. Ken Cockburn (Vienna and Bolzano: Folio, 2006), p. 37. Andreas F. Kelletat, 'Liz Lochheads *What The Pool Said, On Midsummer's Day*: Eine translationsorientierte Annäherung', presented in a poetry translation course (Germersheim: School of Translation, Interpreting, Linguistics and Cultural Studies of Mainz University, 2010).

Chapter 6 – Corbett

1. In this chapter, I refer broadly to Lochhead's 'translations' or 'adaptations', though she herself refers to them all as 'adaptations' or 'versions'.

2. A more minor Molière adaptation, *Patter Merchants* (*Les Précieuses Ridicules*), is not discussed in this chapter; it was performed as part of a double bill in 1989. This chapter deals mainly with the Molière and 'Greek' translations, since *Three Sisters* (performed by the Royal Lyceum Company in 2000) has not been published, to date, and it is therefore difficult for readers to gain access to. Nor does this chapter cover literary adaptations such as *Dracula* and *Blood and Ice*.

3. http://www.lyceum.org.uk/resources_pack/infopack.pdf by Alison Reeves, 2006.

4. See www.theatrebabel.co.uk (accessed 19 January 2012).

5. Graham McLaren, 'Director's Note', in Liz Lochhead, *Educating Agnes* (London: Nick Hern, 2008), p. ii.

6. Susan Bassnett, 'Ways through the Labyrinth: Strategies and Methods of Translating Theatre Texts', in Theo Hermans (ed.), *The Manipulation of Literature: Studies in Literary Translation* (Croom Helms: Routledge, 1985), pp. 87–102; and Susan Bassnett, *Constructing Cultures: Essays on Literary Translation* (Clevedon: Multilingual Matters, 1998), pp. 90–108.

7. This tradition is discussed in Bill Findlay, 'Talking in Tongues: Scottish Translations 1970–1995', in Randall Stevenson and Gavin Wallace (eds), *Scottish Theatre since the Seventies* (Edinburgh: Edinburgh University Press, 1996), pp. 186–97; W. (Bill) Findlay, *Motivation and Method in Scots Translations, Versions and Adaptations of Plays from the Historic Repertoire of Continental European Drama*, 2 vols (unpublished thesis: Queen Margaret University College, Edinburgh, 2000); John Corbett and Bill Findlay (eds), *Serving Twa Maisters* (Glasgow: Association for Scottish Literary Studies, 2005) pp. x–xiii, xvii–xxii; Noël Peacock, *Molière in Scotland* (Glasgow: University of Glasgow French and German Publications, 1993) and 'Robert Kemp's Translations of Molière' in Bill Findlay (ed.), *Frae Ither Tongues: Essays on Modern Translations into Scots* (Clevedon: Multilingual Matters, 2004), pp. 87–105; and Randall Stevenson, 'Triumphant Tartuffication: Liz Lochhead's Translation of Molière's Tartuffe', in Findlay, *Frae Ither Tongues*, pp. 106–22.

8. See Ian Brown, 'Motivation and Politico-Cultural Context in the Creation of Scots Language Versions of Greek Tragedies', in John Kirk and Iseabail Macleod (eds), *Scots: The Language and its Literature* (Amsterdam: Rodopi, forthcoming); John Corbett, '"Nae Mair Pussyfootin: Ah'm Aff, Theramenes": Demotic Neoclassical Drama in Contemporary Scotland', in James McGonigal and Kirsten Stirling (eds), *Ethically Speaking: Voices and Values in Modern Scottish Writing* (Amsterdam: Rodopi, 2006), pp. 1–20; John Corbett, 'Translated Drama in Scotland', in Ian Brown (ed.), *The*

Edinburgh Companion to Scottish Drama (Edinburgh: Edinburgh University Press, 2011), pp. 95–106.

9. Carol Maier and Françoise Massardier-Kenney, 'Introduction', in *Literature in Translation: Teaching Issues and Reading Practices* (Kent: Kent State University Press, 2010) pp. 24–5.

10. Ibid., p. 25.

11. Liz Lochhead, 'Introduction', in *Medea* (London: Nick Hern, 2000), p. iii.

12. Lochhead, *Educating Agnes*, p. 5.

13. Lesley McDowell, 'Hooked on classics', *The Independent*, 5 July 2003.

14. Liz Lochhead, 'Introduction', in *Miseryguts & Tartuffe* (London: Nick Hern, 2002), p. xi.

15. Stevenson, 'Triumphant Tartuffication', p. 106.

16. For further discussion of formal and functional correspondences, see Eugene Nida, 'Principles of Correspondence', in Lawrence Venuti (ed.), *The Translation Studies Reader* (New York and London: Routledge, 2004), pp. 153–67.

17. Lochhead, 'Introduction', *Educating Agnes*, p. i.

18. Brown, 'Motivation'.

19. Lochhead, *Medea*, p. ii.

20. Corbett, '"Nae Mair Pussyfootin: Ah'm Aff, Theramenes": Demotic Neoclassical Drama in Contemporary Scotland'.

21. Lochhead, *Medea*, p. ii.

22. Lochhead, 'Introduction', in *Tartuffe* (London: Nick Hern, 1985), p. i.

23. Stevenson, 'Triumphant Tartuffication', p. 120; see also his 'Re-enter Houghmagandie: Language as Performance in Lochhead's *Tartuffe*', in Robert Crawford and Anne Varty (eds), *Liz Lochhead's Voices* (Edinburgh: Edinburgh University Press, 1993), pp. 109–23.

24. Lochhead, *Miseryguts & Tartuffe*, p. xii.

25. Stevenson, 'Triumphant Tartuffication', p. 121.

26. Lochhead, *Miseryguts*, p. 65.

27. Robert Kemp, *Let Wives Tak Tent*, in Corbett and Findlay (eds), *Serving Twa Maisters*, p. 39.

28. Lochhead, *Educating Agnes*, p. 71.

29. Ibid., p. 6.

30. Liz Lochhead, *Thebans* (London: Nick Hern, 2003), p. 43.

31. Lochhead, *Medea*, p. 17.

32. Lochhead, *Educating Agnes*, pp. 5–6; Lochhead, *Medea*, p.ii.

33. See Ksenija Horvat, 'Liz Lochhead', in Brown (ed.), *The Edinburgh Companion to Scottish Drama*, pp. 177–87; and Crawford and Varty (eds), particularly Alison Smith, 'Speaking in Her Own Voice', pp. 1–16 and Robert Crawford, 'The Two-Faced Language of Lochhead's Poetry', pp. 57–74.

34. Lochhead, *Educating Agnes*, p. 9.

35. J. Dollimore and A. Sinfield, 'Foreword to the First Edition', in *Political Shakespeare: Essays in Cultural Materialism*, 2nd edn (Manchester: Manchester University Press, 1994), p. vii.

36. Lochhead, *Medea*, p.i.

37. Carla Rodriguez González, 'An Interview with Liz Lochhead', *Atlantis* 26.1 (2004), p. 103.

Chapter 7 – Poore

1. Internet searches yield details of several well-publicised school, college and university productions within the last three years, and in Autumn 2010 Sell-A-Door Theatre Company launched an extensive '25th Anniversary' Scottish tour of the play before taking up residence at the Greenwich Playhouse, London.

2. Jan McDonald and Jennifer Harvie, 'Putting New Twists to Old Stories: Feminism and Lochhead's Drama', in Crawford and Varty (eds), *Liz Lochhead's Voices* (Edinburgh: Edinburgh University Press, 1993), p. 130.

3. A. Bennett and N. Royle, *Introduction to Literature, Criticism and Theory* (London: Prentice Hall, 1999), p. 41.

4. W. Hughes, *Dracula: A Reader's Guide to Essential Criticism* (Basingstoke: Palgrave Macmillan, 2008), p. 3.

5. Bram Stoker, *Dracula*, ed. L. S. Klinger (New York: W. W. Norton, 2008), p. 537.

6. Liz Lochhead, *Dracula: Adapted from Bram Stoker's Novel* (London: Nick Hern, 2009), pp. vii–viii.

7. Linda Hucheon, *A Theory of Adaptation* (London: Routledge, 2006), pp. 6–9.

8. Nina Auerbach, *Our Vampires, Ourselves* (Chicago: University of Chicago Press, 1995), p. 115.

9. Ibid., p. 116.

10. Nick Daly, *Modernism, Romance and the Fin de Siècle* (Cambridge: Cambridge University Press, 1999), pp. 46–7.

11. Auerbach, *Our Vampires*, pp. 124, 141–2.

12. K. Khan, producer, *Timeshift: Transylvania Babylon* [2006, compilation of archive footage on vampires], broadcast 3 Oct. 2010, BBC 4, BBC Bristol production.

13. The Pip Simmons Theatre Group had its roots in the Arts Lab and British experimental theatre scene of the late 1960s, and the production of *Dracula* had been touring internationally since 1974.

14. Untitled review of *Dracula* by Pip Simmons Theatre Group, *Sunday Telegraph*, 12 Dec. 1976, Dracula press file, Theatre Museum, London.

15. Milton Shulman, untitled review of *Dracula* by Pip Simmons Theatre

Group, *Evening Standard*, 8 Dec. 1976, p. 15, Dracula press file, Theatre Museum, London.

16. R. Knapp, *The American Musical and the Performance of Personal Identity* (Princeton: Princeton University Press, 2006), p. 240.

17. Ibid., pp. 240–1.

18. Ibid., p. 246. The reviewer of the Pip Simmons *Dracula* for *The Observer* did indeed note that Dracula looked like 'something [. . .] out of "The Rocky Horror Show"', untitled review of *Dracula* by Pip Simmons Theatre Group, *The Observer*, 12 Dec. 1976, Dracula press file, Theatre Museum, London.

19. 'Dracula loses West End vampire stakes', *The Times*, 12 Oct. 1978, Dracula press file, Theatre Museum, London.

20. Untitled review of *Dracula* by Deane and Balderston, *Sunday Telegraph*, 17 Sept. 1978, Dracula press file, Theatre Museum, London; untitled review of *Dracula* by Deane and Balderston, *Financial Times*, 16 Sept. 1978, Dracula press file, Theatre Museum, London.

21. Milton Shulman, 'Out for the Count', *Evening Standard*, 14 Sept. 1978, Dracula press file, Theatre Museum, London.

22. Lochhead, *Dracula*, p. 21.

23. Ibid., p. 25.

24. Ibid., pp. 27–8.

25. Ibid., pp. 33, 62.

26. F. Babbage, 'Heavy Bodies, Fragile Texts: Stage Adaptation and the Problem of Presence', in R. Carroll (ed.), *Adaptation in Contemporary Culture* (London: Continuum, 2009), p. 14.

27. Lochhead, *Dracula*, p. vii.

28. Lauren M. E. Goodlad and Michael Bibby (eds), 'Introduction', in *Goth: Undead Subculture* (Durham, NC and London: Duke University Press, 2007), pp. 14–15.

29. D. Punter and G. Byron, *The Gothic* (Oxford: Blackwell, 2004), p. 61.

30. N. Gagnier, 'The Authentic Dracula: Bram Stoker's Hold on Vampiric Genres', in Goodlad and Bibby (eds), *Goth: Undead Subculture*, p. 303.

31. Lochhead, *Dracula*, p. 34.

32. Indeed, a preference for Stoker, Le Fanu or Polidori's vampires even served as a badge of identity for certain Goth purists who resisted the increasing popularity of Hollywood vampires who looked and behaved like rock stars. Kathryn Bigelow's *Near Dark* (1987) and Joel Schumacher's *The Lost Boys* (1987) both feature vampires as bad boys and rebels, drawing on rock and roll iconography (N. Nixon, 'When Hollywood Sucks, or, Hungry Girls, Lost Boys, and Vampirism in the Age of Reagan', in J. Gordon and V. Hollinger (eds), *Blood Read: The Vampire as Metaphor in Contemporary Culture* (Philadelphia: University of Pennsylvania Press, 1997), pp. 120–3). Meanwhile, the vampire-as-rock-star conceit had been explored in S. P.

Somtow's novel *Vampire Junction* (1984), and in Anne Rice's *The Vampire Lestat* (1985), the sequel to her hugely influential *Interview with the Vampire* (R. Latham, 'Consuming Youth: The Lost Boys Cruise Mallworld', *Blood Read*, pp. 139, 143); and, conversely, rock stars were expressing interest in playing Lestat (Nixon,'When Hollywood Sucks', p. 218). In contrast to this, Lochhead's Dracula, with his bad puns and his solitary bookishness, seems, oddly, rather more human, more ordinary.

33. *Mary Queen of Scots Got Her Head Chopped Off & Dracula* (Harmondsworth: Penguin, 1989), p. 99.
34. Goodlad and Bibby (eds), *Goth: Undead Subculture*, p. 15.
35. Bennett and Royle, *Introduction to Literature*, p. 41.
36. Lochhead, *Dracula*, pp. vii, viii.
37. Ibid., p. vii.
38. Ibid., pp. 73, 42.
39. Jan McDonald, '"The Devil is Beautiful": *Dracula*: Freudian Novel and Feminist Drama', in P. Reynolds (ed.), *Novel Images: Literature in Performance* (London: Routledge, 1993), p. 87.
40. McDonald and Harvie, 'Putting New Twists', in Crawford and Varty (eds), *Liz Lochhead's Voices*, p. 133.
41. McDonald, '"The Devil is Beautiful"', in Reynolds (ed.), *Novel Images*, p. 90.
42. Lochhead, *Dracula*, pp. 4, 6, 7.
43. Ibid., pp. 3, 8–9.
44. Ibid., pp. 13, 14, 12, 14.
45. Ibid., p. 79.
46. D. J. Skal, *Hollywood Gothic: The Tangled Web of Dracula from Novel to Stage to Screen* (New York: Faber and Faber, 2004), pp. 77–161.
47. Lochhead, *Dracula*, pp. 42, 55–6.
48. L. Dryden, *The Modern Gothic and Literary Doubles: Stevenson, Wilde and Wells* (Basingstoke: Palgrave Macmillan, 2003), p. 39.
49. Lochhead, *Dracula*, p. 30.
50. Ibid., p. 58.
51. Skal, *Hollywood Gothic*, pp. 54–5.
52. Lochhead, *Dracula*, p. 79.
53. Ibid., p. 45.
54. McDonald, '"The Devil is Beautiful"', pp. 92–3.
55. See, for instance, ibid., pp. 94–5.
56. W. Greenslade, *Degeneration, Culture and the Novel 1880–1940* (Cambridge: Cambridge University Press, 1994), p. 72.
57. Stoker, *Dracula*, ed. Klinger, pp. 192–8.
58. Lochhead, *Dracula*, p. 66.
59. Ibid., pp. 84–5.
60. Ibid., p. 79.
61. Stoker, *Dracula*, ed. Klinger, pp. 499–500.

62. Lochhead, *Mary Queen of Scots & Dracula*, p. 145; J. Thornton and J. Godber, *Dracula* (London: Warner/Chappell Plays, 1998), p. 96.

63. Thornton and Godber, *Dracula*, pp. 95–6.

64. Lochhead, *Dracula*, pp. 23, 62–3.

65. Dryden, *The Modern Gothic*, pp. 67, 42.

66. K. Miller, *Doubles* (London: Faber and Faber, 1985), p. 213.

67. James Hogg, *The Private Memoirs and Confessions of a Justified Sinner* (Edinburgh: Canongate, 2008), p. 132.

68. Dryden, *The Modern Gothic*, p. 39.

69. R. L. Stevenson, *The Master of Ballantrae*, in *The Scottish Novels* (Edinburgh: Canongate, 1995), pp. 154, 132, 137.

70. McDonald and Harvie, 'New Twists', pp. 137, 131.

71. R. Crawford, 'The Two-Faced Language of Lochhead's Poetry', in Crawford and Varty (eds), *Liz Lochhead's Voices*, p. 68.

72. Qtd in S. J. Boyd, 'The Voice of Revelation: Liz Lochhead and Monsters', in Crawford and Varty (eds), *Liz Lochhead's Voices*, p. 42.

73. M. Germanà, *Scottish Women's Gothic and Fantastic Writing: Fiction since 1978* (Edinburgh: Edinburgh University Press, 2010), p. 5.

74. Ibid., p. 78; Ian Rankin, 'Preface', in James Hogg, *The Private Memoirs and Confessions of a Justified Sinner* (Edinburgh: Canongate, 2008), p. xi.

75. Germanà, *Scottish Women's Gothic and Fantastic Writing*, p. 16.

76. *Blood and Ice* (Edinburgh: Salamander Press, 1982), pp. 26, 28.

77. *Mary Queen of Scots*, p. 12.

78. Ibid., pp. 29, 60.

79. Ibid., pp. 64–5.

80. D. Punter and G. Byron, *The Gothic* (Oxford: Blackwell, 2004), p. 26.

81. *Cuba*, in Liz Lochhead and Gina Moxley, *Cuba / Dog House* (London: Faber and Faber, 1997), p. 41.

82. *Perfect Days* (London: Nick Hern, 1998), p. 4.

83. Ibid., p. 83.

84. *Good Things* (London: Nick Hern, 2004), p. 1.

85. Hogg, *Confessions*, p. 257.

86. Ibid., p. 259.

87. *Medea* (London: Nick Hern, 2000), p. 23.

88. Ibid., p. 45.

89. Ibid., p. 42.

90. Ibid., p. 4.

91. Ibid., p. 16.

92. Ibid., p. 7.

93. D. Glover, *Vampires, Mummies and Liberals: Bram Stoker and the Politics of Popular Fiction* (Durham, NC and London: Duke University Press, 1996), p. 137.

94. The *Journal of Dracula Studies* (www.blooferland.com).

95. Lyndon W. Joslin notes that the film is 'another "reincarnation-romance" interpretation' [where Dracula and Mina have loved each other in a past life] which was 'already old by the time it was spoofed in *Love At First Bite'*. See L. W. Joslin, *Count Dracula Goes to the Movies: Stoker's Novel Adapted, 1922–2003*, 2nd edn (London: MacFarland, 2006), pp. 123, 126.

96. Glover, *Vampires*, p. 149.

97. K. Aubrey, 'In Camera', documentary in *Dracula*, directed by Francis Ford Coppola [1992], DVD, Collector's Edition, Sony Pictures, 2007.

98. Glover, *Vampires*, p. 142.

99. Joslin, *Count Dracula*, pp. 194–210.

100. See, for instance, Carol A. Senf, Elaine Showalter and Sally Ledger's accounts of her, or Christine Ferguson: 'As word conduit rather than vampiric assimilator, Mina Harker epitomizes the novel's logic of linguistic and subjective vitality' (C. Ferguson, *Language, Science and Popular Fiction at the Victorian Fin-de-Siècle*, Aldershot: Ashgate 2006), p. 148; C. A. Senf, 'Dracula: Stoker's Response to the New Woman', *Victorian Studies*, 26.1 (1982), pp. 33–49; E. Showalter, *Sexual Anarchy: Gender and Culture at the Fin de Siècle* (London: Bloomsbury, 1991), pp. 180–2; S. Ledger, *The New Woman: Fiction and Feminism at the Fin de Siècle* (Manchester: Manchester University Press, 1997), pp. 105–6.

101. The novel was published by Harper in 2009; the film is in development, scheduled, at time of writing, for 2012 release.

Chapter 8 – Varty

1. Liz Lochhead, *Times Educational Supplement 2*, 12 May 1995, p. 14.

2. *The Colour of Black and White, Poems 1984–2003* (Edinburgh: Polygon, 2003), pp. 19–34, 40–1.

3. *Dreaming Frankenstein and Collected Poems* (Edinburgh: Polygon Books, 1984), pp. 57–60.

4. *True Confessions and New Clichés* (Edinburgh: Polygon Books, 1985), p. 125.

5. Ibid., pp. 100–1.

6. Two short plays written for the Scottish Youth Theatre, *Disgusting Objects* (1982, performed in summer 1983) and *Rosaleen's Baby* (1984) are not discussed here.

7. Liz Lochhead, 'Introduction', in *Britannia Rules* (Learning and Teaching Scotland, 2003), p. 4. See also Mark Fisher's review of the double bill première at the Royal Lyceum Theatre, Edinburgh in *The Herald*, 14 Sept. 1998.

8. Lochhead, 'Introduction', *Britannia Rules*, p. 5.

9. Ibid., p. 4.

10. Ibid., p. 27.

11. Ibid., pp. 4–5.
12. Ibid., p. 2.
13. Ibid., p. 3.
14. Ibid., pp. 63, 65.
15. Ibid., p. 43.
16. Ibid., p. 108.
17. Ibid., p. 122.
18. *The Herald*, 14 Sept. 1998.
19. Unpublished typescript in my possession, p. 79.
20. *The Independent*, 10 Feb. 1993.
21. Ibid.
22. *The Magic Island*, typescript, p. 1.
23. Ibid., p. 6.
24. *The Tempest*, I, ii, 128–9.
25. *The Magic Island*, p. 12.
26. *Tempest*, I, ii, 341ff.
27. *The Magic Island*, p. 20.
28. Ibid., pp. 20–1.
29. Ibid., p. 23.
30. Ibid., p. 25.
31. Ibid., p. 30.
32. Ibid., p. 32.
33. Ibid., pp. 48–9.
34. Ibid., p. 51.
35. *The Independent*, 10 Feb. 1993.
36. 7 May 1995.
37. http://www.nationalarchives.gov.uk/education/coldwar/g5/cs2/s6_t.htm The autobiographical significance of this moment is confirmed in interview with Chris Small for the *Times Educational Supplement Scotland* on 11 March 2011.
38. Unpublished typescript deposited in the Scottish Theatre Archive, STA RS 18/5, programme produced by Bruce Young, read by Grace Glover.
39. Ibid., p. 1.
40. Ibid., p. 12.
41. 'Sorting Through' is also the title of a poem in *The Colour of Black and White*, p. 39.
42. Liz Lochhead, *Cuba*, Gina Moxley, *Dog House* (London: Faber and Faber, 1997), p. 10.
43. Ibid., p. 25.
44. Ibid., p. 28.
45. Ibid., p. 37.
46. Ibid., p. 41.
47. Ibid.

48. *Jock Tamson's Bairns: Essays on a Scots Childhood*, ed. Trevor Royle (London: Hamish Hamiliton, 1977), p. 121.

49. *Cuba*, p. 10.

Chapter 9 – Scullion

1. Alex Salmond, Scottish Government Video Press Release, 19 January 2011, http://www.youtube.com/watch?v=Y8GPhNqEkyA

2. Alex Salmond, Scottish Government Press Release, 19 January 2011, http://www.scotland.gov.uk/News/Releases/2011/01/19141814

3. Lord McConnell (former First Minister Jack McConnell), Scottish Government Video Press Release, 19 January 2011, http://www.youtube.com/watch?v=Y8GPhNqEkyA

4. Alex Salmond, Scottish Government Press Release, 19 January 2011.

5. See John Hill, 'Towards a Scottish People's Theatre: The Rise and Fall of Glasgow Unity', *Theatre Quarterly*, 7.27 (1977), pp. 61–70; his 'Glasgow Unity Theatre: The Search for a "Scottish People's Theatre"', *New Edinburgh Review*, 40 (1978), pp. 27–31; Douglas Allen, 'Culture and the Scottish Labour Movement', *Journal of the Scottish Labour History Society*, 14 (1980), pp. 30–9; and 'Glasgow Workers' Theatre Group and the Methodology of Theatre Studies', *Theatre Quarterly*, 9.36 (1980), pp. 45–54.

6. Colin Nicholson, 'Knucklebones of Irony: Liz Lochhead', in *Poem, Purpose, Place: Shaping Identity in Contemporary Scottish Verse*, ed. Colin Nicholson (Edinburgh: Polygon, 1992), p. 204.

7. See, inter alia, Ilona Koren-Deutsch, 'Feminist Nationalism in Scotland: *Mary Queen of Scots Got Her Head Chopped Off*', *Modern Drama*, 35 (1992), pp. 424–32; Marilyn Reizbaum, 'Canonical Double Cross: Scottish and Irish Women's Writing', in Karen R. Lawrence (ed.), *Decolonizing Tradition: New Views of Twentieth-Century 'British' Literature Canons* (Urbana and Chicago: University of Illinois Press, 1992), pp. 165–90; Audrey Bain, 'Loose Canons: Identifying a Women's Tradition in Playwriting', in Randall Stevenson and Gavin Wallace (eds), *Scottish Theatre since the Seventies* (Edinburgh: Edinburgh University Press, 1996), pp. 138–45; Jan McDonald, 'Scottish Women Dramatists since 1945', in Douglas Gifford and Dorothy McMillan (eds), *A History of Scottish Women's Writing* (Edinburgh: Edinburgh University Press, 1997), pp. 494–513; Adrienne Scullion, 'Liz Lochhead', in Kate Berney (ed.), *Contemporary Dramatists*, 5th edn (London: St James Press, 1993), pp. 394–5; and 'Contemporary Scottish Women Playwrights', in Janelle Reinelt and Elaine Aston (eds), *The Cambridge Companion to Modern British Women Playwrights* (Cambridge: Cambridge University Press, 2000), pp. 94–118.

8. Reizbaum, 'Canonical Double Cross', p. 165.

9. Ibid., p. 166.

10. See Tom Nairn, *The Break-Up of Britain: Crisis and Neo-Nationalism*

(London: Verso, 1977); David McCrone, *Understanding Scotland: The Sociology of a Stateless Nation* (London: Routledge, 1992); Hugh MacDiarmid after G. Gregory Smith, *Scottish Literature: Character and Influence* (London: MacMillan, 1919).

11. Reizbaum,'Canonical Double Cross', pp. 182–3. See also discussion of this essay in Matt McGuire, *Contemporary Scottish Literature* (Houndsmill: Palgrave MacMillan, 2009).

12. Liz Lochhead, *Mary Queen of Scots Got Her Head Chopped Off & Dracula* (Harmondsworth: Penguin, 1989), p. 16.

13. The two high-profile revivals of *Mary Queen of Scots Got Her Head Chopped Off* have been a touring production for the National Theatre of Scotland in 2009, directed by Alison Peebles, and a production for the Royal Lyceum Edinburgh in 2011, directed by Tony Cownie.

14. Randall Stevenson, 'Perfect Days? Scottish Theatre at the Millennium', in Valentina Poggi and Margaret Rose (eds), *A Theatre that Matters: Twentieth-Century Scottish Drama and Theatre* (Milan: Edizioni Unicopli, 2000), p. 111.

15. Ibid., p. 117.

16. For example, Cairns Craig, 'Constituting Scotland', *Edinburgh Review*, 109 (2002), pp. 5–35; Robert Leach, 'The Short, Astonishing History of the National Theatre of Scotland', *New Theatre Quarterly*, 23.2 (2007), pp. 171–83; Trish Reid, 'From Scenes Like these Old Scotia's Grandeur Springs: The New National Theatre of Scotland', *Contemporary Theatre Review*, 17.2 (2007), pp. 192–201; Adrienne Scullion, 'Home Start: The First Months of the National Theatre of Scotland', *Contemporary Theatre Review*, 16.3 (2006), pp. 373–7; and, 'Gamblers and Speculators: The National Theatre of Scotland Stakes a Claim', *Journal of Irish and Scottish Studies*, 2.2 (2009), pp. 95–108.

17. Lochhead has engaged in these debates as a member of the Scottish Studies Working Group advising on the study of Scottish life and culture in primary and secondary education as well as in her role as Makar. See Scottish Government information on education and training in respect of Scottish Studies, http://www.scotland.gov.uk/Topics/Education/Schools/curriculum/ACE/ScottishStudies; and, Liz Lochhead interviewed by Colin Waters for *The Scottish Review of Books*, 7.4 (2011), http://www.scottishreviewofbooks. org/index.php/back-issues/volume-seven-2011/volume-seven-issue-four/442-liz-lochhead-the-srb-interview

Further Reading

Braun, Anne-Kathrin, *Dramatic Laboratories: Figurations of Subjectivity in Liz Lochhead's Writings* (Cambridge, MA: Galda and Wilch, 2004).

Caretti, Laura, 'Mary Queen of Scots and the "Siren's Song of Tolerance"', in Valentina Poggi and Margaret Rose (eds), *A Theatre that Matters: Twentieth-Century Scottish Drama and Theatre: A Collection of Critical Essays and Interviews* (Milan: Unicopli, 2001), pp. 41–56.

Christianson, Aileen, 'Liz Lochhead's Poetry and Drama: Forging Irony', in Aileen Christianson and Alison Lumsden (eds), *Contemporary Scottish Women Writers* (Edinburgh: Edinburgh University Press, 2000), pp. 41–52.

Colvin, Sarah, 'Disturbing Bodies: Mary Stuart and Marilyn Monroe in Plays by Liz Lochhead, Marie von Ebner-Eschenbach and Gerlind Reinshagen', *Forum for Modern Language Studies*, 35.3 (1999), pp. 251–60.

Crawford, Robert and Anne Varty (eds), *Liz Lochhead's Voices* (Edinburgh: Edinburgh University Press, 1993).

Harvie, Jennifer, 'Desire and Difference in Liz Lochhead's *Dracula*', in *Essays in Theatre/Études Théâtrales*, 11.2 (1993), pp. 133–43.

Horvat, Ksenija, 'Liz Lochhead', in Ian Brown (ed.), *The Edinburgh Companion to Scottish Drama* (Edinburgh: Edinburgh University Press, 2011), pp. 177–87.

Kabitoglou, E. Douka, 'Blood Sisters: Mary Shelley, Liz Lochhead, and the Monsters', in Betty T. Bennett and Stuart Curran (eds), *Mary Shelley in Her Times* (Baltimore: Johns Hopkins University Press, 2000), pp. 214–32.

Koren-Deutsch, Ilona S., 'Feminist Nationalism in Scotland: *Mary Queen of Scots Got Her Head Chopped Off*', *Modern Drama*, 35.3 (1992), pp. 424–32.

May, William, 'Verbal and Visual Art in Twentieth-Century British Women's Poetry', in Jane Dowson (ed.), *The Cambridge Companion to Twentieth-Century British and Irish Women's Poetry* (Cambridge: Cambridge University Press, 2011), pp. 42–61.

McDonald, Jan, '"The Devil is Beautiful": *Dracula*: Freudian Novel and Feminist Drama', in Peter Reynolds (ed.), *Novel Images: Literature in Performance* (London: Routledge, 1993), pp. 80–104.

Mergenthal, Silvia, 'The Dramatist as Reader: Liz Lochhead's Play *Blood and Ice*', in Martin Middeke and Hubert Werner (eds), *Biofictions: The Rewriting of*

Romantic Lives in Contemporary Fiction and Drama (Columbia: Camden House, 1999), pp. 96–105.

Nicholson, Colin, 'Knucklebones of Irony: Liz Lochhead', in *Poem, Purpose and Place: Shaping Identity in Contemporary Scottish Verse* (Edinburgh: Polygon, 1992), pp. 203–23.

Nicholson, Colin, 'Towards a Scottish Theatrocracy: Edwin Morgan and Liz Lochhead', in Berthold Schoene (ed.), *The Edinburgh Companion to Contemporary Scottish Literature* (Edinburgh: Edinburgh University Press, 2007), pp. 159–66.

Poggi, Valentina, 'Mary and her Monster Revisited by Two Contemporary Scottish Writers', in Lilla Maria Crisafulli and Giovanna Silvani (eds), *Mary versus Mary* (Naples: Liguori, 2001), pp. 273–81.

Rodríguez González, Carla, 'An Interview with Liz Lochhead', *Atlantis: Journal of the Spanish Association for Anglo-American Studies*, 26.1 (2004), pp. 101–10.

Todd, Emily B, 'Liz Lochhead Interviewed by Emily B. Todd', *Verse*, 8.3/9:1 (1992), pp. 83–95.

Varty, Anne, 'The Mirror and the Vamp: Liz Lochhead', in Douglas Gifford and Dorothy McMillan (eds), *A History of Scottish Women's Writing* (Edinburgh: Edinburgh University Press, 1997), pp. 641–58.

Watson, Roderick, *The Literature of Scotland: The Twentieth Century*, 2nd edn (Basingstoke: Palgrave Macmillan, 2007).

Woddis, Carole, 'Women's Imaginations: Experimenting with Theatrical Form', in Alexis Greene (ed.), *Women Writing Plays: Three Decades of the Susan Smith Blackburn Prize* (Austin: Texas University Press, 2006), pp. 170–80.

Websites

McCulloch, Margery Palmer, 'Women and Poetry 1972–1999: The Contemporary Scene' http://www.scottishcorpus.ac.uk/corpus/search/document.php?documentid=1435

Scottish Poetry Library http://www.scottishpoetrylibrary.org.uk/poetry/poets/liz-lochhead

Trends and Issues in Contemporary Scottish Theatre (on *Britannia Rules*): http://www.educationscotland.gov.uk/Images/britanniarulesnotes_tcm4-121602.pdf

Walker, Alison and Craig W. McLuckie, 'Liz Lochhead: An Annotated Bibliography' (compiled in 2000) http://www.kalwriters.com/archive/lochhead.html

Notes on Contributors

Joe Ahearne is a writer/director working mainly in UK television since the late 1990s (*This Life, Ultraviolet, Trance, Doctor Who, Apparitions, The Secret of Crickley Hall*). He directed *Latin for a Dark Room* which was broadcast by BBC Scotland on 4 January 1995 and performed by Siobhan Redmond and Neil Pearson.

John Corbett is Professor of English at the University of Macau and an Honorary Research Fellow at the University of Glasgow. He has published widely on Scottish literature and language and language education. Among his books are *Language and Scottish Literature* (1997) and *Written in the Language of the Scottish Nation: A History of Literary Translation into Scots* (1999). With Wendy Anderson, he co-authored *Exploring English with Online Corpora* (2009). He directed two AHRC-funded Scottish corpus projects (www.scottishcorpus.ac.uk).

Robert Crawford is a widely published poet whose collections of poetry include *Full Volume* (2008). His most recent book is *On Glasgow and Edinburgh* (2013). He is Professor of Modern Scottish Literature at the University of St Andrews.

Nancy K. Gish is Professor of English and Women's and Gender Studies at the University of Southern Maine. She is the author of *Hugh MacDiarmid: The Man and His Work* (1984) and editor of *Hugh MacDiarmid: Man and Poet* (1992). She has published numerous articles on MacDiarmid as well as articles and reviews on modern and contemporary Scottish and American authors, including interviews with MacDiarmid, Jackie Kay and Denise Levertov. She has authored two books and many articles on T. S. Eliot and co-edited, with Cassandra Laity, *Gender, Desire, and Sexuality in T. S. Eliot* (2004). She is currently working on the impact of World War One on both English and Scottish poetry.

Andrew Greig is a full-time writer living in Edinburgh and Orkney. He has published nineteen books of fiction, non-fiction and poetry.

Susanne Hagemann teaches at the University of Mainz, Germany. She has written extensively on Scottish literature and on translation. Her latest book, *Übersetzungsränder* (2012, co-edited with Julia Neu) is an anthology of prefaces, afterwords and interviews in which translators of German literature discuss their own work.

Marilyn Imrie has worked in theatre and broadcasting as a producer and director for over thirty years. She chairs the board of the Scottish theatre company Stellar Quines and is on the board of Paines Plough. She has commissioned and directed two original plays from Liz Lochhead for radio – *Fancy You Minding That* and *Mortal Memories* – and five adaptations of her stage plays – *Blood And Ice*, *Quelques Fleurs*, *Cuba*, *Mary Queen of Scots Got Her Head Chopped Off* and *Perfect Days*.

Robyn Marsack joined Carcanet Press in 1982 and, on moving to Scotland in 1987, worked as a freelance editor, translator (from French) and critic, publishing studies of Louis MacNeice and Sylvia Plath, and reviewing poetry regularly for newspapers and journals. She became Director of the Scottish Poetry Library in January 2000, and lives in Glasgow. With Ken Cockburn she co-edited *Intimate Expanses: XXV Scottish Poems 1978–2002* (2004) and with Andrew Johnston, *Twenty Contemporary New Zealand Poets* (2009).

Graham McLaren is currently Associate Director for the National Theatre of Scotland. He is a Glasgow-based theatre artist who has been making theatre for almost two decades. His work ranges from totally improvised and devised pieces to classical texts. In 1994, he established the internationally acclaimed Theatre Babel, remaining Artistic Director until 2008. From 2005 to 2008, he was Artistic and Co-Creative Director at Perth Theatre, Scotland. In 2009 he began creating work for the Toronto based theatre company Necessary Angel as Associate Artist.

Dorothy McMillan is Honorary Senior Research Fellow in English Literature at the University of Glasgow. She has published widely on Women's Writing.

Benjamin Poore is Lecturer in Theatre in the Department of Theatre, Film and Television, University of York. His research interests centre on contemporary representations of the past – especially the Victorians – in British theatre, adaptation from page to stage to screen, and the Gothic. He wrote *Heritage, Nostalgia and Modern British Theatre: Staging the Victorians* (2012).

Laura Severin is Professor of English at North Carolina State University, where she teaches modern and contemporary British literature. She is author of *Stevie Smith's Resistant Antics* (1997) and *Poetry off the Page: Twentieth-Century British Women's Poetry in Performance* (2004), as well as articles on British and women's literature. Her current research focuses on multimedia collaborations between Scottish women poets and visual artists. She also serves as Special Assistant to the Provost for Academic Planning.

Adrienne Scullion publishes widely on Scottish theatre and Scottish women playwrights. She teaches in the School of Culture and Creative Arts at the University of Glasgow.

Anne Varty is Reader and Head of the English Department at Royal Holloway, University of London. Her research interests are in contemporary, modern and Victorian British and European Drama, and Victorian literature. She edited, with Robert Crawford, *Liz Lochhead's Voices* (1993), and she has published *A Preface to Oscar Wilde* (1998), *Eve's Century: A Sourcebook of Writings on Women and Journalism 1890–1918* (1999) and *Children and Theatre in Victorian Britain* (2007).

Index

In the index, LL = Liz Lochhead. Her works are indexed by title alone, works by others have the author's name appended in brackets.

English initial articles are ignored in filing (e.g. *The Bacchae* is indexed as if it were *Bacchae*, *A Choosing* as if it were *Choosing*), but others are not (e.g. 'La Belle Dame Sans Merci' appears under L).

Page numbers suffixed 'n' refer to notes.